Bloom's Modern Critical Views

Bloom's Modern Critical Views

Bloom's Modern Critical Views

EDGAR ALLAN POE
Updated Edition

Edited and with an introduction by
Harold Bloom
Sterling Professor of the Humanities
Yale University

CHELSEA HOUSE
P U B L I S H E R S
An imprint of Infobase Publishing

Bloom's Modern Critical Views: Edgar Allan Poe, Updated Edition

©2006 Infobase Publishing

Introduction © 2006 by Harold Bloom

Chelsea House
An imprint of Infobase Publishing
132 West 31st Street
New York NY 10001

Library of Congress Cataloging-in-Publication Data
Edgar Allan Poe / edited and with an introduction by Harold Bloom
    p. cm — (Bloom's modern critical views)
  Includes bibliographical references and index.
  ISBN 0-7910-8567-8
  1. Poe, Edgar Allan, 1809–1849—Criticism and interpretation. I. Bloom, Harold. II. Series
  S2638.E32 2006
  818'.309—dc   2005027445

Contributing Editor: Pamela Loos
Cover design by Keith Trego
Cover photo © CORBIS

Printed in the United States of America
Bang EJB 10 9 8 7 6 5 4 3 2 1

This book is printed on acid-free paper.

Contents

Editor's Note

My "Introduction" concedes that Edgar Allan Poe is inescapable, if only because he dreamed universal nightmares. Still, I argue, he wrote bad prose and worse poetry, best read in translation, preferably French.

Barbara Johnson, a superb rhetorical critic, juxtaposes Wordsworth and Poe, showing that the great English Romantic sought to save natural passion from the tyranny of style, while Poe gave himself to a passion for repetition.

Our leading historicist of the American Renaissance, David S. Reynolds, places the famous tale, "The Cask of Amontillado" in the contexts of Poe's literary feuds and of contemporary popular literature.

John T. Irwin, whose critical mastery ranges from Faulkner and Hart Crane to detective fiction, analyzes Poe's Platonic fantasy, *Eureka*, as a Pythagorean "mystery," that blends sleuthing and esoteric theology.

Poe's analytic detective stories also are handled by Shawn Rosenheim, for whom Dupin is a narrative therapist who entangles the reader, in a mode prophetic of Sigmund Freud's.

Arthur Gordon Pym, Poe's sole novel, concludes with a menacing white figure who can mean nearly anything, or just the abyss of nothingness. In Scott Peeples' witty reading, all quest for meaning here blinds us, and exposes our desperate reductiveness.

"The Fall of the House of Usher" is adroitly interpreted by Harriet Hustis as an instance of "the Gothic Reading," which exposes us to endless uncertainties.

Poe's indubitable racism is traced in the tales by Leland S. Person, who somewhat ironically finds that the author's sublimely perverse imagination yields us also a reversal of racist values.

The ghastly "Ligeia," extreme even for Poe, is studied by Dorothea E.

von Mücke as a mythology of "the medial woman," no longer alive but still undead.

   "The Fall of the House of Usher" returns in this volume's final essay, where John. H. Timmerman surprisingly judges the story to be a critique both of the Enlightenment and of Romanticism.

HAROLD BLOOM

Introduction

Critics, even good ones, admire Poe's stories for some of the oddest of reasons. Poe, a true Southerner, abominated Emerson, plainly perceiving that Emerson (like Whitman, like Lincoln) was not a Christian, not a royalist, not a classicist. Self-reliance, the Emersonian answer to Original Sin, does not exist in the Poe cosmos, where you necessarily start out damned, doomed, and dismal. But I think Poe detested Emerson for some of the same reasons Hawthorne and Melville more subtly resented him, reasons that persist in the distinguished American writer, Robert Penn Warren, and in many current academic literary critics in our country. If you dislike Emerson, you probably will like Poe. Emerson fathered pragmatism; Poe fathered precisely nothing, which is the way he would have wanted it. Yvor Winters accused Poe of obscurantism, but that truthful indictment no more damages Poe than does tastelessness and tone deafness. Emerson, for better and for worse, was and is the mind of America, but Poe was and is our hysteria, our uncanny unanimity in our repressions. I certainly do not intend to mean by this that Poe was deeper than Emerson in any way whatsoever. Emerson cheerfully and consciously threw out the past. Critics tend to share Poe's easy historicism; perhaps without knowing it, they are gratified that every Poe story is, in too clear a sense, over even as it begins. We don't have to wait for Madeline Usher and the house to fall in upon poor Roderick; they have fallen in upon him already, before the narrator comes upon the place. Emerson exalted freedom, which he and Thoreau usefully called "wildness." No one in Poe is or can be free or wild, and some academic admirers of Poe truly like everything and everyone to be in bondage to a universal past. To begin is to be free, godlike and Emersonian-Adamic, or Jeffersonian. But for a writer to be free is bewildering and even maddening. What American writers and their exegetes half-unknowingly love in Poe is his more-than-Freudian oppressive and curiously original sense and sensation of overdetermination. Walter Pater once remarked that museums depressed him because they made him doubt that anyone ever had once been young. No one in a Poe story ever was young. As D.H. Lawrence angrily observed, everyone in Poe is a vampire—Poe himself in particular.

II

Among Poe's tales, the near-exception to what I have been saying is the longest and most ambitious, *The Narrative of Arthur Gordon Pym*, just as the best of Poe's poems is the long prose-poem *Eureka*. Alas, even these works are somewhat overvalued, if only because Poe's critics understandably become excessively eager to see him vindicated. *Pym* is readable, but *Eureka* is extravagantly repetitious. Auden was quite taken with *Eureka*, but could remember very little of it in conversation, and one can doubt that he read it through, at least in English. Poe's most advanced critic is John T. Irwin, in his book *American Hieroglyphics*. Irwin rightly centers upon *Pym*, while defending *Eureka* as an "aesthetic cosmology" addressed to what in each of us Freud called the "bodily ego." Irwin is too shrewd to assert that Poe's performance in *Eureka* fulfills Poe's extraordinary intentions:

> What the poem *Eureka*, at once pre-Socratic and post-Newtonian, asserts is the truth of the feeling, the bodily intuition, that the diverse objects which the mind discovers in contemplating external nature form a unity, that they are all parts of one body which, if not infinite, is so gigantic as to be beyond both the spatial and temporal limits of human perception. In *Eureka*, then, Poe presents us with the paradox of a "unified" macrocosmic body that is without a totalizing image—an alogical, intuitive belief whose "truth" rests upon Poe's sense that cosmologies and myths of origin are forms of internal geography that, under the guise of mapping the physical universe, map the universe of desire.

Irwin might be writing of Blake, or of other visionaries who have sought to map total forms of desire. What Irwin catches, by implication, is Poe's troubling anticipation of what is most difficult in Freud, the "frontier concepts" between mind and body, such as the bodily ego, the non-repressive defense of introjection, and above all, the drives or instincts. Poe, not just in

Eureka and in *Pym*, but throughout his tales and even in some of his verse, is peculiarly close to the Freudian speculation upon the bodily ego. Freud, in *The Ego and the Id* (1923), resorted to the uncanny language of E.T.A. Hoffmann (and of Poe) in describing this difficult notion:

> The ego is first and foremost a bodily ego; it is not merely a surface entity, but is itself the projection of a surface. If we wish to find an anatomical analogy for it we can best identify it with the "cortical homunculus" of the anatomists, which stands on its head in the cortex, sticks up its heels, faces backwards and, as we know, has its speech-area on the left-hand side.

A footnote in the English translation of 1927, authorized by Freud but never added to the German editions, elucidates the first sentence of this description in a way analogous to the crucial metaphor in Poe that concludes *The Narrative of Arthur Gordon Pym*:

> I.e. the ego is ultimately derived from bodily sensations, chiefly from those springing from the surface of the body, besides, as we have seen above, representing the superficies of the mental apparatus.

A considerable part of Poe's mythological power emanates from his own difficult sense that the ego is always a bodily ego. The characters of Poe's tales live out nearly every conceivable fantasy of introjection and identification, seeking to assuage their melancholia by psychically devouring the lost objects of their affections. D.H. Lawrence, in his *Studies in Classic American Literature* (1923), moralized powerfully against Poe, condemning him for "the will-to-love and the will-to-consciousness, asserted against death itself. The pride of human conceit in KNOWLEDGE." It is illuminating that Lawrence attacked Poe in much the same spirit as he attacked Freud, who is interpreted in *Psychoanalysis and the Unconscious* as somehow urging us to violate the taboo against incest. The interpretation is as extravagant as Lawrence's thesis that Poe urged vampirism upon us, but there remains something suggestive in Lawrence's violence against both Freud and Poe. Each placed the elitist individual in jeopardy, Lawrence implied, by hinting at the primacy of fantasy not just in the sexual life proper, but in the bodily ego's constitution of itself through acts of incorporation and identification.

The cosmology of *Eureka* and the narrative of *Pym* alike circle around fantasies of incorporation. *Eureka*'s subtitle is "An Essay on the Material and

Spiritual Universe" and what Poe calls its "general proposition" is heightened by italics: "*In the Original Unity of the First Thing lies the Secondary Cause of all Things, with the Germ of their Inevitable Annihilation.*" Freud, in his cosmology, *Beyond the Pleasure Principle*, posited that the inorganic had preceded the organic, and also that it was the tendency of all things to return to their original state. Consequently, the aim of all life was death. The death drive, which became crucial for Freud's later dualisms, is nevertheless pure mythology, since Freud's only evidence for it was the repetition compulsion, and it is an extravagant leap from repetition to death. This reliance upon one's own mythology may have prompted Freud's audacity when, in the *New Introductory Lectures*, he admitted that the theory of drives was, so to speak, his own mythology, drives being not only magnificent conceptions but particularly sublime in their indefiniteness. I wish I could assert that *Eureka* has some of the speculative force of *Beyond the Pleasure Principle* or even of Freud's disciple Ferenczi's startling *Thalassa: A Theory of Genitality*; but *Eureka* does badly enough when compared to Emerson's *Nature*, which itself has only a few passages worthy of what Emerson wrote afterwards. And yet Valéry in one sense was justified in his praise for *Eureka*. For certain intellectuals, *Eureka* performs a mythological function akin to what Poe's tales continue to do for hosts of readers. *Eureka* is unevenly written, badly repetitious, and sometimes opaque in its abstractness, but like the tales it seems not to have been composed by a particular individual. The universalism of a common nightmare informs it. If the tales lose little, or even gain, when we retell them to others in our own words, *Eureka* gains by Valéry's observations, or by the summaries of recent critics like John Irwin or Daniel Hoffman. Translation even into his own language always benefits Poe.

I haven't the space, or the desire, to summarize *Eureka*, and no summary is likely to do anything besides deadening both my readers and myself. Certainly Poe was never more passionately sincere than in composing *Eureka*, of which he affirmed: "*What I here propound is true.*" But these are the closing sentences of *Eureka*:

> Think that the sense of individual identity will be gradually merged in the general consciousness—that Man, for example, ceasing imperceptibly to feel himself Man, will at length attain that awfully triumphant epoch when he shall recognize his existence as that of Jehovah. In the meantime bear in mind that all is Life—Life—Life within Life—the less within the greater, and all within the *Spirit Divine*.

To this, Poe appends a "Note":

> The pain of the consideration that we shall lose our individual
> identity, ceases at once when we further reflect that the process,
> as above described, is, neither more nor less than that of the
> absorption, by each individual intelligence of all other
> intelligences (that is, of the Universe) into its own. That God
> may be all in all, *each* must become God.

Allen Tate, not unsympathetic to his cousin, Mr. Poe, remarked of
Poe's extinction in *Eureka* that "there is a lurid sublimity in the spectacle of
his taking God along with him into a grave which is not smaller than the
universe." If we read closely, Poe's trope is "absorption," and we are where
we always are in Poe, amid ultimate fantasies of introjection in which the
bodily ego and the cosmos become indistinguishable. Again, I suspect this
judgment hardly weakens Poe, since his strength is no more cognitive than
it is stylistic. Poe's mythology, like the mythology of psychoanalysis that we
cannot yet bear to acknowledge as primarily a mythology, is peculiarly
appropriate to any modernism, whether you want to call it early, high or
post-modernism. The definitive judgment belongs here to T.W. Adorno,
certainly the most authentic theoretician of all modernisms, in his last book,
Aesthetic Theory. Writing on "reconciliation and mimetic adaptation to
death," Adorno blends the insights of Jewish negative theology and
psychoanalysis:

> Whether negativity is the barrier or the truth of art is not for art
> to decide. Art works are negative *per se* because they are subject
> to the law of objectification; that is, they kill what they objectify,
> tearing it away from its context of immediacy and real life. They
> survive because they bring death. This is particularly true of
> modern art, where we notice a general mimetic abandonment to
> reification, which is the principle of death. Illusion in art is the
> attempt to escape from this principle. Baudelaire marks a
> watershed, in that art after him seeks to discard illusion without
> resigning itself to being a thing among things. The harbingers of
> modernism, Poe and Baudelaire, were the first technocrats of art.

Baudelaire was more than a technocrat of art, as Adorno knew, but Poe
would be only that except for his mythmaking gift. C.S. Lewis may have been
right when he insisted that such a gift could exist even apart from other

literary endowments. Blake and Freud are inescapable mythmakers who were also cognitively and stylistically powerful. Poe is a great fantasist whose thoughts were commonplace and whose metaphors were dead. Fantasy, mythologically considered, combines the stances of Narcissus and Prometheus, which are ideologically antithetical to one another, but figuratively quite compatible. Poe is at once the Narcissus and the Prometheus of his nation. If that is right, then he is inescapable, even though his tales contrast weakly with Hawthorne's, his poems scarcely bear reading, and his speculative discourses fade away in juxtaposition to Emerson's, his despised Northern rival.

III

To define Poe's mythopoeic inevitability more closely, I turn to his story "Ligeia" and to the end of *Pym*. Ligeia, a tall, dark, slender transcendentalist, dies murmuring a protest against the feeble human will, which cannot keep us forever alive. Her distraught and nameless widower, the narrator, endeavors to comfort himself, first with opium, and then with a second bride, "the fair-haired and blue-eyed Lady Rowena Trevanian, of Tremaine." Unfortunately, he has little use for this replacement, and so she sickens rapidly and dies. Recurrently, the corpse revivifies, only to die yet again and again. At last, the cerements are stripped away, and the narrator confronts the undead Ligeia, attired in the death-draperies of her now evaporated successor.

As a parable of the vampiric will, this works well enough. The learned Ligeia presumably has completed her training in the will during her absence, or perhaps merely owes death a substitute, the insufficiently transcendental Rowena. What is mythopoeically more impressive is the ambiguous question of the narrator's will. Poe's own life, like Walt Whitman's, is an American mythology, and what all of us generally remember about it is that Poe married his first cousin, Virginia Clemm, before she turned fourteen. She died a little more than ten years later, having been a semi-invalid for most of that time. Poe himself died less than three years after her, when he was just forty. "Ligeia," regarded by Poe as his best tale, was written a bit more than a year into the marriage. The later Freud implicitly speculates that there are no accidents; we die because we will to die, our character being also our fate. In Poe's myth also, ethos is the daemon, and the daemon is our destiny. The year after Virginia died, Poe proposed marriage to the widowed poet Sarah Helen Whitman. Biographers tell us that the lady's doubts were caused by rumors of Poe's bad character, but perhaps Mrs. Whitman had read "Ligeia"!

In any event, this marriage did not take place, nor did Poe survive to marry another widow, his childhood sweetheart Elmira Royster Shelton. Perhaps she too might have read "Ligeia" and forborne.

The narrator of "Ligeia" has a singularly bad memory, or else a very curious relationship to his own will, since he begins by telling us that he married Ligeia without ever having troubled to learn her family name. Her name itself is legend, or romance, and that was enough. As the story's second paragraph hints, the lady was an opium dream with the footfall of a shadow. The implication may be that there never was such a lady, or even that if you wish to incarnate your reveries, then you must immolate your consubstantial Rowena. What is a touch alarming to the narrator is the intensity of Ligeia's passion for him, which was manifested however only by glances and voice so long as the ideal lady lived. Perhaps this baffled intensity is what kills Ligeia, through a kind of narcissistic dialectic, since she is dominated not by the will of her lust but by the lust of her will. She wills her infinite passion towards the necessarily inadequate narrator and when (by implication) he fails her, she turns the passion of her will against dying and at last against death. Her dreadful poem, "The Conqueror Worm," prophesies her cyclic return from death: "Through a circle that ever returneth in / To the self-same spot." But when she does return, the spot is hardly the same. Poor Rowena only becomes even slightly interesting to her narrator-husband when she sickens unto death, and her body is wholly usurped by the revived Ligeia. And yet the wretched narrator is a touch different, if only because his narcissism is finally out of balance with his first wife's grisly Prometheanism. There are no final declarations of Ligeia's passion as the story concludes. The triumph of her will is complete, but we know that the narrator's will has not blent itself into Ligeia's. His renewed obsession with her eyes testifies to a continued sense of her daemonic power over him, but his final words hint at what the story's opening confirms: she will not be back for long—and remains "my lost love."

The conclusion of Pym has been brilliantly analyzed by John Irwin, and so I want to glance only briefly at what is certainly Poe's most effective closure:

And now we rushed into the embraces of the cataract, where a chasm threw itself open to receive us. But there arose in our pathway a shrouded human figure, very far larger in its proportions than any dweller among men. And the hue of the skin of the figure was of the perfect whiteness of the snow.

Irwin demonstrates Poe's reliance here upon the Romantic topos of the Alpine White Shadow, the magnified projection of the observer himself. The chasm Pym enters is the familiar Romantic Abyss, not a part of the natural world but belonging to eternity, before the creation. Reflected in that abyss, Pym beholds his own shrouded form, perfect in the whiteness of the natural context. Presumably, this is the original bodily ego, the Gnostic self before the fall into creation. As at the close of *Eureka*, Poe brings Alpha and Omega together in an apocalyptic circle. I suggest we read Pym's, which is to say Poe's, white shadow as the American triumph of the will, as illusory as Ligeia's usurpation of Rowena's corpse.

Poe teaches us, through Pym and Ligeia, that as Americans we are both subject and object to our own quests. Emerson, in Americanizing the European sense of the abyss, kept the self and the abyss separate as facts: "There may be two or three or four steps, according to the genius of each, but for every seeing soul there are two absorbing facts—I and the Abyss." Poe, seeking to avoid Emersonianism, ends with only one fact, and it is more a wish than a fact: "I will to be the Abyss." This metaphysical despair has appealed to the Southern American literary tradition and to its Northern followers. The appeal cannot be refuted, because it is myth, and Poe backed the myth with his life as well as his work. If the Northern or Emersonian myth of our literary culture culminates in the beautiful image of Walt Whitman as wound-dresser, moving as a mothering father through the Civil War Washington, D.C. hospitals, then the Southern or countermyth achieves its perfect stasis at its start, with Poe's snow-white shadow shrouding the chasm down which the boat of the soul is about to plunge. Poe's genius was for negativity and opposition, and the affirmative force of Emersonian America gave him the impetus his daemonic will required.

IV

It would be a relief to say that Poe's achievement as a critic is not mythological, but the splendid, and almost complete edition of his essays, reviews and marginalia testifies otherwise. It shows Poe indeed to have been Adorno's "technocrat of art." Auden defended Poe's criticism by contrasting the subjects Baudelaire was granted—Delacroix, Constantin Guys, Wagner—with the books Poe was given to review, such as *The Christian Florist*, *The History of Texas*, and *Poetical Remains of the Late Lucretia Maria Davidson*. The answer to Auden is that Poe also wrote about Bryant, Byron, Coleridge, Dickens, Hawthorne, Washington Irving, Longfellow, Shelley, and Tennyson; a ninefold providing scope enough for any authentic critical consciousness. Nothing that Poe had to say about these poets and storytellers is in any way memorable or at all an aid to reading them. There are no critical insights, no original perceptions, no accurate or illuminating juxtapositions or historical placements. Here is Poe on Tennyson, from his *Marginalia*, which generally surpasses his other criticism:

> Why do some persons fatigue themselves in attempts to unravel such phantasy-pieces as the "Lady of Shalott"? ... If the author did not deliberately propose to himself a suggestive indefinitiveness of meaning, with the view of bringing about a definitiveness of vague and therefore of spiritual *effect*—this, at least, arose from the silent analytical promptings of that poetic genius which, in its supreme development, embodies all orders of intellectual capacity.

I take this as being representative of Poe's criticism, because it is uninterestingly just plain *wrong* about "The Lady of Shalott." No other poem, even by the great word-painter Tennyson, is deliberately so definite in meaning and effect. Everything vague precisely is excluded in this perhaps most Pre-Raphaelite of all poems, where each detail contributes to an impression that might be called hard-edged phantasmagoria. If we take as the three possibilities of nineteenth-century practical criticism the sequence of Arnold, Pater, and Wilde, we find Poe useless in all three modes: Arnold's seeing the object as in itself it really is, Pater's seeing accurately one's own impression of the object, and the divine Oscar's sublime seeing of the object as in itself it really is not. If "The Lady of Shalott" is the object, then Poe does not see anything: the poem as in itself it is, one's impression of the poem as that is, or best of all the Wildean sense of what is missing or excluded from the poem. Poe's descriptive terms are "indefinitiveness" and "vague," but Tennyson's poem is just the reverse:

> She left the web, she left the loom,
> She made three paces through the room,
> She saw the water-lily bloom,
> She saw the helmet and the plume,
>   She looked down to Camelot.
> Out flew the web and floated wide;
> The mirror cracked from side to side;
> "The curse is come upon me," cried
>   The Lady of Shalott.

No, Poe as practical critic is a true match for most of his contemporary subjects, such as S. Anna Lewis, author of *The Child of the Sea and Other Poems* (1848). Of her lyric "The Forsaken," Poe wrote, "We have read this little poem more than twenty times and always with increasing admiration. *It is inexpressibly beautiful*" (Poe's italics). I quote only the first of its six stanzas:

> It hath been said—for all who die
>   there is a tear;
> Some pining, bleeding heart to sigh
>   O'er every bier:
> But in that hour of pain and dread
>   Who will draw near
> Around my humble couch and shed
>   One farewell tear?

Well, but there is Poe as theoretician, Valéry has told us. Acute self-consciousness in Poe was strongly misread by Valéry as the inauguration and development of severe and skeptical ideas. Presumably, this is the Poe of three famous essays: "The Philosophy of Composition," "The Rationale of Verse," and "The Poetic Principle." Having just reread these pieces, I have no possibility of understanding a letter of Valéry to Mallarmé which prizes the theories of Poe as being "so profound and so insidiously learned." Certainly we prize the theories of Valéry for just those qualities, and so I have come full circle to where I began, with the mystery of French Poe. Valéry may be said to have read Poe in the critical modes both of Pater and of Wilde. He saw his impression of Poe clearly, and he saw Poe's essays as in themselves they really were not. Admirable, and so Valéry brought to culmination the critical myth that is French Poe.

V

> Whose head is swinging from the swollen strap?
> Whose body smokes along the bitten rails,
> Bursts from a smoldering bundle far behind
> In back forks of the chasms of the brain—
> Puffs from a riven stump far out behind
> In interborough fissures of the mind ...?

Hart Crane's vision of Poe, in the "Tunnel" section of *The Bridge*, tells us again why the mythopoeic Poe is inescapable for American literary mythology. Poe's nightmare projections and introjections suggest the New York City subway as the new underground, where Coleridge's "deep Romantic chasm" has been internalized into "the chasms of the brain." Whatever his actual failures as poet and critic, whatever the gap between style and idea in his tales, Poe is central to the American canon, both for us and for the rest of the world. Hawthorne implicitly and Melville explicitly made far more powerful critiques of the Emersonian national hope, but they were by no means wholly negative in regard to Emerson and his pragmatic vision of American Self-Reliance. Poe was savage in denouncing minor transcendentalists like Bronson Alcott and William Ellery Channing, but his explicit rejection of Emerson confined itself to the untruthful observation that Emerson was indistinguishable from Thomas Carlyle. Poe should have survived to read Carlyle's insane and amazing pamphlet "The Nigger Question," which he would have adored. Mythologically, Poe is necessary because all of his work is a hymn to negativity. Emerson was a great theoretician of literature as of life, a good practical critic (when he wanted to be, which was not often), a very good poet (sometimes) and always a major aphorist and essayist. Poe, on a line-by-line or sentence-by-sentence basis, is hardly a worthy opponent. But looking in the French way, as T.S. Eliot recommended, "we see a mass of unique shape and impressive size to which the eye constantly returns." Eliot was probably right, in mythopoeic terms.

BARBARA JOHNSON

Strange Fits:
Poe and Wordsworth on the
Nature of Poetic Language

No two discussions of poetry could at first sight appear more different than Wordsworth's "Preface to the *Lyrical Ballads*" and Poe's "Philosophy of Composition."[1] The first has been read as an important Romantic manifesto, sometimes inconsistent, sometimes dated, but always to be taken seriously. The second has been read as a theoretical spoof which, because it cannot be taken at face value, cannot be taken seriously at all. Both, however, can be read as complex texts in their own right—as texts whose very complexities tell us a great deal about the nature of poetic language. I would like to suggest here some directions for such a reading, first by examining the rhetorical slipperiness of each theoretical text, then by invoking for each a poem—Wordsworth's "Strange Fits of Passion" and Poe's "The Raven"— that both exemplifies and undermines the neatness of the explicit theory.

Despite their differences, Poe and Wordsworth do in fact agree on one thing: that the object of poetry is to produce pleasure:

Wordsworth:
The first Volume of these Poems has already been submitted to general perusal. It was published, as an experiment, which, I hoped, might be of some use to ascertain, how far, by fitting to metrical arrangement a selection of the real language of men in a

---

From *A World of Difference*. ©1987 by The Johns Hopkins University Press.

state of vivid sensation, that sort of pleasure and that quantity of pleasure may be imparted, which a Poet may rationally endeavor to impart. (p. 69)

Poe:
Beauty is the sole legitimate province of the poem.... That pleasure which is at once the most intense, the most elevating, and the most pure, is, I believe, found in the contemplation of the beautiful. (p. 1082)

The nature of the pleasure in question, however, is, in both cases, pushed to the edge of trauma: dead women, mad mothers, idiot boys, lugubrious birds—the poems are populated with images that are clearly situated beyond any simple notion of a pleasure principle. Poe indeed goes so far as to make his poem aim for the utmost "luxury of sorrow" to be obtained by "the human thirst for self-torture" (p. 1088). What is at stake in both cases would seem to have something to do with the beyond of pleasure, which for Freud was associated with two highly problematic and highly interesting notions: the repetition compulsion and the death instinct. Questions of repetition and death will indeed be central to our discussion both of Wordsworth and of Poe.

I will begin by outlining, somewhat reductively, the broadest possible differences between the two theoretical texts. Many of the differences are, of course, historical, and can be derived from the type of fashionable poetry each poet is writing against. Poe designs his poetics in opposition to the American tradition of long, sentimental, or didactic poetry associated with such figures as Longfellow or Bryant. Wordsworth is writing against the eighteenth-century British tradition of witty, polished, mock-heroic or rhetorically ornate verse associated with such names as Johnson, Pope, and Gray. But the poetic boundary lines each poet attempts to draw are perhaps of broader applicability, and their attempts can be read as exemplary versions of tensions inherent in the modem Western poetic project as such.

What, then, are the salient differences between these two theories of poetic language? In a well-known passage from the Preface, Wordsworth states that "Poetry is the spontaneous overflow of powerful feelings: it takes its origin from emotion recollected in tranquillity" (p. 85). Poe, on the other hand, writes of his method of composing "The Raven" that it was written backwards, beginning with a consideration of the desired *effect*. "It is my design to render it manifest that no one point in its composition is referrible either to accident or intuition—that the work proceeded, step by step, to its completion with the precise and rigid consequence of a mathematical problem" (p. 1081). Poe's poetic calculus leads him to choose an optimal length of about one hundred lines; then, after consideration of the desired effect and tone (beauty and sadness), he decides that the poem should be structured around a refrain ending in the most sonorous of letters, *o* and *r*. The syllable -*or* is thus the first element of the text of the poem to be written. "The sound of the refrain being thus determined," Poe goes on, "it became necessary to select a word embodying this sound, and at the same time in the fullest possible keeping with that melancholy which I had predetermined as the tone of the poem. In such a search it would have been absolutely impossible to overlook the word 'Nevermore.' In fact it was the very first which presented itself' (pp. 1083–84).

Spontaneous overflow versus calculation, emotion versus rigid consequence, feelings versus letters of the alphabet: a first comparison would lead us to see Wordsworth's poetry as granting primacy to the *signified* while Poe's grants primacy to the *signifier*. This distinction is borne out by the fact that while Wordsworth claims that the language of poetry should be indistinguishable from that of good prose, Poe aims to maximize the difference between prose and poetry, excluding for that reason the long poem from the canon of true poetry. But neither text presents its case as simply as it might appear.

For all his emphasis on emotion, Wordsworth is of course acutely conscious of the centrality of form to the poetic project. He describes the use of verse as a kind of contract made between form and expectation. Form itself constitutes a promise which Wordsworth then claims to have broken:

> It is supposed, that by the act of writing in verse an Author makes a formal engagement that he will gratify certain known habits of association; that he not only apprizes the Reader that certain classes of ideas and expressions will be found in his book, but that others will be carefully excluded. I will not take upon me to determine the exact import of the promise which by the act of writing in verse an Author, in the present day, makes to his reader; but I am certain, it will appear to many persons that I have not fulfilled the terms of an engagement thus voluntarily contracted. (p. 70)

Verse, then, is a contract made by form, a formal promise to include and to exclude certain classes of ideas. Wordsworth's violation of that contract comprises both inclusions and exclusions. He warns the reader that these shifts in boundary lines may produce "feelings of strangeness and awkwardness." Feelings of strangeness are, of course, often the subjects of the poems, as is the case with the poem to which we will later turn, "Strange Fits of Passion." That poem may well tell us something about the nature of strangeness of Wordsworth's poetics, but strangeness is not the only metapoetic expression glossed by the poem. For Wordsworth's first description of his experiment, in the opening paragraph of the Preface, speaks of the poems as "*fitting* to metrical arrangement a selection of the real language of men in a state of vivid sensation." The word "fit," which occurs several times in the preface,[2] thus in the poem takes on the double meaning of both uncontrolled overflow and formal containment. Interestingly, the word "fytt" is also a term for a medieval stanza form. As I will try to show, Wordsworth's entire preface can be read as an attempt to fit all the senses of the word "fit" together.

What does Wordsworth mean by "the real language of men"? In the 1798 "Advertisement to the *Lyrical Ballads*," Wordsworth had spoken of "the language of conversation in the middle and lower classes of society." These, then, are the "classes of ideas" that poetry had previously excluded. But Wordsworth includes them only to again exclude them; the substitution of the expression "the real language of men" for "the conversation of the middle and lower classes" acts out an erasure of "class," a gesture of dehistoricization and universalization. Poetic inclusions and exclusions clearly operate on more than one level at a time. Others are more qualified than I am to comment on Wordsworth's tendency to pastoralize away the historical reality of the rural along with the urban and the industrial, grounding "*human* nature" instead in a state of congruence with "the beautiful and permanent forms" of *external* Nature. Let it suffice here to suggest that, in the discussion that follows, the complex fate of the word "mechanical" may not be unconnected to a set of attitudes toward the industrial revolution.

There is one type of exclusion about which Wordsworth's preface is very dear—or at least it tries to be. The crucial exclusion for Wordsworth would seem to be the exclusion of personification.

> The reader will find that personifications of abstract ideas rarely occur in these volumes; and, I hope, are utterly rejected as an ordinary device to elevate the style, and raise it above prose. I have proposed to myself to imitate, and, as far as possible, to adopt the very language of men; and assuredly such personifications do not make any natural or regular part of that

language. They are, indeed, a figure of speech occasionally prompted by passion, and I have made use of them as such; but I have endeavored utterly to reject them as a mechanical device of style. (p. 74)

The operative opposition here is the opposition between the "natural" and the "mechanical." Personifications, says Wordsworth, are not "natural," but rather "a mechanical device of style." But already there is an exception: they are sometimes naturally prompted by passion. If poetry is located at a point of vivid sensation, if it is defined as always being in some sense a strange fit of passion, then where does Wordsworth draw the line? Are personifications natural or mechanical? How natural is the natural language of passion?

Let us look further at Wordsworth's attempts to distinguish between the natural and the mechanical. Since his whole sense of value and originality seems to depend on his making that distinction clear, we would expect him to clarify it in the essay. One of the ways in which Wordsworth works the distinction over is by telling it as a story. He tells it twice, once as a story of degradation, and once as a story of recollection. The first is a history of abuse; the second, a history of recovery. What we will do is look closely at the rhetorical terms in which the two stories are told. They are both, of course, stories of rhetoric, but what we will analyze will be the rhetoric of the stories.

First, from the "Appendix on Poetic Diction," the history of abuse:

The earliest Poets of all nations generally wrote from passion excited by real events; they wrote *naturally*, and as men: feeling powerfully as they did, their language was daring, and figurative. In succeeding times, Poets, and men ambitious of the fame of Poets, perceiving the influence of such language, and desirous of producing the same effect, without having the same animating passion, set themselves to a *mechanical* adoption of those figures of speech, and made use of them, sometimes with propriety, but much more frequently applied them to feelings and ideas with which they had *no natural connection* whatsoever. A language was thus insensibly produced, differing materially from the real language of men in *any situation* [original emphasis]. The Reader or Hearer of this *distorted language* found himself in a perturbed and unusual state of mind: when affected by the genuine language of passion he had been in a perturbed and unusual state of mind also: in both cases he was willing that his common judgment and understanding should be laid asleep, and he had no instinctive and infallible perception of the true to make him reject the false.... This *distorted language* was received with admiration; and Poets, it is probable, who had before contented themselves for the most part with *misapplying* only expressions which at first had been dictated by real passion, *carried the abuse still further*, and introduced phrases composed apparently in the spirit of the original figurative language of passion, yet altogether of their own invention, and distinguished by various degrees of *wanton deviation* from good sense and *nature*.... In process of time metre became a symbol or promise of this unusual language, and whoever took upon him to write in metre, according as he possessed more or less of true poetic genius, introduced less or more of this *adulterated phraseology* into his compositions, and the true and false became so inseparably interwoven that the taste of men was gradually *perverted*; and this language was received as a *natural* language; and at length, by the influence of books upon men, did to a certain degree really become so. (pp. 90–91; emphasis mine unless otherwise indicated)

In this history of abuse, the natural and the mechanical, the true and the false, become utterly indistinguishable. It becomes all the more necessary—but all the more difficult—to restore the boundary line. Each time Wordsworth attempts to do so, however, the distinction breaks down. The natural becomes unnatural, life imitates art, and mechanical inventions are mistaken for the natural language of passion.

Wordsworth's other developmental narrative is one that leads not to degradation but to amelioration. This time the story takes place in a temporality of the self, the temporality expressed by the juxtaposition of the two clauses: "Poetry is the spontaneous overflow of powerful feelings," and "it takes its origin from emotion recollected in tranquillity." For Wordsworth, in other words, the poet is a man who attempts to write in obedience to the classic example of the double bind: "be spontaneous." In an early paragraph in the preface, Wordsworth makes the double bind into a developmental narrative, in which the acrobatics of grammar—the sustained avoidance of any grammatical break—mimes the desire for seamless continuity. If the whole story can be told in one breath, Wordsworth implies, then nothing will be lost, the recuperation of the spontaneous will be complete.

For all good poetry is the spontaneous overflow of powerful feelings: but though this be true, Poems to which any value can be attached, were never produced on any variety of subjects but by a man, who being possessed of more than usual organic sensibility, had also thought long and deeply. For our continued influxes of feeling are modified and directed by our thoughts, which are indeed the representatives of all our past feelings; and, as by contemplating the relation of these general representatives to each other we discover what is really important to men, so, by the repetition and continuance of this act, our feelings will be connected with important subjects, till at length, if we be originally possessed of much sensibility, such habits of mind will be produced, that, by obeying blindly and mechanically the impulses of those habits, we shall describe objects, and utter sentiments, of such a nature and in such connection with each other, that the understanding of the being to whom we address ourselves, if he be in a healthful state of association, must necessarily be in some degree enlightened, and his affections ameliorated. (p. 72)

The astonishing thing about this story is that it uses the word "mechanical"—which has been the name of a negative value everywhere else in the preface—as the height of poeticity. "Obeying blindly and mechanically the impulses of habits" was exactly what produced abuse and corruption in the other story, but here it produces health, enlightenment, and amelioration. What can be said about the relation between the two stories?

Both stories are designed to define and judge the relation between an original moment of feeling and utterance and its later repetition. Wordsworth's task is to distinguish between good repetition and de graded, hollow repetition. In describing his own creative process, he speaks of the art of developing habits that will lead to a "blind, mechanical" reproduction of the original emotion. In describing the poetic degradations he wants to condemn, he again speaks of a "mechanical" adoption of figures of speech. For Wordsworth's theory to stand, it is urgent for him to be able to distinguish between good and bad repetition. Yet the good and the bad are narrated in almost the same terms. Wordsworth again and again repeats the story of repetition, but is never able to draw a reliable dividing line. He can *affirm* good repetition, but he can't tell a story that will sufficiently distinguish it from bad. What Wordsworth's essay shows is that talking about poetry involves one in an urgent and impossible search for that distinction, for a recipe for reliable blindness. This is not an inability to get it right, but rather the acting out of an insight into the nature of poetry and the poetic process. For what, indeed, is the problem in any modern theory of poetic language, if not the problem of articulating authenticity with conventionality, originality and continuity, freshness with what is recognizably "fit" to be called poetic?

While Wordsworth is thus attempting to instate the naturalness of "genuine" repetition, Poe would seem to be doing just the opposite: mechanical repetition is clearly in some sense what "The Raven" is all about. In turning to Poe, we can therefore expect some sort of inversely symmetrical plea for the poeticity of the mechanical, the empty, and the hollow. It is as though a talking bird were the perfect figure for the poetic parroting of personification that Wordsworth would like to leave behind. But before moving on to Poe, let us look at Wordsworth's "Strange Fits of Passion" as another inscription of the theories expounded by the preface.

It has already become clear in our discussion that the phrase "Strange Fit of Passion" can be read in at least two ways as a summary of Wordsworth's poetic project: poetry is a fit, an outburst, an overflow, of feeling;[3] and poetry is an attempt to fit, to arrange, feeling into form. The poem would seem to be about an example of an experience fit to be made into poetry:

> Strange fits of passion have I known:
> And I will dare to tell,
> But in the Lover's ear alone,
> What once to me befell.
>
> When she I loved looked every day
> Fresh as a rose in June,
> I to her cottage bent my way,
> Beneath an evening-moon.
>
> Upon the moon I fixed my eye,
> All over the wide lea;
> With quickening pace my horse drew nigh
> Those paths so dear to me.
>
> And now we reached the orchard-plot;
> And, as we climbed the hill,

The sinking moon to Lucy's cot
Came near, and nearer still.

In one of those sweet dreams I slept,
Kind Nature's gentlest boon!
And all the while my eyes I kept
On the descending moon.

My horse moved on; hoof after hoof
He raised, and never stopped:
When down behind the cottage roof,
At once, the bright moon dropped.

What fond and wayward thoughts will slide
Into a lover's head!
'O mercy!' to myself I cried,
'If Lucy should be dead!'

The lovers alarm at his wayward thought indicates that he does not know what put it into his head, that he sees no connection between that thought and any part of his waking or dreaming life. The obvious connection the poem invites us to make is between the moon dropping and Lucy dying. But in the poem, that connection is elided, replaced by a mere discontinuity. That connection can in fact be made only in a world that admits the possibility of personification. The moon must be seeable as a correlative, a personification of Lucy.[4] And the hiatus marks the spot where that possibility is denied. The strange fit depicted in the poem can in some sense be read, therefore, as the revenge of personification, the return of a poetic principle that Wordsworth had attempted to exclude. The strangeness of the passion arises from the poem's uncanny encounter with what the theory that produced it had repressed.[5] Indeed, this is perhaps why the *Lyrical Ballads* are so full of ghosts and haunting presences. It is as though poetry could not do without the figures of half-aliveness that the use of personification provides. Or perhaps it is the other way around: that personification gives us conventionalized access to the boundary between life and death which Wordsworth, by repressing explicit personification, uncovers in a more disquieting way.[6]

It is doubtless no accident that a by-product of this fit is the death of a woman. In speaking to the lover's ear alone, Wordsworth is profoundly, as he says in the preface, "a man speaking to men." Even when Wordsworth speaks of or as a woman, the woman tends to be abused, mad, or dead. If Wordsworth's aim in these poems is to undo the abuse of dead poetic figures and recover a more natural language, he seems to have transferred the abuse from personifications to persons.

Poe makes the connection between poetry and dead women even more explicit when he writes, "The death of a beautiful woman is, unquestionably, the most poetic topic in the world—and equally is it beyond doubt that the lips best suited for such topic are those of a bereaved lover" (p. 1084). The work of poetry may well be the work of mourning, or of murder—the mourning and murder necessitated by language's hovering on the threshold between life and death, between pleasure and its beyond, between restorative and abusive repetition. But why, in Poe's case, does the male mourner require a talking bird to make his grief into a poem?

The raven, as Poe explains it in "The Philosophy of Composition," is chosen as a plausible vehicle for the repetition of the refrain—the word "nevermore." The bird is thus a figure for mechanical poetic repetition. The purveyor of the burden has to be a bird: the intentional relation to a signified is denied through the nonhuman repetition of a pure signifier. The word "nevermore," offered here as the most poetical of words, in fact crops up uncannily in Wordsworth's essay too as a distinguishing poetic mark. In differentiating between admirable and contemptible uses of "real language," Wordsworth juxtaposes two short stanzas, one by Dr. Johnson, the other from "Babes in the Wood." Johnson's contemptible stanza goes:

> I put my hat upon my head,
> And walked into the Strand,
> And there I met another man
> Whose hat was in his hand.

The admirable stanza reads:

> These pretty Babes with hand in hand
> Went wandering up and down;
> But never more they saw the Man
> Approaching from the Town.

It is hard to see what Wordsworth considers the key distinction between the two if it is not the expression "never more." In choosing to have the raven repeat the single word "nevermore," Poe may well have put his finger on something fundamental about the poetic function as a correlative, precisely, of loss.

If the word "nevermore" stands in Poe as a figure for poetic language as such, a number of theoretical implications can be drawn. Since the bird is not human, the word is proffered as a pure signifier, empty of human intentionality, a pure poetic cliché. The empty repetition of the word therefore dramatizes the theoretical priority of the signifier over the signified which Poe claimed when he said that he began the text of the poem with the letters *o* and *r*. The plot of "The Raven" can be read as the story of what happens when the signifier encounters a reader. For the narrator of the poem first introduces himself as a reader, not a lover—a reader of "quaint and curious forgotten lore." Poe's claim, in "The Philosophy of Composition," that the poem was written backwards (commencing with its *effect*) applies both to the poem and to the essay about it: both are depictions not of the writing but of the reading of "The Raven."

The poem's status as mechanical repetition is signified in another way as well. It would be hard to find a poem (except perhaps "Strange Fits of Passion") which is packed with more clichés than "The Raven": ember, remember, December, midnight, darkness, marble busts—all the bric-a-brac of poetic language is set out in jangling, alliterative trochees to hammer out a kind of ur-background of the gothic encounter. And the conversation begins in pure politeness: "Tell me what thy lordly name is," asks the speaker of the bird, and the bird says, "Nevermore."

The poem within the poem—the single word "nevermore"—has at this point finally been spoken and the reader sets out to interpret it. He begins by finding it obscure:

> Much I marveled this ungainly fowl to hear discourse so plainly,
> Though its answer little meaning—little relevancy bore.

Then he tries a little biographical criticism:

> "Doubtless," said I, "what it utters is its only stock and store
> Caught from some unhappy master whom unmerciful Disaster
> Followed fast and followed faster....

Sinking onto a velvet couch, the reader then turns to free association "linking fancy unto fancy"—until the air grows denser and the reader sees the bird as a messenger of forgetfulness (psychoanalytic criticism), to which the Raven's "nevermore" comes as a contradiction. It is at this point that the reader begins to ask questions to which the expected "nevermore" comes as a ferociously desired and feared answer. The reader cannot leave the signifier alone. Reader-response criticism has set in. In this way, he writes his own story around the signifier, letting it seal the letter of his fate until, finally, it utterly incorporates him:

> And my soul from out that shadow that lies floating on the floor
> Shall be lifted—nevermore.

Sense has been made through the absorption of the subject by the signifier. The poem has sealed, without healing, the trauma of loss. What began as a signifier empty of subjectivity has become a container for the whole of the reader's soul. A poetry of the pure signifier is just as impossible to maintain as a poetry of the pure signified. Repetition engenders its own compulsion-to-sense. Poetry works *because* the signifier cannot remain empty—because, not in spite, of the mechanical nature of its artifice.

Paradoxically, then, Poe is writing a highly artificial poem that describes the signifier as an artifice that somehow captures the genuine. Yet generations of American readers have responded to it backwards: rejecting it for the artifice its own genuineness is demystifying. It cannot communicate its insight about how poems work if it does not work as a poem. Yet if the poem worked better, it would not carry the insight it carries.

Wordsworth and Poe are thus telling symmetrically inverse stories about the nature of poetic language. Wordsworth attempts to prevent the poetic figure from losing its natural passion, from repeating itself as an empty, mechanical device of style. But the formula for recollection in tranquillity involves just such a blind, mechanical repetition of the lost language. Poe writes a poem packed with clichés in order to show that those clichés cannot succeed in remaining empty, that there is also a natural passion involved in repetition, that the mechanical is of a piece with the profoundest pain. Yet the poem's very success in embodying its message entails its failure to make it true. If it were possible to differentiate clearly between the mechanical and the passionate, between the empty and the full, between the fit and the fit, between "real" language and "adulterated phraseology," there would probably be no need for extensive treatises on the nature of poetic language. But there would also, no doubt, be no need for poetry.

Notes

1. I shall refer to the 1805 version of the preface, as printed in *Wordsworth's Literary Criticism*, ed. W.J.B. Owen (London: Routledge & Kegan Paul, 1974). The "Philosophy of

Composition" appears in *The Unabridged Edgar Allan Poe* (Philadelphia: Running Press, 1983).

2. E.g.: "I hope that there is in these Poems little falsehood of description, and that my ideas are expressed in language *fitted* to their respective importance" (p. 75); "If the Poet's subject be judiciously chosen, it will naturally, and upon *fit* occasion, lead him to passions the language of which, if selected truly and judiciously, must necessarily be dignified and variegated, and live with metaphors and figures" (p. 77); "As it is impossible for the Poet to produce upon all occasions language as exquisitely *fitted for the passion* as that which the real passion suggests, it is proper that he should consider himself as in the situation of a translator" (p. 79). The question then becomes, "Is every fit that fits fit?"

3. In addition to its meaning of "outburst," *fit* can also refer to an arrest, a stroke, a hiatus. Silas Marner's strange fits, for example, freeze him in stop-action stillness while the rest of life continues around him. That the notion of "fits" carries with it a suggestion of the supernatural or the mysterious is indicated by George Eliot's report of folk belief: "Some said that Marner must have been in a 'fit,' a word which seemed to explain things otherwise incredible." *Silas Marner* (Penguin ed.), p. 55.

4. Cf. Geoffrey Hartman: "To take the moon's drop as the direct cause of the thought assumes that the lover has identified his beloved with the moon." *Wordsworth's Poetry* (New Haven: Yale University Press, 1964), p. 23. The imputation of a suppressed personification here implies that Lucy herself is a person. But is she? The long-standing and unresolved debate over the identity of Wordsworth's Lucy would suggest that Lucy is already in fact not a person but a personification. For a fascinating conceptualization of the question of rhetorically mediate, "naturalized" personifications (that is, those that are made to seem real, "found" rather than allegorically made) and their relation to eighteenth-century allegory, see Steven Knapp, *Personification and the Sublime* (Cambridge: Harvard University Press, 1985). At one point Knapp essentially uses the notion of a "strange fit" to refer to the Wordsworthian sublime: "Sometimes—and most strikingly in episodes of naturalized personification—the gap between two moments is replaced by a curious *lack of fit* between two ways of perceiving a single object" (p. 100).

5. It might be objected that this is not the type of personification Wordsworth had in mind, that what he wished to avoid was personifications of abstract ideas, not celestial bodies. Yet the example of bad personification Wordsworth cites in the preface *does* in fact involve celestial bodies, not abstract ideas. In the sonnet by Gray in which Wordsworth italicizes only the parts he considers valuable, it is the personification of the sun and of the natural world ("reddening Phoebus lifts his golden fire," etc.) that Wordsworth does *not* italicize.

6. A very suggestive gloss on what is unsettling in Wordsworth's rejection of personification is given by Frances Ferguson: "The insistence of the cottage girl in 'We are Seven' that she and her dead siblings are not separated from one another by death involves a kind of personification, but it is personification pushed to such an extreme that it becomes a virtual anti-type to personification. This girl personifies *persons*, and the radically disquieting element in her remarks is the growing consciousness in the poem that persons should need to be personified, should need to be reclaimed from death by the imagination. Her version of personification revolves around death as the essential abstract idea behind personification. Persons and personifications become united members in the community of the living and the dead." Frances Ferguson, *Wordsworth: Language as Counter-Spirit* (New Haven: Yale University Press, 1977), pp. 26–27.

DAVID S. REYNOLDS

Poe's Art of Transformation:
"The Cask of Amontillado" in Its Cultural Context

"The Cask of Amontillado" is a prime example of Poe's ability to sculpt materials from popular literature and culture into a masterwork of terror. At once derivative and freshly individualistic, the tale enacts Poe's belief that "the truest and surest test of originality is the manner of handling a hackneyed subject."[1]

It has long been surmised that this story of murderous revenge reflects Poe's vindictive hatred of two prominent New York literary figures, the author Thomas Dunn English and the newspaper editor Hiram Fuller.[2] If "The Cask" is, on some level, a retaliatory document, surely Poe could not have envisioned a more ghoulish type of retaliation. Seen against the background of the war of the literati, the narrator Montresor (Poe) gets back at his enemy Fortunato (English) for a recent insult, using their mutual friend Luchesi (Fuller) as a foil in his scheme. Although we know from the start that Montresor is bent on revenge, and we have ominous feelings as he takes his foe into the depths of his skeleton-filled wine vaults, the tale's atmosphere is deceptively convivial; the two connoisseurs banter and drink as they go in search of the cask of Amontillado (a fine Spanish sherry) Montresor says he has received. Only when Montresor lures Fortunato into a small niche, quickly chains up his stupefied victim, and proceeds to wall up the niche with bricks and mortar are we overwhelmed by the horrifying fact of live burial.

From *New Essays on Poe's Major Tales*, edited by Kenneth Silverman. ©1993 by Cambridge University Press.

Poe's animus against the literati may have motivated the revenge theme, but it fails to account for specific details of plot, character, and imagery. For those we must look to the tale's popular cultural context. Poe was a great borrower, and he had an eye on the popular market. On one level, his terror tales were clearly designed to cater to a public increasingly enamored of horror and sensationalism.[3] Writing in the era of the crime-filled penny papers and mass-produced pamphlet novels, he was well aware of the demands of the sensation-loving public. His letters are peppered with excited boasts about some work of his that has made a "sensation" or a "hit." In his tale "The Psyche Zenobia," he had the editor of a popular magazine declare: "Sensations are the great thing after all. Should you ever be drowned or hung, be sure and make a note of your sensations—they will be worth to you ten guineas a sheet" (340). Following the lead of the sensation mongers, Poe made use of some of the wildest situations imaginable.

One such situation was live burial. In "The Premature Burial" Poe wrote that "*no* event is so terribly well adapted to inspire the supremeness of bodily and of mental distress, as is burial before death," a topic that creates "a degree of appalling and intolerable horror from which the most daring imagination must recoil" (961). The specific work which established the premise of "The Cask of Amontillado" was Joel Tyler Headley's "A Man Built in a Wall," first published in the *Columbian Magazine* in 1844 and collected in Headley's *Letters from Italy* (1845).[4] Headley reports having visited an Italian church containing a niche in which was discovered the skeleton of a man who had been buried alive by a workman under the direction of the man's smirking archenemy. After a detailed description of the grotesque posture of the skeleton, suggesting an excruciatingly painful death, Headley recreates the murder:

> The workman began at the feet, and with his mortar and trowel built up with the same carelessness he would exhibit in filling any broken wall. The successful enemy stood leaning on his sword—a smile of scorn and revenge on his features—and watched the face of the man he hated, but no longer feared.... It was slow work fitting the pieces nicely, so as to close up the aperture with precision.... With care and precision the last stone was fitted in the narrow space—the trowel passed smoothly over it—a stifled groan, as if from the centre of a rock, broke the stillness—one strong shiver, and all was over. The agony had passed—revenge was satisfied, and a secret locked up for the great revelation day.

Several details in Headley's piece—the premise of live burial in a hidden niche, the careful placement of the bricks, the revenge motive, the victim's agonized groaning and numbed stillness—anticipate "The Cask of Amontillado."

Also analogous to Poe's story is Honoré de Balzac's "La Grande Bretêche," an adaptation of which appeared in the *Democratic Review* in November 1843. Balzac describes a jealous husband who, on discovering that his wife's lover is hiding in her closet, has the closet walled up as the lady watches. Poe most likely also knew the story "Apropos of Bores" (*New-York Mirror*, December 2, 1837), in which a man at a party tells of going with a porter into the vast wine vaults of Lincoln's Inn to view several pipes of Madeira that were stored there. They found the pipes in good condition but had a terrifying accident: When their candle was extinguished, they groped to the cellar door only to have the key break off in the lock. They impulsively decided to forget their sorrows by staving in a wine pipe and getting drunk in order to forget "the horrible death that awaits us." Giving up this impulse, they soberly faced the fact that their remains would not be discovered until all traces of identity were destroyed. We never learn the outcome of the tale, for the narrator and his listeners are called to tea before he is finished.

Another predecessor of Poe's tale, hitherto unacknowledged, was the sensational best-seller *The Quaker City; or The Monks of Monk Hall* (1845) by George Lippard, Poe's friend from his Philadelphia days.[5] Monk Hall, a huge mansion where Philadelphia's prominent citizens gather in secret revels and debauchery, has below it a so-called "dead-vault," a vast cellar with labyrinthine passages and hidden recesses. The cellar is anticipatory of the vast vault beneath Montresor's mansion in several ways: It is lined with countless skeletons, its walls are clammy with moisture, and it is the scene of live burial. One critic has called "absurd" Poe's notion in "Cask" of "an ossuary ... gruesomely combined with the appurtenances of a wine cellar,"[6] but many of Poe's contemporary readers had been prepared for such an odd coupling by the description of Monk Hall, where not only are the wine cellar and dead-vault side-by-side but the dead-vault is littered with liquor bottles strewn amid the skeletons. In a scene that presages Montresor's long descent with his victim into the catacombs, Devil-Bug, the sadistic keeper of Monk Hall, slowly takes a victim, Luke Harvey, down an extensive staircase into the depths of the dead-vault. Hardly as subtle as Montresor, Devil-Bug mutters to his victim, "I am a-goin' to bury you alive! D'ye hear that? I'm a-goin' to bury you alive!"[7] Just as Montresor howls and laughs at the enchained Fortunato, so Devil-Bug takes noisy pleasure in the sufferings of his victim. "He shrieked forth a horrible peal of laughter, more like the howl of a hyena, than the sound of a human, laugh." Unlike Montresor, Devil-Bug does not succeed in his murderous scheme; his intended victim escapes. Devil-Bug, however, is haunted by the vision of a previous murder victim, just as (according to one reading) Montresor is tortured by the recollection of his crime.

A larger cultural phenomenon that influenced Poe was the temperance movement, which produced a body of literature and lectures filled with the kinds of horrifying images that fascinated him. Poe's bouts with the bottle, leading eventually to his death, are well known. Less familiar is Poe's ambiguous relationship with the American temperance movement. In the 1830s Poe had befriended the Baltimore writer John Lofland, who delivered temperance lectures even though, like several other backsliding reformers of the period, he drank and took drugs in private. Another of Poe's acquaintances, Timothy Shay Arthur, wrote some of the most popular (and darkest) temperance tales of the day, including *Six Nights with the Washingtonians* (1842) and *Ten Nights in a Bar-room* (1854). In the early 1840s, the rise of the Washingtonians—reformed drunkards who told grisly tales of alcoholism in an effort to frighten listeners into signing a pledge of abstinence—brought to temperance rhetoric a new sensationalism. Walt Whitman's novel *Franklin Evans* (1842), for example, written on commission for the Washingtonians, luridly depicts the ill results of alcohol, including shattered homes, infanticide, crushing poverty that leads to crime, and delirium tremens with its nightmare visions. Poe had direct association with the Washingtonians. In 1843, after a period of heavy drinking, he promised a temperance friend from whom he hoped to gain a political appointment that he would join the Washingtonians. Whether or not he did so at that time, he did join a related group, the Sons of Temperance, in the last year of his life. When on August 31, 1849 the *Banner of Temperance* announced Poe's initiation into the order, it said: "We trust his pen will sometimes be employed in its behalf. A vast amount of good might be accomplished by so pungent and forcible a writer."[8]

What the *Banner of Temperance* neglected to say was that Poe had already written temperance fiction, or more precisely, his own version of what I would call dark temperance, a popular mode that left didacticism behind and emphasized the perverse results of alcoholism. Following the lead of many dark temperance writers who portrayed once-happy families ripped asunder by a husband's inebriety, Poe in "The Black Cat" (1843) dramatized alcohol's ravages on an initially peaceful couple. The narrator tells us that he had once been known for his docility and gentleness but that his character—"through the instrumentality of the Fiend Intemperance—

had (I blush to confess it) experienced a radical alteration for the worse. I grew, day by day, more moody, more irritable, more regardless of the feelings of others" (851). As in popular temperance literature, the first sip is followed by escalating pathological behavior. The narrator declares that "my disease grew upon me—for what disease is like Alcohol!" (851). One night a "fiendish malevolence, gin-nurtured" impels him to cut out the eye of his cat with a pen-knife, a deed he tries unsuccessfully to drown in wine. Before long he has been driven by alcohol to paranoia and crime, even to the extent of murdering his wife.

"The Cask of Amontillado" also studies the diseased psyche associated with alcohol. Everything in the story revolves around alcohol obsession. The object of the descent into the vault is a pipe of wine. Both of the main characters are wine connoisseurs, as is their mentioned friend Luchesi. The narrator, Montresor, boasts, "I was skilful in the Italian vintages myself, and bought largely whenever I could."[9] As for Fortunato, he is so vain about his knowledge of wine and so fixated on the supposed Amontillado that he goes willingly to his own destruction. When we meet him, we learn "he had been drinking much" in the carnival revelry, and as he walks unsteadily into the vault his eyes look like "two filmy orbs that distilled the rheum of intoxication." He gets drunker after sharing the bottle of Médoc that Montresor breaks open in the cellar, and even more so when he subsequently gulps down the flacon of De Grave (one of several puns that point to his fate).

Fortunato's name has a double meaning: from his perspective, he is "fortunate" to have an opportunity to show off his expertise in wines; from the reader's viewpoint, it is his bad "fortune" to be sucked to doom by his overriding interest in liquor.[10] Poe's contemporary readers, accustomed to dark temperance rhetoric, would have found special significance in the interweaving of alcohol and death images in passages like this:

> The wine sparkled in his eyes and the bells jingled.
> My own fancy grew warm with Médoc. We had passed through walls of piled bones, with casks and puncheons intermingling, into the inmost depths of the catacombs.

The jingling of the bells reminds us of the fool Fortunato has become because of his destructive obsession. The wine-instilled agitation of Montresor's fancy reflects his role in this devilish communion, while the intermingled casks and bones, besides recalling Lippard's Monk Hall, enhance the eerie dark temperance atmosphere. After Montresor chains

Fortunato to the wall, their dialogue takes on a dreary circularity that shows once again the importance of alcohol obsession to the story. "The Amontillado!" exclaims the victim; "True, the Amontillado," replies the murderer. Even after he has been walled in, the hapless Fortunato, in a desperate attempt to pass off the situation as a joke, returns to the subject of drinking:

> "We will have many a rich laugh about it at the palazzo—he! he! he!—over our wine—he! he! he!"
> "The Amontillado!" I said.
> "He! he! he!—he! he! he!—yes, the Amontillado!"

The dark temperance mode gives the tale a grim inevitability and another cultural phenomenon—anti-Masonry—contributes to its black humor and mysterious aura. At the center of the story is a dialogue that shows Poe tapping into his contemporaries' concerns about the Masons, a private all-male order widely thought to be involved in heinous crime. After drinking the bottle of De Grave, Fortunato throws it upward with a grotesque gesture Montresor does not understand.

> "You do not comprehend?" he said.
> "Not I," I replied.
> "Then you are not of the brotherhood."
> "How?"
> "You are not of the masons."
> "Yes, yes," I said, "yes, yes."
> "You? Impossible! A mason?"
> "A mason," I replied.
> "A sign," he said.
> "It is this," I answered, producing a trowel from beneath the fold of my *roquelaire*.
> "You jest," he exclaimed, recoiling a few paces. "But let us proceed to the Amontillado."

This marvelous moment of black humor has a range of historical associations rooted in the anti-Masonry mania that had swept America during Poe's apprentice period. The pun on "mason" (referring both to the fraternal order and to a worker in brick and stone) seems to have a specific historical referent. At the center of the Masonry controversy was one William Morgan, a brick-and-stone mason of Batavia, New York, who in 1826, after thirty years of membership in the Masons, was determined to publish a harsh exposé of the order but was silenced before he could, most likely by vindictive members of the order. Morgan's disappearance was wreathed in mystery. One night in September 1826 he was seized, gagged, and spirited away in a carriage to the Niagara frontier, where all trace of him was lost. The story spread that a group of Masons, viewing Morgan as a traitor, had drowned him in the Niagara River. (It is perhaps meaningful, in this context, that Montresor leads his victim "below the river bed.") Anti-Masonry sentiment snowballed and became a substantial political movement, peaking in the mid-1830s and then feeding into the ascendant Whig party. The Masonic order was viewed as undemocratic and as a tangible threat to American institutions. In particular, its oath, whereby members swore to uphold rational secular values (without reference to God or Christianity), was seen as sacrilegious. When Poe has Fortunato make a "grotesque" movement signaling membership in the order, he is introducing a sign that many of his readers would have regarded as demonic. When Montresor gives the sign of the trowel, he is not only foretelling the story's climax but is also summoning up the associations of brick-and-stone masonry, murderous revenge, and mysterious disappearance surrounding American Masonry.

So central is the Masonic image that the tale has been interpreted as an enactment of the historical conflict between Catholics and Masons. In this reading, Fortunato's real crime is that he is a Mason, whereas Montresor, a Roman Catholic, assumes a perverted priestly function in his ritualistic murder of his Masonic foe.[11] It should be pointed out, however, that in the predominantly evangelical Protestant America of Poe's day *both* Masons and Catholics were held suspect. If anti-Masonic feeling feeds into the portrait of Fortunato, anti-Catholic sentiment lies behind several of the grim images in the tale. In the 1830s and 1840s, American Protestant authors, fearful of the rapid growth of the Catholic church with the sudden flood of immigrants arriving from abroad, produced a large body of lurid literature aimed at exposing alleged depravity and criminality among Catholics. In 1838 one alarmed commentator wrote of the "tales of lust, and blood, and murder ... with which the ultra-protestant is teeming."[12] Of special interest in connection with Poe's tale is Maria Monk's best-selling *Awful Disclosures of ... the Hotel Dieu Nunnery at Montreal* (1836), which featured a huge cellar that served as both a torture chamber and a tomb, where priests had killed some 375 people and cast their remains into a lime pit. Whether or not Poe had Maria Monk and her ilk in mind when he concocted his tale of torture behind cellar walls, it is notable that he made use of Catholic images: The story is set during the *Carnivale*, a Catholic season just before Lent; Montresor's family motto about the heel crushing the serpent refers to

Genesis 3:14 (the curse upon the serpent) and historically symbolizes the Church militant triumphing over the forces of evil; the early history of the Church is recalled when the underground passages are called "catacombs"; and the final words, "*In pace requiescat!*" are the last words of a requiem mass. The Catholic connection is further strengthened if we accept the idea that Poe derived the name Montresor from an old French Catholic family.[13] Although not explicitly anti-Catholic, the tale combines religious and criminal imagery in a way reminiscent of the anti-Catholic best-sellers of the day.

Though grounded in nineteenth-century American culture, "The Cask of Amontillado" transcends its time-specific referents because it is crafted in such a way that it remains accessible to generations of readers unfamiliar with such sources as anti-Catholicism, temperance, and live-burial literature. The special power of the tale can be understood if we take into account Poe's theories about fiction writing, developed largely in response to emerging forms of popular literature that aroused both his interest and his concern. On the one hand, as a literary professional writing for popular periodicals ("Cask" appeared in the most popular of all, *Godey's Lady's Book*) Poe had to keep in mind the demands of an American public increasingly hungry for sensation. On the other hand, as a scrupulous craftsman he was profoundly dissatisfied with the way in which other writers handled sensational topics. John Neal's volcanic, intentionally disruptive fiction seemed energetic but formless to Poe, who saw in it "no precision, no finish ... —always an excessive force but little of refined art."[14] Similarly, he wrote of the blackly humorous stories in Washington Irving's *Tales of a Traveller* that "the interest is subdivided and frittered away, and their conclusions are insufficiently *climacic* [sic]" (*ER*, 586–7). George Lippard's *The Ladye Annabel*, a dizzying novel involving medieval torture and necrophilic visions, struck him as indicative of genius yet chaotic. A serial novel by Edward Bulwer-Lytton wearied him with its "continual and vexatious shifting of scene," while N.P. Willis's sensational play *Tortesa* exhibited "the great error" of "*inconsequence*. Underplot is piled on underplot," as Willis gives us "vast designs that terminate in nothing" (*ER*, 153, 367).

In his own fiction Poe tried to correct the mistakes he saw in other writers. The good plot, he argued, was that from which nothing can be taken without detriment to the whole. If, as he rightly pointed out, much sensational fiction of the day was digressive and directionless, his best tales were tightly unified. Of them all, "The Cask of Amontillado" perhaps most clearly exemplifies the unity he aimed for.

The tale's compactness becomes instantly apparent when we compare it with the popular live-burial works mentioned earlier. Headley's journalistic "A Man Built in a Wall" begins with a long passage about a lonely Italian inn and ends with an account of the countryside around Florence; the interpolated story about the entombed man dwells as much on the gruesome skeleton as on the vindictive crime. Balzac's "La Grande Bretêche" is a slowly developing tale in which the narrator gets mixed accounts about an old abandoned mansion near the Loire; only in the second half of the story does he learn from his landlady that the mansion had been the scene of a live burial involving a husband's jealous revenge. The entombment in "Apropos of Bores" is purely accidental (two unlucky men find themselves trapped in a wine vault) and is reduced to frivolous chatter when the narrator breaks off at the climactic moment and his listeners crack jokes and disperse to tea. Closest in spirit to Poe, perhaps, is the "dead-vault" scene in Lippard's *The Quaker City*: There is the same ritualistic descent into an immense cellar by a sadistic murderer intent on burying his victim alive. Lippard, however, constantly interrupts the scene with extraneous descriptions (he's especially fascinated by the skeletons and caskets strewn around the cellar). In addition, this is just one of countless bloodcurdling scenes in a meandering novel light-years distant, structurally, from Poe's carefully honed tale.

So tightly woven is "The Cask" that it may be seen as an effort at literary one-upsmanship on Poe's part, designed pointedly as a contrast to other, more casually constructed live-burial pieces. In his essays on popular literature, Poe expressed particular impatience with irrelevancies of plot or character. For instance, commenting on J.H. Ingraham's perfervid best-seller *Lafitte, the Pirate of the Gulf*, he wrote: "We are surfeited with unnecessary details.... Of outlines there are none. Not a dog yelps, unsung" (*ER*, 611).

There is absolutely no excess in "The Cask of Amontillado." Every sentence points inexorably to the horrifying climax. In the interest of achieving unity, Poe purposely leaves several questions unanswered. The tale is remarkable for what it leaves out. What are the "thousand injuries" Montresor has suffered at the hands of Fortunato? In particular, what was the "insult" that has driven Montresor to the grisly extreme of murder by live burial? What personal misfortune is he referring to when he tells his foe, "you are happy, as I once was"? Like a painter who leaves a lot of suggestive white canvas, Poe sketches character and setting lightly, excluding excess material. Even so simple a detail as the location of the action is unknown. Most assume the setting is Italy, but one commentator makes a good case for France.[15] What do we know about the main characters? As discussed, both are bibulous and proud of their connoisseurship in wines. Fortunato, besides being a Mason, is "rich, respected, admired, beloved," and there is a Lady Fortunato,who will miss him. Montresor is descended from "a great and numerous family" and is wealthy enough to sustain a palazzo, servants, and extensive wine vaults.

Other than that, Poe tells very little about the two. Both exist solely to fulfill the imperatives of the plot Poe has designed. Everything Montresor does and says furthers his strategy of luring his enemy to his death. Everything Fortunato does and says reveals the fatuous extremes his vanity about wines will lead him to. Though limited, these characters are not what E.M. Forster would call flat. They swiftly come alive before our eyes because Poe describes them with acute psychological realism. Montresor is a complex Machiavellian criminal, exhibiting a full range of traits from clever ingratiation to stark sadism. Fortunato, the dupe whose pride leads to his own downfall, nevertheless exhibits enough admirable qualities that one critic has seen him as a wronged man of courtesy and good will.[16] The drama of the story lies in the carefully orchestrated interaction between the two. Poe directs our attention away from the merely sensational and toward the psychological.

Herein lies another key difference between the tale and its precursors. In none of the popular live-burial works is the *psychology* of revenge a factor. In Headley and Lippard, the victim is unconscious and thus incognizant of the murderer's designs; similarly, in Balzac there is no communication at all between the murderer and the entombed. In Poe, the relationship between the two is, to a large degree, the story. Montresor says at the start, murder is most successful if the victim is made painfully aware of what is happening: "A wrong is unredressed ... when the avenger fails to make himself felt as such to him who has done the wrong."[17] By focusing on the process of vanity falling prey to sly revenge, Poe shifts attention to psychological subtleties ignored by the other live-burial writers.

Particularly intriguing are the brilliantly cruel ploys of Montresor. An adept in what today is called reverse psychology, Montresor never once invites Fortunato to his home or his wine vaults. Instead, he cleverly plays on his victim's vanity so that it is Fortunato who is always begging to go forward into the vaults. Montresor merely says he has received a pipe of "what passes for Amontillado," that he has his doubts, and that, since Fortunato is engaged, he is on his way to consult another connoisseur, Luchesi. By arousing vanity and introducing the element of competition ("Luchesi cannot tell Amontillado from Sherry," grumbles Fortunato[18]), Montresor never needs to push his victim toward destruction. It is the victim who does all the pushing, while the murderer repeatedly gives reasons why the journey into the cellar should be called off. This ironic role reversal begins when Fortunato, whose curiosity is piqued, demands: "Come, let us go."

> "Whither?" [asks Montresor.]
> "To your vaults."
> "My friend, no; I will not impose on your good nature. I perceive you have an engagement. Luchesi—"
> "I have no engagement;—come."
> "My friend, no. It is not the engagement, but the severe cold with which I perceive you are afflicted. The vaults are insufferably damp. They are encrusted with nitre."
> "Let us go, nevertheless. The cold is merely nothing."

And so, as Montresor tells us, "I suffered him to hurry me to my palazzo." Reverse psychology governs even Montresor's advance preparations for the murder: The palazzo is empty because he has told his servants they should not stir from the house since he would be away all night—an order "sufficient, I well knew, to insure their immediate disappearance, one and all, as soon as my back was turned." As he and Fortunato enter the vaults, he points out the white web-work of niter gleaming on the cavern walls. The mention of the niter makes Fortunato cough convulsively, at which Montresor makes a show of compassion: "'Come,'" I said, with decision, "'we will go back; your health is precious.'" Fortunato is resolved to go on, however, even when they pass by piles of bones. Montresor again tells him: "'Come, we will go back ere it is too late. Your cough—,'" but Fortunato doggedly drags forward. Only when he is chained to the wall does the savage irony of the situation become clear. Montresor invites him to feel the damp niter of the wall and repeats: "Once more let me *implore* you to return. No? Then I must positively leave you. But I must first render you all the little attentions in my power." Montresor's show of concern for Fortunato is at last revealed as a craftily designed cover for murderous resolve.

There is a rigorous logic about the imagery Poe deploys in the tale. By far the most important image is the carnival. Virtually the only fact made known to us exterior to the central action or characters is that it is carnival season. When we consider the effect Poe is trying to create, we see how shrewd a choice the carnival is as a central image. To celebrate the carnival, Fortunato is dressed in motley, with a tight parti-colored costume and a conical cap and bells. His clownish dress is an apt symbol of his obtuseness as he becomes Montresor's willing dupe. The bells on his fool's cap jingle at key moments: when he first enters the catacombs; when he drinks the Médoc; and after he has been completely walled in and has given up hope. For Montresor, the carnival provides the opportunity for a perfect disguise. Before returning to his palazzo with Fortunato; Montresor dons a black silk mask and draws about him a cape, beneath which, we later learn, he has concealed a rapier and a trowel. His costume not only reflects his villainous intent but also facilitates his announced plan of murdering Fortunato with impunity: Who would know Montresor was with Fortunato the night of the latter's disappearance if both were in carnival disguise?

Yet another effect of the carnival image is to highlight, by way of contrast, Poe's terrifying climax. Fortunato's haughtiness and high spirits at the beginning of the tale bespeak a noted man of society enjoying the pleasures of the season with his wife and friends. By the end, Fortunato is in precisely the opposite of a carnival atmosphere. He faces the prospect of total isolation, degradation, and death by starvation or suffocation. Nothing could be more pathetic than his attempt to revive a carnivalesque conviviality. He calls his predicament a fine joke that will raise many a laugh over wine at the palazzo. The carnival image is now a bitter mockery of the horrid fate he confronts.

Other tokens of Poe's craftsmanship are the puns and double meanings that abound in the tale, puns that take on full significance only in retrospect, when we reach the gruesome ending. Montresor's initial greeting—"My dear Fortunato, how luckily you are met"—makes an ironic pun on Fortunato's name ("lucky") and underscores how *un*lucky Fortunato actually is. Another black joke comes when in the vault Fortunato shrugs off his bad cough: "it will not kill me. I shall not die of a cough." In light of the story's conclusion, Montresor's response is at once funny and foreboding: "True—true." It is ironic that Fortunato should raise a toast to "the buried that repose around us" (he will soon be joining them!) and equally so that Montresor replies with a toast "to your long life." A final devastating pun comes when the enchained Fortunato, in his pathetic effort to escape, says with feigned casualness, "Let us be gone." Montresor's loaded reply rings like a death knell: "Yes, let us be gone."

The double meanings surrounding the discussion of Montresor's family arms are especially telling. The arms has two contrasting meanings, dependent on perspective. The "huge human foot d'or, in a field of azure" that crushes a "serpent rampant" could stand for Fortunato, whom Montresor views as an oppressive weight to be gotten rid of: from this vantage point, the serpent's fangs embedded in the heel are symbolic of the vengeful Montresor. From a different perspective, the huge destructive foot may be said to represent Montresor's present murderous act, and the embedded fangs are the pangs of conscience he will have to live with for the rest of his life. The two perspectives illuminate different sides of Montresor's character, which is more complicated than it first appears. One side of Montresor tells him that his act of revenge is completely justified in light of the "thousand injuries" he has suffered. This side prompts his sham compassion, his wicked puns, and his sadistic behavior once Fortunato is chained up. The other side of him, which manifests itself three times toward the end of the tale, says that he himself will have to suffer as much as his victim. When the enchained Fortunato lets out a series of loud, shrill screams, Montresor recalls, "For a brief moment I hesitated—I trembled." He then reassumes his sadistic posture, screaming even louder than his victim. Soon he pauses again, hearing the low laugh that "erected the hairs upon my head" and the "sad voice" hardly recognizable as Fortunato's. He becomes cruel again, drily repeating Fortunato's vain jokes about returning to the palazzo. But when his final call to his victim is answered only by a jingling of bells, "My heart grew sick," a confession only partly retrieved from actual compassion by the half-hearted explanation "—on account of the catacombs."

These moments when Montresor second-guesses himself have led some commentators to predict an unhappy future for him. "*In pace requiescat!*" Montresor says in conclusion, but, as Thomas O. Mabbott points out, these words may be ironic: "Fortunato had rested in peace for fifty years; Montresor must always have feared being found out" (1265–6). Does Montresor become the haunted criminal fearful of discovery, or does his callousness intensify and smother any residual feelings of remorse? Is the tale a moral exemplum on the wages of crime, or is it a gleeful portrait of a successful murder? One group of critics sees the tale as the deathbed confession of a criminal who has been tortured by guilt for fifty years.[19] According to them, Montresor's stated goal of punishing his foe with impunity is an ironic comment on the fact that Montresor himself has never been able to escape the punishment of his own conscience. In contrast, another group sees Montresor as an unrepentant pathological killer whose crime is a source of power for him and a source of vicarious satisfaction for Poe and the reader.[20]

Is "The Cask of Amontillado" intensely moralistic or frighteningly amoral? These questions, I would say, are finally unresolvable, and their very unresolvability reflects profound paradoxes within the antebellum cultural phenomena that lie behind the tale. A fundamental feature of anti-Catholic novels, dark temperance literature, and reform novels like Lippard's *The*

Quaker City is that they invariably proclaimed themselves pure and moralistic but were criticized, with justification, for being violent and perverse. Many popular American writers of Poe's day Wallowed in foul moral sewers with the announced intent of scouring them clean, but their seamy texts prove that they were more interested in wallowing than in cleaning. This paradox of immoral didacticism, as I have called it elsewhere,[21] helps account for the hermeneutic circularities of "The Cask of Amontillado." On the one hand, there is evidence for a moral or even religious reading: The second sentence, "You, who know so well the nature of my soul," may be addressed to a priest to whom Montresor, now an old man, is confessing in an effort to gain deathbed expiation. On the other hand, there is no explicit moralizing, and the tale reveals an undeniable fascination with the details of cunning crime. Transforming the cultural phenomenon of immoral didacticism into a polyvalent dramatization of pathological behavior, Poe has it both ways: He satisfies the most fiendish fantasies of sensation lovers (including himself, at a time when revenge was on his mind), still retaining an aura of moral purpose. He thus serves two types of readers simultaneously: the sensationally inclined, curious about this cleverest of killers, and the religiously inclined, expectant that such a killer will eventually get his due. In the final analysis, he is pointing to the possibility that these ostensibly different kinds of readers are one and the same. Even the most devoutly religious reader, ready to grab at a moral lesson, could not help being intrigued by, and on some level moved by, this deftly told record of shrewd criminality.

Poe had famously objected to fiction that struck him as too allegorical, fiction in which imagery pointed too obviously to some exterior meaning, and had stressed that the province of literary art was not meaning but effect, not truth but pleasure. Effect is what a tale like "The Cask of Amontillado" is about. An overwhelming effect of terror is produced by this tightly knit tale that reverberates with psychological and moral implications. Curiosity and an odd kind of pleasure are stimulated by the interlocking images, by the puns and double meanings, and, surprisingly, by the ultimate humanity of the seemingly inhuman characters. Fortunato's emotional contortions as he is chained to the wall are truly frightening; they reveal depths in his character his previous cockiness had concealed. Montresor's moments of wavering suggest that Poe is delving beneath the surface of the stock revenge figure to reveal inchoate feelings of self-doubt and guilt. Unlike his many precursors in popular culture, Poe doesn't just entertain us with skeletons in the cellar. He makes us contemplate ghosts in the soul.

NOTES

1. *Collected Works of Edgar Allan Poe*, ed. Thomas Ollive Mabbott (Cambridge: Harvard University Press, 1978), p. 802. Hereafter most references to the *Collected Works* will be cited parenthetically in the text.

2. Poe's acerbic commentary on the current literary scene in "The Literati of New York City," a six-part series that ran in *Godey's Lady's Book* from May through September 1846, prompted a violent rejoinder from Fuller, editor of the *New-York Mirror* and the *New-York Evening Mirror*. When Poe's derogatory article on English appeared in the July issue of *Godey's*, English wrote a slashing reply (published in Fuller's *Evening Mirror*) which heaped insults on Poe. After additional sallies in the press, Poe filed suit for libel against English on July 23, 1846. A few weeks after the suit was filed, English's novel *1844, or the Power of the 'S.F.'* began to appear serially in Fuller's newspaper. The novel contained a satirical portrait of Poe as Marmaduke Hammerhead, a drunken, pretentious literary fop. In this bitter atmosphere "The Cask of Amontillado" was written; the tale appeared in the November issue of *Godey's*. Poe won the libel suit on February 17, 1847, and was awarded $225. See Francis P. Dedmond, "'The Cask of Amontillado' and the War of the Literati," *Modern Language Quarterly* 15 (1954): 137–46. A rather overstated Freudian reading of the literary battles surrounding the tale is offered in Marie Bonaparte, *The Life and Works of Edgar Allan Poe: A Psycho-Analytic Interpretation* (London: Hogarth, 1971), pp. 505–6.

3. See my discussion of popular sensational literature in *Beneath the American Renaissance: The Subversive Imagination in the Age of Emerson and Melville* (New York: Knopf, 1988), pp. 169–248.

4. The August 1844 issue of the *Columbian Magazine* in which the Headley piece appeared also contained Poe's "Mesmeric Revelation." Poe reviewed Headley's *Letters from Italy* in the August 9, 1845, issue of the *Broadway Journal*. Headley's volume was the third in Wiley and Putnam's "Library of American Books," the second being Poe's *Tales* (1845). See Joseph S. Shick, "The Origin of 'The Cask of Amontillado,'" *American Literature*, 6 (1934): 18–21. See also Mabbott's introduction to "Cask" in *Collected Works*, pp. 1253–4.

5. Poe probably met Lippard in 1842 when he was working for *Graham's Magazine*, across the street from the Philadelphia *Spirit of the Times*, where Lippard was working at the time. Lippard's satirical series "The Spermaceti Papers," published in 1843 in the Philadelphia *Citizen Soldier*, singled Poe out for praise in his generally derisive portrait of the Graham group. For his part, Poe wrote Lippard a letter on February 18, 1844, praising Lippard's novel *The Ladye Annabel* as "richly inventive and imaginative—indicative of genius in its author." The friendship between the writers was still strong in the summer of 1849, when Poe, penniless and hungover, struggled up to Lippard's newspaper office begging for help. Although there is no record of Poe's having read *The Quaker City*, he very likely knew of this, his friend's most significant and most popular work, which sold some sixty thousand copies in 1845, the year before Poe wrote "Cask." See *George Lippard, Prophet of Protest: Writings of an American Radical, 1822–1854*, ed. David S. Reynolds (New York: Peter Lang, 1986), pp. 256–67, and Reynolds, *George Lippard* (Boston: Twayne, 1982), pp. 8–9, 18–19, 102–10.

6. Burton R. Pollin, *Discoveries in Poe* (Notre Dame: University of Notre Dame Press, 1970), p. 29.

7. Lippard, *The Monks of Monk Hall*, ed. Leslie Fiedler (New York: Odyssey, 1970), p. 301. The next quotation in this paragraph is from p. 310.

8. *The Poe Log: A Documentary Life of Edgar Allan Poe, 1809–1849*, ed. Dwight Thomas and David K. Jackson (Boston: G.K. Hall, 1987), p. 830.

9. Quotations from the "The Cask of Amontillado" are from *Collected Works*, pp. 1252–63.

10. The connection between Fortunato and self-destructive drunkenness is further underscored by Burton Pullin's discovery that Poe may have derived this character's name from a passage about a drunken man referred to as "*Fortunate senex*" in Victor Hugo's *Noire-Dame de Paris*. See Pollin, *Discoveries in Poe*, p. 31.

11. Kathryn Montgomery Harris, "Ironic Revenge in Poe's 'The Cask of Amontillado,'" *Studies in Short Fiction*, 6 (1969): 333–5.

12. David Meredith Reese, *Humbugs of New-York: Being a Remonstrance against Popular Delusion, Whether in Science, Philosophy, or Religion* (New York: John S. Taylor, 1838), p. 217.

13. See Pollin, *Discoveries in Poe*, p. 35. The Catholic connection is strengthened by yet another Montresor Poe may have been aware of: Jacques Montresor, a French officer in one of Benjamin Franklin's bagatelles who is depicted addressing a confessor just before his death. See William H. Shurr, "Montresor's Audience in 'The Cask of Amontillado,'" *Poe Studies*, 10 (1977): 28–9. However, E. Bruce Kirkham suggests the name comes from Captain John Montresor, a wealthy British engineering officer for whom New York's Montresor's island (now known as Randall's island) was named. See Kirkham, "Poe's 'Cask of Amontillado' and John Montresor," *Poe Studies*, 20 (1987): 23.

14. Poe, *Essays and Reviews* (New York: Library of America, 1984), p. 1151. This volume is hereafter cited parenthetically in the text as *ER*.

15. Pollin, *Discoveries in Poe*, pp. 29–33. Pollin points out that when Poe compares Montresor's crypts with "the great catacombs of Paris" he is revealing his awareness of contemporary accounts of the great necropolis under the Faubourg St. Jacques, in which the skeletal remains of some three million former denizens of Paris were piled along the walls. One such account had appeared in the "Editor's Table" of the *Knickerbocker Magazine* for March 1838. Pollin also develops parallels between "The Cask" and Victor Hugo's *Notre-Dame de Paris*, a novel Poe knew well.

16. Joy Rea, "In Defense of Fortunato's Courtesy," *Studies in Short Fiction*, 4 (1967): 57–69. I agree, however, with William S. Doxey, who in his rebuttal to Rea emphasizes Fortunato's vanity and doltishness; see Doxey, "Concerning Fortunato's 'Courtesy,'" *Studies in Short Fiction*, 4 (1967): 266. Others have pointed out that there may be an economic motive behind the revenge scheme. Montresor, who calls the wealthy Fortunato happy "as I once was," seems to feel as though he has fallen into social insignificance and to think delusively he can regain his "fortune" by the violent destruction of his supposed nemesis, who represents his former socially prominent self. See James Gargano, "'The Cask of Amontillado': A Masquerade of Motive and Identity," *Studies in Short Fiction*, 4 (1967): 119–26. That economic matters would be featured in this tale is not surprising, since Poe was impoverished and sickly during the period it was written. His preoccupation with money is reflected in the names Montresor, Fortunato, Luchesi ("Luchresi" in the original version)—"treasure," "fortune," and "lucre"—which, as David Ketterer points out, all add up to much the same thing (*The Rationale of Deception* [Baton Rouge: Louisiana State University Press], p. 110).

17. It is ambiguous, though, whether Montresor's stated goal is finally achieved. Jay Jacoby argues that Fortunato dies prematurely, since he is silent at the end and does not cry out in pain when Montresor's flaming torch is thrust at his head and falls at his feet.

Thus the avenger's plan of making himself known to the victim as an avenger is foiled. See Jay Jacoby, "Fortunato's Premature Demise in 'The Cask of Amontillado,'" *Poe Studies*, 12 (1979): 30–1.

18. Through this statement, Poe may be trying to show just how fatuous Fortunato is, for Amontillado is a sherry. Moreover, the fact that it is Spanish brings into question Montresor's vaunted expertise about "the Italian vintages." It is conceivable Poe himself did not know the facts about Amontillado, though one would think as a devoted drinker he would have.

19. See G.R. Thompson, *Poe's Fiction: Romantic Irony in the Gothic Tales* (Madison: University of Wisconsin Press, 1973), pp. 13–14; Thomas Pribek, "The Serpent and the Heel," *Poe Studies*, 20 (1987): 22–3; James E. Rocks, "Conflict and Motive in 'The Cask of Amontillado,'" *Poe Studies*, 5 (1972): 50–1; Kent Bales, "Poetic Justice in 'The Cask of Amontillado,'" *Poe Studies*, 5 (1972): 51; Ketterer, *The Rationale of Deception in Poe*, p. 112; J. Gerald Kennedy, *Poe, Death, and the Life of Writing* (New Haven: Yale University Press, 1987), p. 142; and Mabbott, *Collected Works*, p. 1266.

20. See Marvin Felheim, *Notes and Queries*, 199 (1954): 447–8; Vincent Buranelli, *Edgar Allan Poe* (New York: Twayne, 1961), p. 72; Edward Wagenknecht, *Edgar Allan Poe: The Man Behind the Legend* (New York: Oxford University Press, 1963), p. 161; Edward H. Davidson, *Poe: A Critical Study* (Cambridge: Harvard University Press, 1964), p. 202; Stuart Levine, *Edgar Allan Poe: Seer and Craftsman* (Deland, Florida: Everett Edwards, 1972), p. 87; Walter Stepp, "The Ironic Double in Poe's 'The Cask of Amontillado,'" *Studies in Short Fiction*, 13 (1976): 447–53; and Eric Mottram, "Law, Lawlessness, and Philosophy in Edgar Allan Poe," in *Edgar Allan Poe: The Design of Order*, ed. Robert E. Lee (London: Vision, 1987), p. 160.

21. *Beneath the American Renaissance*, Chapter 2.

JOHN T. IRWIN

A Platonic Dialogue; Eureka as Detective Story; Marked with a Letter; The Tetractys and the Line of Beauty; Letter as Nodal Point; A Shared Structure; Thematizing the Act of Reading

That reflexiveness is associated with infinity in Poe's figurations of self-consciousness should not surprise anyone familiar with his writings, for Poe was intrigued by the subject of infinity and dealt with it in several works, including his late mystical-mathematical treatise on cosmology, *Eureka*. Of his various discussions of the topic, the one most significant for our present purposes is the imaginary dialogue entitled "The Power of Words" (1845) published less than a year after the appearance of "The Purloined Letter." The fact that "The Power of Words" is a Platonic dialogue between two spirits named Oinos and Agathos (the One and the Good) is especially relevant to Poe's detective stories, given the Platonic trajectory that we suggested runs across the three tales. (Regarding the name Agathos, recall that the goal of the journey from the cave to the realm of pure light is the idea of the good.)

The dialogue between Oinos and Agathos takes place in the future, after the destruction of the world. Oinos, a recent inhabitant of the earth, is "a spirit new-fledged with immortality" seeking instruction about the afterlife from the angel Agathos, who informs him that this questioning is only proper since "not in knowledge is happiness, but in the acquisition of knowledge." But Oinos wonders whether, if a spirit's happiness consists in acquiring knowledge, there must eventually be a limit to such happiness, for

From *The Mystery to a Solution: Poe, Borges, and the Analytic Detective Story*. ©1994 by The Johns Hopkins University Press.

"must not *at last* all things be known," the mind and the objects of its knowledge absolutely coincide? In reply Agathos invites Oinos to look around himself at the "infinity of matter"—an infinity whose "*sole* purpose," Agathos speculates, "is to afford infinite springs, at which the soul may allay the thirst to *know* which is for ever unquenchable within it—since to quench it, would be to extinguish the soul's self" (3:1211–12).

The shape of this argument is not essentially different from the one underlying the detective stories (the contention that the analytic power is itself "but little susceptible of analysis"). In one case, Agathos claims that the object of knowledge (the universe) is infinite and thus the process of knowing this object unending; in the other, Poe implies that the process of knowing the self absolutely resists closure and that consequently this object of knowledge (the self) is for all practical purposes infinite. Were such an absolute coincidence ever to be effected it would, like the possibility of Oinos's exhausting the objects of knowledge in the universe, "extinguish the soul's self" by doing away with the difference that constitutes identity.

What makes "The Power of Words" particularly interesting for our purposes is the explicit connection Poe subsequently makes between infinity and algebraic analysis, between the infinite objects of knowledge and the indefinite advancement of mathematics as a means of comprehending that infinity. Noting that "as no thought can perish, so no act is without infinite result," Agathos continues,

> The mathematicians who saw that the results of any given impulse were absolutely endless—and who saw that a portion of these results were accurately traceable through the agency of algebraic analysis— ... saw, at the same time, that this species of analysis itself, had within itself a capacity for indefinite progress—that there were no bounds conceivable to its advancement and applicability, except within the intellect of him who advanced or applied it. (3:1213–14)

And he adds, "It was deducible from what they knew, that to a being of infinite understanding—one to whom the *perfection* of the algebraic analysis lay unfolded—there could be no difficulty in tracing every impulse given the air—and the ether through the air—to the remotest consequences at any even infinitely remote epoch of time." Agathos says that "this faculty of referring at all epochs, *all* effects to *all* causes" is "in its absolute fulness and perfection" the "prerogative of the Deity alone," although in every degree "short of the absolute perfection" the "power itself" is "exercised by the whole host of the Angelic Intelligences" (3:1214–15).

Yet only four years later, in *Eureka*, Poe imagines an ultimate goal in which this "absolute fulness and perfection" of the analytic power will no longer be solely a prerogative of the deity, since at that period all individual intelligences will have merged with the divine intelligence. According to Poe, God "passes his Eternity in perpetual variation of Concentrated Self and almost Infinite Self-Diffusion," the current state of the universe being simply his "present expansive existence," in which all his creatures are but "infinite individualizations of Himself." These creatures are more or less conscious intelligences, "conscious, first, of a proper identity; conscious, secondly and by faint indeterminate glimpses, ... of an identity with God." Poe predicts that of these two classes of consciousness the former will grow weaker "during the long succession of ages," and the latter will grow stronger, until "the sense of individual identity will be gradually merged in the general consciousness" and man, "ceasing imperceptibly to feel himself Man, will at length attain that awfully triumphant epoch when he shall recognize his existence as that of Jehovah" (*P*, 16:314–15).

Eureka is, of course, relevant to a discussion of the Dupin stories because of the numerous similarities between the cosmological treatise and the detective tales. The first and most obvious of these is that *Eureka* is structured like a detective story: The question of the essence, origin, and end of the universe is presented as a cosmic mystery to be solved by a combination of rational analysis and imaginative intuition. Indeed, at one point in *Eureka* Poe explicitly likens his analytic speculations in cosmology to Dupin's detective work: Noting the resemblance (in terms of their shared peculiarity) between the problem of the unequal distribution of matter in the universe and the "outré character" (2:547) of the crime in "The Murders in the Rue Morgue," Poe argues that it is precisely by "such peculiarities—such protuberances above the plane of the ordinary—that Reason feels her way ... in her search for the True" (*P*, 16:228). *Eureka* is, of course, written in a voice that one immediately recognizes as Dupin's. And, predictably enough, the solution this voice seeks to the mystery of the universe must be both mathematically correct and aesthetically satisfying, both true and beautiful, a solution that will always remain beyond the power of those who are "mathematicians *solely*" (*P*, 16:223) and reveal itself only to those with the instinct for mathematics and poetry (indeed, Poe represents the mathematical/metaphysical speculations of *Eureka* as being "an Art-Product alone: ... a Poem" [*P*, 16:183]).

According to Poe, such a solution must also explain the universe in terms of the interplay of simplicity and complexity. It must account for the complexity of matter through the simplicity of mathematical and geometrical principles, which is to say, account for the complexity of the universe's present state in terms of the absolute simplicity of its origin. And it is in this connection that we confront the most striking resemblance between *Eureka* and the Dupin stories; for just as Poe makes the ongoing mystery at the heart of his three detective tales the mystery of the self's structure, the puzzle of self-consciousness, so in *Eureka* by presenting the universe as an apotheosized self, he makes this same mysterious structure the central puzzle of the universe. For the universe in its present state is nothing but God's self in a condition of "almost Infinite Self-Diffusion," nothing but "his present expansive existence." And just as God's self passes through eternity in a "perpetual variation" between "Concentrated Self" and "Infinite Self-Diffusion," between ultimate self-contraction and ultimate self-expansion, original simplicity and final complexity, so in that model of the human self evoked in "The Purloined Letter" (the figure of a square folded and unfolded along its diagonal) we find adumbrated this same interplay between simplicity and complexity, the figure's unfolding foreshadowing its infinite progression or expansion and its folding foreshadowing its infinite regression or contraction. Moreover, as we identified this reflexive fold with the notion of infinity (as Russell says, "Whenever we can 'reflect' a class into a part of itself, the same relation will necessarily reflect that part into a smaller part, and so on *ad infinitum*"), so Poe in *Eureka* links the concept of infinity to the reflexive structure of self-consciousness by claiming that "the word, 'Infinity'" as applied to the physical universe represents simply "the *thought of a thought*" (P, 16:200).

Given that the central mystery in both the Dupin stories and *Eureka* is the structure of the self (whether human or divine), we should note one further resemblance between "The Purloined Letter" and Poe's cosmological treatise, a resemblance that brings us back to our discussion of the alphabetic characters impressed on the purloined letter's seals. For just as Poe inscribes this symbol of reflexiveness, in its folded and refolded states, with the characters *S* and *D*, so he notes in *Eureka* that our galaxy, a symbol of the gigantic self that is the universe (God's self), also seems to be inscribed with an alphabetic character. Remarking that "in nearly all our astronomical treatises" the "*shape* of the Galaxy ... is said to resemble that of a capital *Y*" (P, 16: 271), Poe explains that the galaxy's *Y* shape is simply an appearance based on our earthly perspective, that is, a function of human self-consciousness. Yet despite this qualification, he still goes on to use the alphabetic figure as the most effective means of describing our solar system's astronomical location.

Just as the meanings of the letters *S* and *D* inscribed on Poe's symbol of the human self are overdetermined, so the meaning of the letter *Y* inscribed on his symbol of the divine self is equally overdetermined. For though it might seem at first glance that *Y* is simply the initial of the deity whose self the universe is (Yahweh), an appearance reinforced by Poe's closing remark about man's ultimately recognizing his existence as that of Jehovah, there is at least one other relevant meaning that critics have found in the letter—the capital *Y* being interpreted as the so-called *littera Pythagorae*. Thus Joan Dayan in her reading of *Eureka* identifies "Poe's Y" as "the Samian letter used by Pythagoras as an emblem of the two roads of Virtue and Vice."[1] Called the Samian letter from the place usually associated with Pythagoras (the island of Samos), the *Y* was said to have been regarded by him as "a symbol of human life (Servius, on Vergil, *Aeneid* vi.136)" (*EB*, 28:890). Poe would undoubtedly have known of the Pythagorean significance of the letter from references to it in English and Latin poetry. Dayan, for example, points to the lines from Pope's *Dunciad* (4, 151–52): "When Reason doubtful, like the Samian letter, / Points him two ways, the narrower is the better" (Dayan, 238 n. 44). Given Poe's proficiency in Latin, he would probably have known as well the original on which Pope's lines are based, a passage from the third satire of Persius:

> Et tibi quae Samios diduxit littera ramos
> surgentem dextro monstravit limite callem. (*EB*, 28:890)

> ... the Samian's parable, Y
> Displaying its two forks, revealed to you
> The stone climb which rises to the Right.[2]

(There was, of course, a readily available translation of Persius's third satire by Dryden that Poe could also have known.) It is interesting to note, in light of our earlier discussion of the cultural coding of directionality, that in the Latin poem the righteous path is literally the path to the right, and that, given the way the letter *Y* is usually printed by hand with a single straight line slanted toward the right and a second line that deviates from it to the left, the righteous path was also the straight one.

A Pythagorean significance for Poe's *Y* seems more than likely considering the tone of Poe's mathematical-mystical speculations in *Eureka*. And the likelihood of the letter's being an allusion to the notion of human existence as a decision at a crossroads is increased by Poe's description of our solar system's astronomical position in the *Y*-shaped galaxy: "Our Sun" is "actually situated at that point of the Y where its three component lines unite" (*P*, 16:272). The sun is, of course, a traditional symbol of self-consciousness, and Poe's description of its location as being the point where the *Y*'s "three component lines unite" creates an image that resonates backward and forward in time across several texts concerned with human self-awareness that we have discussed: backward first to the figure of Oedipus and that epiphany of self-consciousness that turns upon his understanding what happened at a place where three roads meet; backward as well to the figure of Theseus and the innumerable crossroads composing the labyrinth, a place where self-definition (the differentiation of the human) is figured as a problem of self-location; and backward also to Sir Thomas Browne and the quincuncial network as an image of man's place in the world; and then forward to Borges and "The Garden of Forking Paths," in which the human condition is evoked in terms of a labyrinth whose paths branch endlessly in time.

Given the structural resemblance between Poe's marking of the purloined letter with alphabetic characters and his noting that our galaxy is shaped like a letter, we should not be surprised that as one of the significances of the galactic Y seems to be Pythagorean, so too does one of the significances of the purloined letter's *D*. As we noted earlier, our capital *D* derives from the Greek capital delta (Δ), a three-sided letter that, as the fourth character in the Greek alphabet, is used as a sign for the number four. And this same combination of a delta-like triangular shape and the number four recalls the most sacred symbol of the Pythagoreans—the tetractys or "four-group," the "kernel of Pythagorean wisdom,"[3] the brotherhood's "shibboleth or *symbolon*," as the classicist Walter Burkert describes it (Burkert, 187).

The symbol was composed of "the numbers, 1, 2, 3, 4 ... represented in a pebble figure, in the form of the 'perfect triangle'" (Burkert, 72), which is to say, an equilateral triangle each of whose sides contains four points, a triangle of fours. The highest oath that a Pythagorean could take was to swear by the tetractys, since it emblemized for Pythagoras's followers their

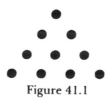

Figure 41.1

belief that "number is the essence of all things," as Aristotle says in the *Metaphysics* (Aristotle, 17:41). And indeed the tetractys served as a compendium of number symbolism: The four numbers 1, 2, 3, 4 add up to 10, the root of the decimal system and the Pythagorean perfect number (as evidenced, for example, in the original decad of oppositions that make up the Pythagorean table of opposites). Further, these four numbers contain not only the basic musical intervals of fourth (4:3), fifth (3:2), and octave (2:1), "but also, according to the Platonic pattern, point, line, plane, and solid" (Burkert, 72). That is, the figure exhibits the way in which the material world, considered in terms of dimensionality, is built up out of numbers: Beginning at the triangle's apex with the geometric point, we move downward to the next level, the two points that are the minimum number needed to determine a line; then to the next level, the three points that are the minimum needed to determine a plane; and then to the last level, the four points that are the minimum needed to determine a solid.

In making the tetractys a symbol of the material world's origin from the realm of numbers, the Pythagoreans simply substituted for the four basic elements of earth, air, fire, and water (considered as the building blocks of all things) the first four numbers, and they arranged then) so as to show the origin of all things in unity as well as the way that unity flows out or falls down into multiplicity. (One is reminded of the opening of Borges's story "The Book of Sand," which combines the symbolism of dimensionality [contained in the tetractys] with the concept of infinity to create an image of beginning a tale with the most basic elements: "The line is made up of an infinite number of points; the plane of an infinite number of lines; the volume of an infinite number of planes; the hypervolume of an infinite number of volumes.... No, unquestionably this is not —*more geometrico*—the best way of beginning my story" [*BS*, 117].) Since, as Burkert points out, "The harmonic ratios, the 'perfection' of 10, and the role of the pebble figures are all part of what Aristotle attributes to the Pythagoreans" (Burkert, 72), Poe's knowledge of the tetractys's significance would not have required much more than an acquaintance with Book I of Aristotle's *Metaphysics*.

There is one further significance of the tetractys that seems to have a tantalizing connection with the Dupin stories. Burkert notes that the Neoplatonic philosopher Iamblichus, whose work is a principal source of our knowledge of Pythagorean lore, links the Pythagoreans' sacred number symbol to the oracle of Delphi: In his *De Vita Pythagorica* Iamblichus responds to the question "What is the oracle of Delphi?" with the answer "The tetractys; that is, the harmony in which the Sirens sing" (Burkert, 187).

As Burkert explains, since the tetractys contains within itself "the harmonic ratios of fourth, fifth, and octave" and since

> the Sirens produce the music of the spheres, the whole universe is harmony and number.... The tetractys has within it the secret of the world; and in this manner we can also understand the connection with Delphi, the seat of the highest and most secret wisdom. Perhaps Pythagorean speculation touched upon that focal point, or embodiment, of Delphic wisdom, the bronze tripod of Apollo. Later sources speak of its mysterious ringing, which must have been "daemonic" for Pythagoreans. (Burkert, 187)

This bit of Pythagorean lore about the tetractys and the Sirens' song reminds us of the epigraph to "The Murders in the Rue Morgue," taken from the fifth chapter of Browne's *Urn Burial*: "What song the Syrens sang, or what name Achilles assumed when he hid himself among women, although puzzling questions, are not beyond all conjecture" (2:527). Since Poe uses this quotation as an introduction to the first of three related stories, stories whose whole point is that puzzling questions can indeed be solved through rational conjecture; it seems only appropriate for him to allude in the last of these stories to just such a conjectural answer to the famous question of the Sirens' song, which is to say, to allude, through the letter D and the three/four oscillation associated with it, to the ancient dictum identifying the Sirens' song with the harmonic ratios contained in the tetractys (the triangle of fours), one of these ratios being, of course, that of 4:3 (a fourth). Moreover, since the Pythagorean lore in question not only links the tetractys to the Sirens' song but also both of these to the oracle of Delphi, there is a further appropriateness in Poe's epigraphically invoking the Sirens' song in his first detective story. For, as we saw, the figure from Greek mythology whose story represents the archetypal pattern for the detective genre is Oedipus, and the Delphic oracle is central to his story. It is on the way from Delphi that Oedipus meets Laius and his retinue at the crossroads. And when Oedipus, as king of Thebes, sets out to solve the mystery of Laius's murder, the problem presents itself as a puzzle built upon the four numbers contained in the tetractys.

Of course, the general appropriateness of Poe's having in mind a Pythagorean significance for one of the meanings of the letter D stems from what we have described as the Pythagorean tone of his discussion of analysis and algebra, his sense of the true mathematician as someone who combines the resolvent and the creative powers, at once mathematician and poet. But if we are correct in seeing a reference to the Pythagorean tetractys among the possible meanings Poe associates with the letter *D*, then this raises a further question. For with the two earlier significations suggested for the letter (the initial of "Difference" and the sign for the differential in calculus), there was a reciprocal signification in each case for the letter *S* (the initial of "Sameness" and the sign for the integral in calculus), so that one naturally wonders whether, in a similar fashion, there exists for the letter *S* a meaning that is the reciprocal of the Pythagorean significance proposed for *D*.

Since the letter *D* evokes in a Pythagorean context a symbolic figure (the triangle of fours) rather than the initial of a word, we should probably seek the significance of the letter *S* in terms of its graphic symbolism as well. And indeed there does exist a symbolic association of the letter that immediately comes to mind, an association originating with a graphic artist whose work Poe admired—William Hogarth. In his art treatise *The Analysis of Beauty* (1753) Hogarth, discussing the serpentine line or elongated *S* curve, notes that in the frontispiece to the 1745 edition of his engraved works he had drawn "a serpentine line lying on a painter's pallet, with these words under it, THE LINE OF BEAUTY," a designation that caused widespread curiosity in the art world, with painters and sculptors applying to him "to know the meaning of it."[4] In his preface Hogarth cites various authorities to support his view that the serpentine line is the most beautiful in painting and design because it is the most fit to express motion, "the greatest grace and life that a picture can have," and he quotes a passage from the sixteenth-century painter Giovanni Lomazzo citing Michelangelo's advice to a young artist to "*alwaies make a figure Pyramidall, Serpentlike, and multiplied by one two and three*" (Hogarth, v–vi). As we noted earlier, the pyramidal shape had been associated with the tip of a flame since at least the time of the ancient Egyptians, and this same association is made by Lomazzo, who notes that "the forme of the flame ... is most apt for motion: For it hath a *Conus* or sharpe pointe ... that so it may ascende to his proper sphere," and by the seventeenth-century French painter Dufresnoy, whom Hogarth quotes to the effect that "a fine figure and its parts ought always to have a serpent-like and flaming form" because these sorts of lines have a "life and seeming motion in them, which very much resembles the activity of the flame and of the serpent" (Hogarth, vi–vii).

This linking of the images of pyramid, serpent, and flame has a Pythagorean/Platonic ring to it, and Hogarth goes on to note that for the painters and sculptors of ancient Greece "Pythagoras, Socrates, and Aristotle, seem to have pointed out the right road in nature" for their study

(Hogarth, xii). Indeed, on the specific subject of Pythagoras, Hogarth cites the translator's preface to Ten Kate's *Beau Ideal* and its discussion of "the Analogy of the ancient Greeks." The translator says that this "Analogy" is "the true key for finding all harmonious proportions in painting, sculpture, architecture, musick, etc." and that it was "brought home to Greece by Pythagoras ... after this great philosopher had travell'd into Phoenicia, Egypt and Chaldea, where he convers'd with the learned" (Hogarth, xiii). Of what this Analogy consists, the translator does not say, but clearly it seems to be based on the sense that harmony or proportion in the arts is a function of mathematical ratios—a notion the ancient world associated with Pythagoras. Not only were the harmonic ratios in music (such as those contained in the tetractys) thought to be Pythagorean discoveries, but also certain proportions in painting and architecture, the most famous of these being the "golden section." Burkert notes that "Euclid gives the construction of the golden section ... in book 4, which is ascribed 'as a whole' to the Pythagoreans" (Burkert, 452).

The golden section or golden mean is the Euclidean problem of dividing a straight line in extreme and mean ratios, and it enters into ancient painting and architecture as the notion of a perfect proportion achieved by dividing "a straight line or rectangle ... into two unequal parts" such that "the ratio of the smaller to the greater part is the same as that of the greater to the whole."[5] Like "the mathematical value pi," the ratio of the golden section "cannot be expressed as a finite number, but an approximation is 8:13 or 0.618:1" (*ODA*, 210). Indeed, some historians of mathematics such as G.J. Allman have suggested that "it was rather in connexion with the line cut in extreme and mean ratio than with reference to the diagonal and side of a square that the Pythagoreans discovered the incommensurable" (Heath, 3:19). Suffice it to say that like the incommensurability of the diagonal, the incommensurability of the golden section has been associated since antiquity with the Pythagoreans in their legendary capacity as discoverers of the irrational. And undoubtedly part of the aura of the golden section's mysterious perfection for the ancients was its irrationality, the fact that its exact numerical determination vanished in infinity. Besides its importance in Euclid, Plato, and Vitruvius (who used it in his work *De architectura* "to establish architectural standards for the proportions of columns, rooms, and whole buildings"[6]), the golden section was a topic of intense study in the Renaissance and the subject of a book entitled *Divina Proportione* (1509) by Luca Pacioli, the best-known mathematician of the period and a friend of Leonardo and Piero della Francesca. Maintaining that this "divine proportion" possesses mystical properties, Pacioli explains that the ratio "cannot be expressed by a number and, being beyond definition, is in this respect like God, 'occult and secret'; further, this three-in-one proportion is symbolic of the Holy Trinity" (*ODA*, 210), the "three-in-one proportion" referring to the three lengths compared in the figure—the smaller segment, the larger, and the whole line.

It is precisely in the spirit, then, of an inquiry into hidden ancient wisdom, into Pythagorean lore, that Hogarth invokes the translator's preface to Ten Kate's *Beau Ideal*, with its reference to the "Analogy of the ancient Greeks" as a "*great key of knowledge*," and in this vein he continues, "As every one has a right to conjecture what this discovery of the ancients might be, it shall be my business to chew it was a key to the thorough knowledge of variety both in form, and movement" (Hogarth, xv–xvi). Quoting Shakespeare, Hogarth sums up "all the charms of beauty in two words, INFINITE VARIETY," the sense being that beauty inheres in "an *infinite variety of parts*" (Hogarth, xvi–xvii) brought together in a single, harmonious whole, the effect of an interplay of complexity and simplicity, difference and sameness. (One is immediately reminded of Poe's reference in the *Marginalia* to "Pythagoras' definition of beauty" as "the reduction of many into one.") In a distinctly Pythagorean tone, Hogarth continues, "The ancients made their doctrines mysterious to the vulgar, and kept them secret from those who were not of their particular sects ... by means of symbols, and hieroglyphics" (Hogarth, xvii), and indeed Hogarth may have had in mind those two recognition symbols used by members of the Pythagorean brotherhood—the tetractys and the pentagram or star-pentagon, which the Pythagoreans called Health (Interestingly enough, the relationship between the pentagram and the pentagon seems to have involved for the Pythagoreans a problem in geometric construction that depended for its solution on another problem, that of the golden section [Heath, 2:99].)

Hogarth invokes the notion of ancient wisdom concealed in symbols and hieroglyphical emblems here because he is about to give an oblique gloss on the emblem that appears on the title page of *The Analysis of Beauty*, an emblem constructed from the shapes of a pyramid and serpentine line and from the word variety. Hogarth begins his explanation of the figure with a quotation from Lomazzo: "The Grecians in imitation of antiquity searched out the truly renowned proportion, wherein the exact perfect ion of most exquisite beauty and sweetness appeareth; dedicating the same in a triangular glass unto Venus the goddess of divine beauty" (Hogarth, xvii). And he adds, giving the quotation specific reference to the figures he has discussed, "The symbol in the triangular glass, might be similar to the line Michael Angelo recommended; especially, if it can be proved, that the triangular form of the

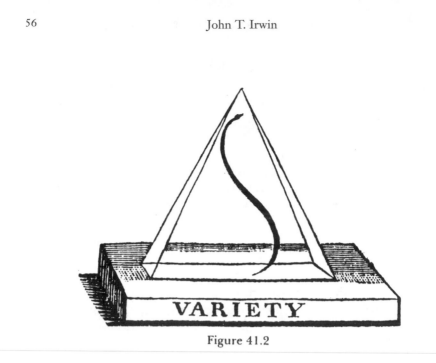

Figure 41.2

glass, and the serpentine line itself, are the two most expressive figures that can be thought of to signify not only beauty and grace, but the whole *order of form*" (Hogarth, xvii).

We know that at the University of Virginia Poe had something of a local reputation for his talent in drawing, one of his classmates remarking that so great was his artistic skill his fellow students were "in doubt whether Poe in future life would be Painter or Poet" (*Log*, 69). And we also know that at the university in May 1826 Poe came upon "a rare edition of Hogarth's prints" in a second-hand shop and tried to buy it (*Log*, 71). Although the edition ultimately went to someone else, Poe had apparently examined it with great care. In later years, Poe was fond of quoting approvingly Hogarth's remark that genius is "but *diligence* after all" (3:1145, 1149 n. 47), suggesting that his early regard for the artist's work stayed with him all his life. And certainly if Poe knew Hogarth's work, he would have known of his association with the serpentine line. For as Hogarth himself points out in the preface to *The Analysis of Beauty*, the self-portrait published as a frontispiece to his engraved works showed "a serpentine line, lying on a painter's pallet" and beneath it the words "THE LINE OF BEAUTY." Finally, it seems hard to believe that anyone as interested as Poe was in questions of analysis and in the subject of the sublime and beautiful would not have made it a point to read a work entitled *The Analysis of Beauty*, particularly if it had been written by an artist whose work he admired.

The question is, then, if Poe did know *The Analysis of Beauty*, as seems more than likely, what would he have made of the emblem Hogarth had created for the title page, an emblem combining a "triangular form" and a "serpentine line" as the "two most expressive figures" to signify "not only beauty and grace, but the whole order of form." I would suggest that, given Poe's taste for deciphering cryptograms, he would have almost certainly seen the two combined shapes as letters, the "triangular form" evoking the Greek capital *D* (the legend on which the emblem is based is, after all, Greek in origin, according to Lomazzo) and the "serpentine line" evoking the letter *S*. Moreover, given the Pythagorean resonances in Hogarth's preface, Poe might well have assimilated these letters to the two powers he associated with the true mathematician—the resolvent and the creative, the analytic and the poetic—the *D* evoking the triangular tetractys as a figure of the mathematical component of reality and the *S* evoking the line of beauty as a figure of the aesthetic, the two together (one inscribed within the other) presenting an emblem of the conjunction of these two orders in the creation of the universe. Indeed, the sexual resonances of these conjoined symbols (the phallic serpent within the pubic triangle) suggest the image of a sacred marriage, a *hieros gamos* of beauty and mathematics. (Hogarth had, of course, quoted Lomazzo to the effect that the Greeks placed the perfect aesthetic shape "in a triangular glass" and dedicated it "unto Venus," the goddess of love.) And certainly a sexual resonance is present as well in the conjunction of these two alphabetic characters on the seals of the purloined letter. Not only are the two states of the letter gender-coded (the address on the original letter written in a bold, masculine hand; that on the refolded letter in a diminutive, feminine one), but the letter itself is undoubtedly an amorous communication between the duke of S—— (or some male member of his family) and the queen, a form of written intercourse meant to evoke another form of intercourse—hence the letter's susceptibility to being used for blackmail by the minister and hence the appropriateness, in Lacan's reading of the tale, of associating the letter with the phallic signifier, with the linking third term that both unites and differentiates masculine and feminine.

So far we have suggested three sets of possible significations for the *S* and *D* impressed on the purloined letter's seals, and there is at least one more we should note, a set that bears directly on the nature of the fold, specifically, on the turning of the letter inside out like a glove. For, as we noted, the everting of a glove reverses its handedness, and certainly Poe with his knowledge of Latin would have noticed that *S* and *D* are the initials of the words for left and right in that language—*sinistra* and *dextra*—a signification that reinforces the sense of mirror-image reciprocity between the terms in the other differential pairs and that points once again to the V-shaped fold of the hand as the bodily given that grounds a linguistic system of differential oppositions.

What becomes clear, then, is that in making the purloined letter a figure of the reflexive nature of the self, Poe has made it a nodal point at which a series of differential oppositions intersect—oppositions that are presented either through the manipulation of the letter (inner/outer, depth/surface), through the handwriting of the address (masculine/feminine), or through the possible significances of the initials on the seals (such as sameness/difference). But to grasp the full point of Poe's evoking the letter as the intersection of these oppositions, we must understand its position within the overall structure of the tale, a structure that "The Purloined Letter" shares with the myths of Oedipus and Theseus and with the first Dupin story.

Taking the myth of Oedipus as the general form of this scenario, we can identify its recurring elements as follows: There is a protagonist (Oedipus) whose fated task is to enact the mysterious relationship of sameness and difference that constitutes self-identity, enact it by confronting an antagonist (the Sphinx) who poses the internal problem of self-identity or self-difference (a problem figured within the self as the mind/body difference) as the external problem of differentiating human from animal. The antagonist, a physical embodiment of the external problem, is literally a monster, a combination of animal and human parts in which the feral predominates. But the antagonist poses the problem in a form that, although it bears an animal sanction for failure (death by being devoured), demands a human (i.e., mental) solution. When Oedipus answers the riddle correctly, the Sphinx kills herself. But Oedipus, having successfully confronted the general question of human identity, must now face the individual problem of personal identity, enacting the dark half of the riddle's truth by discovering not the difference that separates human from animal but the sameness that unites them, a discovery ultimately made through a scenario structured around the same set of numbers that governs the Sphinx's riddle of human differentiation. Since the incest taboo is a traditional cultural marker of the difference between animal and human, incest functions in the Oedipus myth as a structural means of linking the general problem of human differentiation within the natural world to the specific problem of personal identity within a human community (i.e., the recognition of kinship and its rules). This same broad structure is repeated in the Theseus myth with slight modifications.

The protagonist is Theseus, his half-animal, half-human antagonist the Minotaur, and the mental problem associated with the antagonist the labyrinth. Unlike the Sphinx's riddle (a puzzle of words and numbers), the labyrinth poses the problem of human differentiation in terms of oppositions such as right/left and inner/outer that figure self-consciousness as self-location.

In the first Dupin story Poe adapts these mythic structures to his own ends. The protagonist is Dupin, and the antagonist the manlike killer ape, or more precisely, a combination of the ape's human master (the sailor and his animal slave (the orangutan). The mental problem linked with the antagonist (the locked-room puzzle) is, as we noted earlier, a variant of the labyrinth, employing in its figuration of the self's structure many of the same oppositions associated with the Minotaur's dwelling and presenting at the same time (as in Poe's manipulation of the word *clew*, for example) a self-conscious commentary on its mythic antecedents. For of course what characterizes the Dupin stories is precisely the degree of self-consciousness they exhibit about their *own* literary origin, tradition, and structure as they pursue the task of reflecting on the structure of self-consciousness. The major change Poe makes in adapting the Oedipus/Theseus scenario for the first Dupin story concerns the transition from the general problem of differentiating the human to the individual one of self-identity within the family unit, a transition effected, as we said, in terms of the incest taboo as a cultural marker of the difference *animal/human*. For in "The Murders in the Rue Morgue" the incest motif and the element of familial violence are not associated with the protagonist Dupin but with the protagonist's creator, the killing of a mother and daughter within a claustrophobic family setting suggesting the more or less conscious translation of Poe's ambivalent feelings about his own semi-incestuous family circle evident in the dying woman stories.

We should note, in moving from the first to the last Dupin story, that the absence from "Marie Rogêt" of the structure we have been discussing is probably due to Poe's abandoning his original design for the tale in order to parallel the real case of Mary Cecilia Rogers. But with the third Dupin story, the scenario appears once more. The protagonist is again Dupin and the antagonist the Minister D——, whose character Poe presents as a combination of animal and human traits. The prefect describes the minister as one "who dares all things, those unbecoming as well as those becoming a man" (3:976); while Dupin refers to him as "that *monstrum horrendum*, an unprincipled man of genius" (3:993). As a figure of superior human intelligence in the service of base instincts, the minister culminates the structure's genealogy of "horrifying monsters." Similarly, the incest taboo and the element of familial violence characteristic of the structure are evoked by the substitutive Oedipal triangle (king, queen, and minister) in the original scene in the royal boudoir. The coding of the minister's role within the triangle is accomplished, first, by his taking possession of the phallic communication from the queen's lover and using it against her (the mental violence of blackmail), and second, by Dupin's inscribing a quotation from Crebillon's *Atrée* in the letter he leaves at the minister's house. The quotation in effect compares the minister's scheme to the ancient tale of Atreus and Thyestes: As Thyestes seduced the wife of his brother King Atreus, so the minister has tried to blackmail the king's wife with evidence of an adulterous affair. Atreus punishes his brother by having Thyestes' two children boiled and served to their unwitting father. And when Thyestes discovers the truth, he curses the house of Atreus, a curse that ends up consuming his brother's offspring for generations to come.

There is, of course, a natural appropriateness to the punishment Atreus inflicts on his brother, for in most cultures the taboos against incest and cannibalism, considered as markers of the animal/human difference, are structurally linked. Which is to say that just as human beings are forbidden to mate with their own kin, so they are forbidden to eat their own kind. Indeed, we can even see a faint trace of this connection between the two taboos running through the Oedipus myth, starting with the animal threat of the Sphinx to devour Oedipus if he fails to answer her riddle and ending with the self-devouring fates of Oedipus's incestuous offspring.

As the minister fills the role in the third Dupin story of the part-human, part-animal antagonist, so the mental puzzle associated with this role is the hidden-object problem. And just as the first Dupin story's locked-room problem is a conscious reworking of the labyrinthine puzzle associated with the Minotaur (as well as a commentary on the meaning of such puzzles), so the hidden-object problem is Poe's summation of this commentary. In effect, Poe makes the purloined letter a compendium of the oppositions and motifs connected with these mental tests—to which he adds his own interpretive embellishments, as, for example, when the inner/outer opposition associated with the labyrinth is translated into the endless reversibility of inner and outer as a figure of mind; or when the numbers governing the Sphinx's riddle become associated with the figure of a square folded along its diagonal as an image of self-consciousness; or when the right/left opposition from the labyrinth is linked, through the image of the quincuncial network, to the body's mirror asymmetry and the V-shaped fold of the hand. For Poe, the purloined letter figures the point of intersection in the self's structure where reflexiveness, infinity, and incommensurability are joined. And like the V shape in Browne's *Garden of Cyrus*, the purloined letter with its myriad associations is meant to evoke the interface between mind and body as the point where alphabetic characters, numbers, and geometric shapes can be converted into one another on the basis of a common physical form—a bilateral or bipolar, mirror-image relationship figured as a fold.

The self is, then, for Poe essentially a structure of number and geometry (number spatially extended as relation) within language. It is an identity in difference, a unity that is halved and doubled, an always-about-to-be-accomplished evenness constituted by its being originally and essentially at odds with itself, a shifting marker of positions within geometrical as well as grammatical relationships—indeed, one could go on indefinitely multiplying its numerical expressions within speech. Small wonder, then, that as Poe attempts to analyze the analytic power in the Dupin stories the amount of mathematical reference and imagery increases almost exponentially from tale to tale. And small wonder, too, that in pursuing a Pythagorean/Platonic trajectory in the stories Poe is ultimately led to the task of distinguishing the true mathematician (in the Pythagorean sense of the term) from the mere mathematician, of distinguishing analysis from algebra. For what Poe has done is to take the task of differentiating the human that he found in the myths of Oedipus and Theseus and reflect its mind/body opposition into one of the two differential terms (mind). Which is simply to say that just as there is a difference between mind and body, so there is a difference between the aspects of mind related to each, between a mental power reflecting the mind's abstract structure and one reflecting the body's physical instincts. Poe makes this distinction at the very start of the Dupin stories with the narrator's remark about "the Bi-Part Soul" and his notion of "a double Dupin—the creative and the resolvent." These powers, personified later in the figures of poet and mathematician, represent respectively the intuitive and the ratiocinative aspects of mind: the former concerned with the sensual, the emotional, the aesthetic—translating into consciousness the realm of animal instinct and bodily knowledge; the latter concerned with the ideal, the abstract, the logical—reflecting into consciousness the mind's own numerical/geometrical form: the two together as necessary to the definition of a true poet as to that of a true mathematician. For just as Poe believes that the true mathematician must possess powers of imagination and aesthetic insight, so he also believes—as "The Philosophy of Composition," "The Rationale of Verse," and "The Poetic Principle" make clear—that the true poet must be literally a man of numbers, in that ancient sense of verse as a kind of counting.

In "The Purloined Letter" Poe is able to take this structure of self-consciousness (in which the whole is reflected into a part of itself) one step further by naming the story after the central symbolic object the story presents and by making that symbolic object a text—an identity-in-difference that allows Poe to embody the theme of analyzing the analytic power iii the tale's oblique analysis of its own ontological/epistemological status. Indeed, the notion of the text's describing its own status suggests one of the practical concerns that may have led Poe to the invention of the detective story. Poe supported himself for most of his adult life as a writer for and editor of literary magazines during a period when the reading public in America was growing and its character changing. As both writer and editor, Poe undoubtedly tried to learn as much as he could about the composition of his audience, about its interests and its taste in reading, in order to give his work as broad an appeal as possible. We know that Poe prided himself on the fact that as an editor he dramatically increased the circulation of all the magazines with which he was associated. And in this regard one can well imagine Poe asking himself whether there existed a single interest or activity shared by all readers, one that a writer or editor could take advantage of. To which one can equally well imagine Poe replying, in one of those mental shortcuts that constitute genius, that, obviously, there does exist one activity that all readers share and that, one assumes, they are all interested in—the act of reading itself. Consequently, if one were to invent a type of story that thematized the act of reading, that presented reading as the analytic interpretation, the decipherment, of a text contained within the framing text of the tale, then one would have created a form of both universal interest and unparalleled immediacy for readers, a form in which the emotional energy generated by the reader's effort to interpret the text would flow directly into the main character's activity of solving the mystery, a genre in which the reader would be asked to interpret the author's intentions by participating in the detective's attempt to interpret the criminal's.

Poe makes this thematization of the act of reading explicit in the first two Dupin stories by having Dupin and the narrator analyze lengthy newspaper accounts of the cases. In "The Murders in the Rue Morgue" the entire presentation of the crime is accomplished by two excerpts (running to eight pages in the Mabbott edition) from the "Gazette des Tribunaux," excerpts from which Dupin extracts a crucial clue by noting that each witness identifies the killer as speaking a different foreign language, but always one that that particular witness does not himself speak. And as the entire exposition phase in the first story is accomplished through Dupin's reading newspaper reports before visiting the scene of the crime, so in "The Mystery of Marie Rogêt" the entire investigation is carried out without Dupin ever viewing the crime scene. In effect, the story consists of nothing but Dupin's analysis of written reports of the case. The narrator tells us that he "procured, at the Prefecture, a full report of all the evidence elicited, and, at the various newspaper offices, a copy of every paper in which, from first to last, had been published any decisive information in regard to this sad affair" (3:728–29). With Poe once again introducing lengthy journalistic excerpts into the text, Dupin and the narrator sift through the various accounts of the crime, comparing versions, eliminating various theories of the murder advanced by different reporters, rejecting seemingly important clues as red herrings, and singling out details that may lead somewhere. Pausing midway in this exercise in textual analysis (an analysis that demonstrates who didn't commit the crime), Dupin sends the narrator out to verify certain details and adds, "I will examine the newspapers more generally than you have as yet done. So far, we have only reconnoitred the field of investigation; but it will be strange indeed if a comprehensive survey ... of the public prints, will not afford us ... a *direction* for inquiry" (3:752).

With this flourish, Poe emphasizes that Dupin's vaunted powers of detection amount in the first two stories to little more than a highly developed form of close reading; and in thus heightening the reader's awareness of the text-within-a-text motif in the first two tales, Poe prepares the reader to notice the change he makes in the motif in the final tale. For while in the first two, the actual words of the self-included text (the newspaper accounts of the crime) appear within the framing tale, in the third story it is simply a description of the self-included text that appears, the text-within-a-text being made to signify not in its own words (we are never shown the contents of the letter) but in ways more elliptical and problematic (i.e., the oppositions associated with its manipulation, the gender of the hand in which it is addressed, the initials on the seals, and so on). Indeed, in some sense it is the verbal "blankness" of the self-included text (the purloined letter with its letters purloined), its empty, mirror-like quality, that makes it possible for Poe to superimpose on it the framing tale that bears its name, to fold that framing tale back into itself so that it becomes its own content. And this move, which sets up a ceaseless oscillation of outer and inner figuring the reflexive structure of the self, seems to lead immediately to the use of mathematical and geometrical images as the most natural and accurate means of representing the necessary intersection of reflexiveness, infinity, and incommensurability—a not unpredictable transition from the imagery of letters to that of numbers and geometrical shapes reflecting the way the V-shaped fold, as a figure of reflexiveness, forms a graphic conversion point for these three registers of signification or inscription.

In understanding that the structure of self-consciousness involves a necessary relationship among reflexiveness, infinity, and incommensurability, Poe in effect reproduced an insight of the ancient Greeks, and in choosing to snake the analysis of the analytic power the central mystery in the Dupin stories, he committed himself to a notion of mystery best characterized as "Pythagorean." Poe's aesthetic task, like that of the creators of the myths of Oedipus and Theseus, was to find mysteries that would serve as dramatic correlatives for the central mystery of the human condition, and the fact that the mysteries he created were ones associated with the commission of crimes simply evokes the ancient sense that the structure of self-consciousness, as something constituted by an original and essential oddness, is basically transgressive.

NOTES

1. Joan Dayan, *Fables of Mind: An Inquiry into Poe's Fiction* (New York: Oxford University Press, 1987), 238 n. 44. Subsequent citations of this volume in text as Dayan.

2. *Latin Poetry in Verse Translation*, ed. L.R. Lind (Boston: Houghton Mifflin, 1957), 251.

3. Walter Burkert, *Lore and Science in Ancient Pythagoreanism*, trans. Edwin L. Minar, Jr. (Cambridge: Harvard University Press, 1972), 72. Subsequent citations of this volume in text as Burkert.

4. William Hogarth, *The Analysis of Beauty* (London: Scolar Press, 1974), x–xi. Subsequent citations of this volume in text as Hogarth.

5. *The Oxford Dictionary of Art*, ed. Ian Childers and Harry Osborne (Oxford: Oxford University Press, 1988), 210. Subsequent citations of this volume in text as *ODA*.

6. Ralph Mayer, *A Dictionary of Art Terms and Techniques* (New York: Crowell, 1969), 169–70.

SHAWN ROSENHEIM

Detective Fiction, Psychoanalysis, and the Analytic Sublime

"We have gone so far as to combine the ideas of an agility astounding, a strength superhuman, a ferocity brutal, a butchery without motive, a grotesquerie in horror absolutely alien from humanity, and a voice foreign in tone to the ears of men of many nations, and devoid of all distinct or intelligible syllabification.... What impression have I made upon your fancy?" I felt a creeping of the flesh as Dupin asked me the question. "A madman," I said, "has done this deed—some raving maniac escaped from a neighboring Maison de Santé."

—Edgar Allan Poe, "The Murders in the Rue Morgue"

Though "The Murders in the Rue Morgue" may be said to have initiated the genre of detective fiction, many twentieth-century fans have been put off by what seems like Poe's capricious violation of an implicit narrative convention. The ape, it is alleged, represents an instance of bad faith, since no reader could reasonably be expected to include animals in a list of potential murderers. More generally, we may take Poe's ape story as an index of a deeper bad faith on the part of the whole genre, in its frequent imbalance between the detective story's protracted narrative setup and its often unsatisfying denouement. There is often an embarrassing sense on the part of readers of detective fiction that its typically Gothic revelations are incommensurate with the moral weight suggested by the genre's narrative

From *The American Face of Edgar Allan Poe*, edited by Shawn Rosenheim and Stephen Rachman. ©1995 by The Johns Hopkins University Press.

form. In this sense, too, Poe's orangutan is an emblem of readers, who—their attention solicited by an unworthy narrative dilemma—find that the real crime has been practiced on their own sensibility. In the words of Geoffrey Hartman:

> The trouble with the detective novel is not that it is moral but that it is moralistic; not that it is popular but that it is stylized; not that it lacks realism but that it picks up the latest realism and exploits it. A voracious formalism dooms it to seem unreal, however "real" the world it describes.... The form trusts too much in reason; its very success opens to us the glimpse of a mechanized world, whether controlled by God or Dr. No or the Angel of the Odd. (Hartman 1975, 225)

Though well taken, Hartman's caution is hardly original: already in the first detective story, Poe recognized the problem. As Poe indicated in a letter to Phillip Cooke, he was aware that the promise of detective fiction to unriddle the world was ultimately tautological: "Where is the ingenuity of unravelling a web which you yourself have woven for the express purpose of unravelling? These tales of ratiocination owe most of their popularity to being something in a new key. I do not mean to say that they are not ingenious—but people think they are more ingenious than they are—on account of the method and air of method" (Poe 1966, 2:328).

Poe's comment interests me because, while he demystifies the detective story, insisting that the narrator's solution to the crime is, in fact, no "solution" at all, but a *coup de théâtre* staged by the author from behind the scenes, he also recognizes the willingness of readers to be deceived by the story's "method and air of method." Such an air of method might also be described as the genre's penchant for analysis, a term that recurs throughout the Dupin stories.[1] "Rue Morgue" begins with a discussion of "analysis," and in a letter describing "Marie Rogêt," Poe emphasizes the same term: "under the pretense of showing how Dupin ... unravelled the mystery of Marie's assassination, I, in fact, enter into a very rigorous analysis of the real tragedy in New York" (Poe 1969–78, 3:718). Though it may at first seem curious that the literary genre most vocally devoted to the powers of the ratiocinative mind should vex those powers on the mindless acts of Poe's orangutan, on consideration, Poe's use of the ape in "Rue Morgue" emerges as something more than a simple narrative miscalculation or mere sideshow. In brief, the ape permits Poe to elaborate a cryptographic argument about language and human identity, in which the extreme contrast between the ape's physicality and Dupin's inhuman reason tells us something about the constitutive oppositions of the genre. And since detective fiction in general, and Poe's more particularly, has enjoyed a long and privileged relation to psychoanalytic reading, Poe's experiments with the monkey may tell us something about how we, as readers, are ourselves made to ape his ape.

"Analysis" in several senses has been a key to the theoretical ubiquity of "The Purloined Letter." But while that story is unquestionably a great achievement, Poe purchases the analytic force of his narrative only by purging the text of any attempt at realist representation (Limon 1990, 103). Hence, Barbara Johnson's too-familiar claim that Minister D—'s letter is "not hidden in a geometrical space, where the police are looking for it ... but is instead located 'in' a *symbolic* structure" is correct only because of Poe's refusal to engage the difficult project of representing the texture of social experience (Johnson 1980). In sharp contrast to the outdoor settings of "Marie Rogêt," or even to the street scenes in "Rue Morgue," "The Purloined Letter" retreats from the boulevards, parks, and waterways of the teeming city, with their social and sexual ambiguities, into the enclosed and private spaces of Minister D—'s chambers. Hence, the remarkable success of "The Purloined Letter" as a locus for literary and psychoanalytic theory— indeed, as one of *the* venues by which French theory has translated itself into America—begins to seem the consequence of playing cards with a stacked deck. The tale's theoretical richness derives from the fact that Lacan, Derrida, Johnson, and the others who have written in their wake have chosen a text that is already supremely two-dimensional, already overtly concerned with allegorizing the operations of the signifier.

In fact, the semiotic purity of "The Purloined Letter" is an exception in Poe's detective fiction, which focuses more generally on the tension between representations of three-dimensional bodies and language, which is either two-dimensional in its printed form or, as speech, proves uncannily disembodied and invisible. The dominant form of the genre is far closer to "Rue Morgue" or, in its true-crime mode, to "The Mystery of Marie Rogêt," in which Poe is less concerned with the "itinerary of the signifier" narrowly conceived than he is with the problems posed by the difficult intersection between the human capacity for language and the brute fact of incarnation. Poe's obsession with corpses, especially prominent in the late fiction, reveals his continuing anxiety over the body's refusal to suffer complete encipherment into language. Significantly enough, Poe's deaths are almost invariably associated with injuries to the organs of speech. The horror of Valdemar's mesmeric dissolution in "The Facts in the Case of M. Valdemar" stems from the grotesque contrast between his putrefying body and his "wonderfully, thrillingly distinct—syllabification" (Poe 1984b, 839–40), as "ejaculations of 'dead! dead!'" burst "from the tongue and not the lips of the sufferer" (ibid., 842). In "Rue Morgue" the strangled Camille L'Espanaye's tongue is "bitten partially through" (ibid., 410). Marie Rogêt bears "bruises and impressions of fingers" about her throat, and "a piece of lace was found tied so tightly around the neck as to be hidden from sight; it was completely buried in the flesh, and was fastened by a knot which lay just under the left ear" (ibid., 513). And in "Thou Art the Man," often considered Poe's fourth detective story, the narrator ("Mr. P.") exposes and destroys the murderer Charley Goodfellow by confronting him with the speaking corpse of his victim, who bursts out of a wine cask with impressive consequences:

> There sprang up into a sitting position, directly facing the host, the bruised, bloody and nearly putrid corpse of the murdered Mr. Shuttleworthy himself. It gazed for a few moments ... with its decaying and lack-lustre eyes ... uttered slowly, but clearly and impressively the words, "Thou art the man!" and then, falling over the side of the chest as if thoroughly satisfied, stretched out its limbs quiveringly. (Ibid., 740)[2]

Such obsessive instances of mutilated language suggest that for Poe the disjunction between linguistic and physical identity was always traumatic. As in so much detective fiction, the violence attendant on social relations in "Rue Morgue" results from the represented encounter between two-dimensional signs and three-dimensional bodies, and might properly be described as cryptonymic. I borrow the term from Nicholas Abraham and Maria Torok, who in their reinterpretation of Freud's case study hypothesize that the Wolf Man's physical symptoms stem from a punning, multilingual "verbarium" of key (or code) words, which indirectly name the principal traumas of his life. The words are "encrypted" in the self to avoid analysis by the self, for whom they pose insoluble psychic double binds. In consequence, it becomes an essential but impossible task to say whether the words name a real event or whether in themselves they produce the symptoms they are meant to explain.[3] Derrida describes the Wolf Man in language equally well suited to the involutions of psychic space manifested in, say, Roderick Usher: he had "edified a crypt within him: an artifact, an artificial unconscious in the Self, an interior enclave, partitions, hidden passages, zigzags, occult and difficult traffic" (Abraham and Torok 1986, xliv); the only passage through this Gothic architecture of the mind is through the magic words of the verbarium, coded translingually across English, Russian, and German, to keep the crypt, that "monument of a catastrophe," impermeable (ibid., xlv). As the comparison to Usher suggests, cryptonymy involves an unambiguously Gothic understanding of language. Not only Derrida's diction but the case study's corresponding themes of paralysis, violation, and unspeakability are common property of the Gothic novel and of nineteenth-century hysteria.

As I have noted elsewhere (Rosenheim 1989), to an extraordinary degree cryptography provides secret organizing principles for Poe's trilogy of detective stories. The cryptograph reflects on the level of the sign what Dupin embodies on the level of character, and what the form of detective fiction implies on the level of narrative: the fantasy of an absolutely legible world. As it is encountered in Poe's essays on secret writing, cryptography is the utopian inverse of cryptonymy, since in it reader and writer are fully present to one another within their two-dimensional cipher. Conceptually, analysis is closely associated with cryptography. Both depend on the "separating or breaking up of any whole into its parts so as to find out their nature, proportion, function, relationship, etc.,"[4] and both emphasize the abstract, symbolic force of mind over matter, which provides a form of mental leverage over the world. But already in the moment of creating the genre of detective fiction, Poe suggests that the only "analysis" it can offer may itself be a fiction. While cryptography seems to propose a detour around the Gothic aspects of cryptonymy—a way of avoiding its disturbing physicality—cryptography takes on disturbing cryptonymy features whenever Poe attempts to represent actual bodies. The problem is that cryptography provides an *alternative body* in conflict with one's corporeal investment; since even in cryptography language is never truly free of the material shell of the signifier, this linguistic self finds itself in tension with one's embodied identity.

Despite the story's promise of legibility, "Rue Morgue" intimates that the triumph of the detective's analytics cannot be clearly distinguished from the effects of the analytics on the reader's body. To the degree that the reader invests his belief in this formal drive toward legibility, he becomes Poe's dupe, for should the reader attempt to imitate Dupin, he quickly finds that his analysis devolves into mere repetition.[5] And yet, to that same degree, these stories threaten to become meaningful: if the uncanny anticipation of the story's own interpretation is at all significant, it is so because the text discloses in the reader's body the nature of the interpretive desires that initiate one's reading. Like the purloined letter, the lesson of "Rue Morgue" is hidden in plain sight, announced in the story's first lines: "The mental features discoursed of as the analytical are, in themselves, but little susceptible of analysis. We appreciate them only in their effects" (Poe 1984b, 397). While our readings certainly produce "effects," the desire to discover the right relation of analysis to literature is ultimately doomed by the impossibility of establishing a metalanguage uncontaminated by the materiality of signification. In this respect, the narrator's attempt in "Rue Morgue" to keep his analytic discourse free from the corporeal opacity of his subject resembles Freud's procedure in his case studies. If detective fiction is notoriously susceptible to psychoanalytic interpretation, this is only because psychoanalysis, too, has often seemed to presume the separation of its analytical procedures from the materiality of its objects—a separation between language and the body that "Rue Morgue" both constructs and, finally, destroys.

II

Following Richard Wilbur, critics have long recognized speech in "Rue Morgue" as a symbolic expression of identification, noting that Dupin's use of a high and a low register links him with the high and low voices of the sailor and the ape (Wilbur 1967). But Poe is finally less interested in pitch than in syllabification, which runs on a continuum from the orangutan's grunts to Dupin's "rich tenor," with its "deliberateness and entire distinctness" of enunciation (Poe 1984b, 410–12). Hence Poe's own deliberation in staging the ape's crime within earshot of such a polyglot group of auditors, each of whom hears in the orangutan's voice someone speaking an unfamiliar language. Henri Duval: "The shrill voice, this witness thinks, was that of an Italian.... Was not acquainted with the Italian language." William Bird: the voice "appeared to be that of a German.... Does not understand German." Alfonzo Garcia: "The shrill voice was that of an Englishman—is sure of this. Does not understand the English language, but judges by intonation" (Poe 1984b, 409–10). Similarly, Isidore Muset, "—Odenheimer," and Alberto Montani, respectively attribute the voice to Spanish, French, and Russian speakers. Poe even has Dupin supplement his references to the "five great divisions of Europe" with mention of "Asiatics" and "Africans," in what amounts to a Cook's Tour of the varieties of human speech:

> Now, how strangely unusual must that voice have really been, about which such testimony as this *could* have been elicited!—in whose *tones*, even, denizens of the five great divisions of Europe could recognize nothing familiar! You will say that it might have

been the voice of an Asiatic—of an African.... Without denying the inference, I will now merely call your attention to [the fact that] ... no words—no sounds resembling words—were by any witness mentioned as distinguishable. (Ibid., 416)

What is at stake in this inventory? As with the case studies of deaf-mutes and feral children that appeared toward the end of the eighteenth century, the orangutan offered Enlightenment thinkers a liminal figure of the human at a time when language was crucially involved in the definition of humanity. By the 1840s, however, the ape had been reduced to a comic or grotesque image. But given Poe's insistence on the syllabic nature of speech, it is also important to recognize the orangutan's affiliation with a tradition of philosophical inquiry.[6] The most comprehensive discussion of the orangutan's relation to language is given in *The Origin and Progress of Language*, by James Burnet, Lord Monboddo, who devotes sixty pages to this question in order to understand "the origin of an art so admirable and so useful as language," a subject "necessarily connected with an inquiry into the original nature of man, and that primitive state in which he was, before language was invented" (Burnet 1974, 1:267). Monboddo hypothesizes that the orangutan is actually a species of humankind, being "a barbarous nation, which has not yet learned the use of speech" (ibid., 270). The taxonomic name of the orangutan, *Homo sylvestris*, is merely a translation of the Malay "Ourang-Outang," which, according to the naturalist Buffon, "signifies, in their language, a wild man" (ibid., 272). According to Monboddo, orangutans use tools, grow melancholy when separated from their tribes, and are capable of conjugal attachment and even shame. Monboddo cites an explorer who saw a female orangutan that "shewed signs of modesty ... wept and groaned, and performed other human actions: So that nothing human seemed to be wanting in her, except speech" (ibid., 272–73).

By enlisting orangutans in the same species as humans, Monboddo intends to demonstrate that what separates the two is less biology than culture, epitomized by the possession of language. For Buffon, this lack of speech discredits the orangutan's evolutionary pretensions. Monboddo ridicules Buffon, however, for making "the faculty of speech" part of the essence of humanity, and for suggesting that "the state of pure nature, in which man had not the use of speech, is a state altogether ideal and imaginary" (ibid., 293). Buffon thus anticipates the current association of language and human origins. For Poe as for Buffon, the "state of pure nature" is "altogether ideal" and precisely "imaginary," since, ontogenetically if not phylogenetically, human consciousness is a function of the subject's mirroring in language.

This tradition provides a context for understanding the dramatic process by which the narrator discovers the identity of the killer. From the start, Poe has planted clues: the crime is "brutal," "inhuman," "at odds with the ordinary notions of human conduct." Now Dupin remarks on the crime's strange combination of features:

> "We have gone so far as to combine the ideas of an agility astounding, a strength superhuman, a ferocity brutal, a butchery without motive, a *grotesquerie* in horror absolutely alien from humanity, and a voice foreign in tone to the ears of men of many nations, and devoid of all distinct or intelligible syllabification.... What impression have I made upon your fancy?"
>
> I felt a creeping of the flesh as Dupin asked me the question. "A madman," I said, "has done this deed—some raving maniac escaped from a neighboring *Maison de Santé*." (Poe 1984b, 423)

The narrator's suggestion is close, but "the voices of madmen, even in their wildest paroxysms ... have always the coherence of syllabification" (ibid., 558). Identification of the criminal depends, again, on Dupin's understanding of language; in fact, the testimony of the crime's auditors constitutes an *aural cryptogram*. The origin of this moment goes back to "A Few Words on Secret Writing," in which Poe remarked that of the hundred ciphers he received, "there was only one which we did not immediately succeed in solving. This one we *demonstrated* to be an imposition—that is to say, we fully proved it a jargon of random characters, having no meaning whatsoever." Poe's ability to interpret signs requires him to recognize when a set of signs violates the "universal" rules of linguistic formation. The claim to cryptographic mastery depends on the logically prior ability to recognize when a set of characters is not even language. By having the solution to the crime in "Rue Morgue" turn on the aural cryptogram, Poe simultaneously dramatizes both the power of human analysis and his fear of what life without language might be like.

After its recapture the orangutan is lodged in the *Jardin des Plantes*. Until his death in 1832, the *Jardin* was Georges Cuvier's center of research; as the repeated juxtaposition of Cuvier and Dupin indicates, Poe finds in the zoologist's mode of analysis an analogue to his own technique of detection.[7] Cuvier was famous for his ability to reconstruct an animal's anatomy from fragmentary paleontological remains, through systematic structural comparison. As a contemporary of Poe's wrote: "Cuvier astonished the world by the announcement that the law of relation which existed between the various parts of animals applied not only to entire systems, but even to parts of a system; so that, given an extremity, the whole skeleton might be known ... and even the habits of the animal could be indicated" (*Review* 1851).[8] Like Cuvier's bones, and in implicit analogy with them, syllables are for Poe linguistic universals, basic morphological units that form the necessary substrate to thought. Individual words possess meaning for the linguist only through their participation in a global system: "the word is no longer attached to a representation except insofar as it is previously a part of the grammatical organization by means of which the language defines and guarantees its own coherence" (Foucault 1973, 280–81).

Cuvier seems to provide a methodological justification for Poe's cryptographic reading of the world. But if this is so, what should we make of Cuvier's key role in revealing the true nature of the murderer? Having teased the reader's narrative appetite with oblique clues concerning the killer's nature, Dupin introduces the text of Cuvier with a theatrical flourish, sure that his revelation will produce its intended effect: "It was a minute anatomical and generally descriptive account of the large fulvous Ourang-Outang of the East Indian Islands. The gigantic stature, the prodigious strength and activity, the wild ferocity, and the imitative propensities of these mammalia are sufficiently well known to all. I understood the full horrors of the murder at once" (Poe 1984b, 424). This is a curious passage, not least because in Poe's version, the description of the orangutan virtually reverses Cuvier's actual claims. Not content to note that the orangutan is "a mild and gentle animal, easily rendered tame and affectionate," Cuvier disparages "the exaggerated descriptions of some authors respecting this resemblance" to humans (Cuvier 1832, 54–55); he at once deflates both the ape's anthropic pretensions and its wildness. That Poe knew this text seems almost certain: M'Murtrie, who translated Cuvier's book, seven years later published with Poe and Thomas Wyatt *The Conchologist's First Book*, with "Animals according to Cuvier." Yet evidently Poe's intellectual allegiance to Cuvier was subservient to his need to magnify the melodramatic and Gothic aspects of the murders. In the final analysis, it is not the crime but the solution that produces the reader's uncanny shiver, not the violence but the minute and clinical attention that Dupin requires of the narrator. To understand why the killer's simian origins produce "the full horrors" of which the narrator speaks, we need first to examine the effects of the revelation that Poe's narrative produces.

III

Throughout the Dupin stories, Poe offers models for the nature of analysis, including games of odd and even, theories of mental identification, and the elaborate comparison of the respective merits of chess and whist. Yet as we discover in "Rue Morgue," analysis itself must remain disappointingly invisible to the reader, except through its intensely pleasing effects:

> We know of them, among other things, that they are always to their possessor, when inordinately possessed, a source of the liveliest enjoyment. As the strong man exults in his physical ability, delighting in such exercises as call his muscles into action, so glories the analyst in that moral activity which *disentangles*. He derives pleasure from even the most trivial occupations bringing his talent into play. He is fond of enigmas, of conundrums, of hieroglyphics. (Poe 19846, 397)

In its basic narrative structure, "Rue Morgue" is itself an enigma whose effects, according to its own logic, should clarify the nature of analysis. But the opening discussion reverses the ordinary process of interpretation: the crime and its solution "will appear to the reader somewhat in the light of a commentary upon the [analytic] propositions just advanced" (ibid., 400), rather than the other way around. Nor is it clear exactly why we should experience "the liveliest enjoyment" from the ensuing tale of violence. Might we understand the tale as an allegory of the superiority of brain to brawn, in which Dupin handily defeats both the sailor's evasions and the ape's brute difference? Certainly; but the pleasure of such a reading is not itself analytical, and hence brings us no closer to understanding the properties that the narrative so ostentatiously foregrounds. Since the narrator has compared analytic pleasure to that enjoyed by the strong man, we ought perhaps to consider the two "strong men" of the tale as guides. The first of these is the orangutan (*Homo sylvestris*), possessed of "superhuman" strength; the second is its owner, "a tall, stout, and muscular-looking person" who comes equipped, as in a fairy tale, with "a huge oaken cudgel" (ibid., 426). But these figures seem to exercise their powers only in violence: the elder L'Espanaye's head is "nearly severed" "with one determined sweep" of the ape's "muscular arm" (ibid., 430), and though the sailor seems amicable by comparison, even he spends his energy whipping the ape into submission, and his muscles tense at the thought of killing Dupin ("The sailor's face flushed.... He started to his feet and grasped his cudgel" [ibid., 427]). In practice, while the pleasures of the analyst seem only figurally related to those of his muscular counterpart ("As the strong man exults ... so glories the analyst"), the narrative that follows demonstrates that the relation between the two is causal: the analyst's skills are called for because of the strong man's exertion, as Dupin pits his thought against the unwitting power of the ape and the sailor's potential for violence.

According to Peter Brooks, any given story has a central metaphor that, however dissolved into the thread of the narrative, articulates the story's primary relationships. And since all narrative can be mapped rhetorically as a relation between the poles of metaphor and metonymy, we can describe the narrative's duration as a metonymy "acting out of the implications of metaphor," which at once reveals the meaning of the impacted initial metaphor and transforms it through its narrative embodiment (Brooks 1985, 13).

Citing the example of Conan Doyle's "Musgrave Ritual," Brooks shows that the obscure and apparently meaningless ritual practiced by the Musgraves is actually a metaphor that condenses and shapes the action of the story. Regardless of whether Brooks is right to contend that the relation between initial metaphor and narrative metonymy holds for all stories, it is undeniably true of detective fiction in general, and of its founding text as well. The first rhetorical figure encountered in "Rue Morgue"—the analogy between the pleasures of analysis and those of strength—provides the story's structuring metaphor; in fact, the tale has everything to do with the proper way of understanding the relationship between the physical and the mental, and the pleasures associated with each.

Take as an emblem of this disjunction the difficulty that the Mmes L'Espanaye find in keeping head and body together: Camille L'Espanaye is strangled; her mother's throat is "so entirely cut that upon an attempt to raise her, the head fell off" (Poe 1984b, 411, 406). "Rue Morgue" repeatedly stages the violent separation of heads and bodies, literal and figurative, and while Dupin and the orangutan are the most visibly polarized emblems of this split, the form of the tale repeats this pattern, joining its analytic head to the fictive body through the most insecure of narrative ligatures: "The narrative to follow will appear to the reader somewhat in the light of a commentary upon the propositions just advanced" (ibid., 400). However one wishes to allegorize this relation of heads to bodies—as an opposition between spirit and matter, analysis and effects, or ego and id—it is the distinguishing structural feature of the text at every level. But though "Rue Morgue" formally repeats the opposition between body and head in the relationship of narrative and commentary, we can identify Brooks's initial metaphor only in retrospect, since Poe's text conceals its metaphors as metonymies until the narrative's climactic revelation, by which time we as readers have been thoroughly implicated in a scene at which we imagined ourselves only spectators.

Generically, this implication has already been built into the text through its combination of the Gothic with what I call the analytic sublime. Besides its extravagant setting in a "time-eaten and grotesque mansion, long deserted through superstitions into which we did not inquire, and tottering to its fall" (ibid., 400–401), "Rue Morgue" reveals its generic debt in the sensational violence of the killings, the segmentation of space into barely permeable vesicles, and the uncanniness of the crime's resolution. Although Eve Sedgwick argues compellingly that as a genre the Gothic is preeminently concerned with male homosocial desire, Poe's detective stories find their activating tension less in the closeting of sexual difference than in the closeting of consciousness within the body. Despite its overt disavowal of the Gothic ("let it not be supposed," the narrator reminds us, "that I am detailing any mystery, or penning any romance" [ibid., 402]), Poe employs an aura of analytical reason only to intensify the reader's experience of violence and disorder.

In the Gothic's implicit spatial model, Sedgwick suggests, an "individual fictional 'self'" is often "massively blocked off from something to which it ought normally to have access": air, personal history, a loved one. Regardless of the specific lack, it is the unspeakability of this occlusion that is generically distinctive: "The important privation is the privation exactly of language, as though language were a sort of safety valve between the inside and the outside which being closed off, all knowledge, even when held in common, becomes solitary, furtive, and explosive" (Sedgwick 1986, 17).[9] Thus although the detective story, with its long retrospective reconstructions, seems par excellence the genre in which language is adequate to its task of description, in the end, the apparent rationality of the detective is a device used to create Sedgwick's Gothic division. Far from offering a safety valve between inner and outer, language itself separates the analyst from the object, thereby creating the pressure differential between self and world that language is pressed to describe. The impalpable tissue separating inside and outside is consciousness itself, which can never be identical either with itself or with the body. The more intensely Poe thematizes disembodied reason (the analytic sublime), the more powerfully Gothic will be the moment in which our identification with the body of the ape is revealed.

This use of reason against itself appears with particular clarity in the

episode in which Dupin discovers the exit by which the killer escaped from
the quarters of the Mmes L'Espanaye. In this first instance of the locked-
room mystery, the doors to the L'Espanaye home are locked; there are no
secret passages or "preternatural events"; and the condition of the bodies
rules out suicide. The two windows are shut, each fastened by "a very stout
nail" pushed into a gimlet hole drilled through frame and casement. Yet on
visiting the house, Dupin displays absolute confidence in his logical powers:
"The impossibility of egress, by means already stated, being thus absolute,
we are reduced to the windows. It is only left for us to prove that these
apparent 'impossibilities' are, in reality, not such." Reasoning that "the
murderers *did* escape from one of these windows," Dupin decides that the
sashes

> *must*, then, have the power of fastening themselves. There was no
> escape from this conclusion. I had traced the secret to its ultimate
> result—and that result *was the nail*. It had, I say, in every respect,
> the appearance of its fellow in the other window, but this fact was
> an absolute nullity (conclusive as it might seem to be) when
> compared with the consideration that here, at this point,
> terminated the clew. "There *must* be something wrong," I said,
> "about the nail." I touched it; and the head, with about a quarter
> of the shank, came off in my fingers. The rest of the shank was in
> the gimlet-hole, where it had been broken off. (Poe 1984b, 419)

This is what Freud called the "omnipotence-of-consciousness" with a
vengeance: the evidence of the senses is "an absolute nullity" against the
locked room of Dupin's logic ("There was no escape from this conclusion").
As predicted, and in apparent confirmation of his hypothesis, the nail-head
pops off at Dupin's touch, as if his analysis was a type of narrative
thaumaturgy, able to bring about changes in the world through mere
enunciation ("'There must be something wrong,' I said, 'about the nail'").
Such confusion of causes and effects is a version of the tale's split between
analysis and action, an indication that Poe's analytical sublime contains the
seeds of its own undoing. The abstract introduction to a tale of horror (also
familiar from "The Imp of the Perverse") intensifies the shock of the
narrative by increasing the contrast between the narrative's ratiocinative calm
and the brutality to follow. And since excessive contrast is itself a Gothic
convention, "Rue Morgue" stages the relation between the story's
introduction and its main body as another instance of the Gothic. Indeed, the
nail itself anticipates my conclusion: its status as a token of the power of

reason is immediately undermined by Dupin's recognition that the nail itself is fractured. Like everything else in "Rue Morgue," the nail—an apparent integer—splits into head and body.

IV

This constant recurrence of heads and bodies is structurally parallel to the separation in detective fiction of the metonymy and metaphoric poles of language. Working with clues associated with the narrative's originating crime, the detective's analytical method is primarily a form of metonymy, which is, in turn, associated with the frame narrative of the detective's analysis, and with its origins in cryptography. Conversely, the core narrative of most detective stories obsessively concerns itself with bodies, most commonly with their violation and murder. Metonymy, Lacan suggests, is evidence of the displacement of desire for the mother onto the signifying chain itself. As the law of the signifier, the law of the father separates the infant from the mother at the moment when Oedipal injunctions manifest themselves in, and as, the child's newly acquired language. The child attempts to recapture its original plenitude through the use of language, but this displaced search turns into an identification of suspended desire with the process of signification itself:

> And the enigmas that desire seems to pose for a "natural philosophy"—its frenzy mocking the abyss of the infinite, the secret collusion with which it envelops the pleasure of knowing and of dominating with a jouissance, these amount to no other derangement of instinct than that of being caught in the rails— eternally stretching forth towards the *desire for something else*—of metonymy. (Lacan 1977, 166–67)

In place of the child's imaginary, there are only the "rails" of metonymic linkage, which, far from leading back to the mother, constitute the bars separating one from her being. But this "desire for something else" is not without compensatory pleasures, chief among which is the "jouissance" of employing language to structure the observable world, investing it with the sense of an almost tangible approach to the object of desire. The rails teeter constantly along the edge of remembrance, "at the very suspension-point of the signifying chain" (ibid.).

In its concern with evidence, the detective's search is a variation on the metonymic suspension displayed by the narrator of the Gothic romances, who tends "to muse, for long unwearied hours, with [his] attention riveted to some frivolous device on the margin or in the typography of a book" (Poe 1984b, 227). This obsessive attention is a defense mechanism designed to turn the mind away from something that must seem to be repressed, but which, in fact, hovers teasingly close to consciousness:

> There is no point, among the many incomprehensible anomalies of the science of mind, more thrillingly exciting than the fact ... that in our endeavors to recall to memory something long forgotten, we often find ourselves *upon the very verge* of remembrance, without being able, in the end, to remember. And thus how frequently, in my intense scrutiny of Ligeia's eyes, have I felt approaching the full knowledge of their expression—felt it approaching—yet not quite be mine—and so at length entirely depart! (Ibid., 264–65)

Compare this to the narrator's reaction to Dupin's description of the strength, ferocity, and "harsh and unequal voice" possessed by the orangutan: "At these words a vague and half-formed conception of the meaning of Dupin flitted over my mind. I seemed to be upon the verge of comprehension, without power to comprehend—as men, at times, find themselves upon the brink of remembrance without being able, in the end, to remember" (ibid., 421). In both cases, the quality of this near-memory, and the habits of both excessively attentive narrators, correspond to Lacan's metonymic subject "perversely" fixated "at the very suspension-point of the signifying chain, where the memory-screen is immobilized and the fascinating image of the fetish is petrified" (Lacan 1977, 167).

Lacan's rhetorical analysis permits us to see how completely the metonymic frame narrative of the tale disembodies both analyst and reader, even as the Gothic narrative core of the detective story foregrounds metaphors of the body.[10] This metaphoric pull toward embodiment is crystallized in the basic scenario of "Rue Morgue," which, as Marie Bonaparte noted long ago, is a particularly nasty Oedipal triangle. For Bonaparte, the orangutan represents the infant, whose obsession with the question of the mother's sexual difference is only settled through the symbolic castration involved in Mme L'Espanaye's decapitation. Bonaparte's reading depends on a style of anatomical literalization now out of fashion, discredited in an era in which psychoanalytic critics rightfully prefer textual and rhetorical criticism to readings that, as Brooks notes, mistakenly choose as their objects of analysis "the author, the reader, or the fictive persons of the text" (Brooks 1987, 2). The problem is that "Rue Morgue" continually solicits what can only be described as bad Freudian readings. Bonaparte's biographical interpretation of Poe's fiction is, in the main, enjoyably unconvincing, but her monomaniacal inventory of sexual symbols (of, for instance, the L'Espanayes' chamber as a gigantic projection of the interior female anatomy) is difficult to dismiss. From the rending of the double doors of the L'Espanaye home ("a double or folding gate ... bolted neither at bottom nor top" forced "open, at length, with a bayonet"), to the ape's futile ransacking of Mme L'Espanaye's private drawers ("the drawers of a *bureau* ... were open, and had been, apparently, rifled, although many articles still remained in them" [Poe 1984b, 421]), to the identification of the broken and the whole nail, the story overcodes its anatomical symbols. Discovered in its crimes, the orangutan's "wild glances" fall on "the head of the bed, over which the face of its master, rigid with horror, was just discernible." The ape stuffs Camille "head-down" in the chimney; the L'Espanayes live in a room "at the head of the passage"; the nail in the window behind the bed is fixed "nearly to the head"; Dupin looks over "the head-board minutely"; the other nail too is "driven in nearly up to the head." The ape flees from its master's bed to the L'Espanayes, where it swings itself through the window "directly upon the headboard of the bed." "Head" is used twenty times, "bed," "bedstead," or "bedroom" seventeen times; as well as rhyming aurally, "head" and "bed" continually chime through their contiguity in the text, inviting the reader to link them through metaphor. Even the fractured window-nail can represent the mother's phallus: "Il y a le mystère du clou mutilé d'une des fenêtres, sans doute symbole, sur le mode 'mobilier,' de la castration de la mère." Dupin's inductions about the broken nail constitute a *fort-da* game in which he resolves the question of the maternal phallus by both denying its presence ("'There *must* be something wrong,' I said, 'about the nail.' I touched it; and the head ... came off in my fingers") and affirming it ("I now carefully replaced this head portion and ... the fissure was invisible"). Such an explanation helps clarify why the analysis of the nail musters such weird intensity: "There *must* ... be something wrong with the nail" (Bonaparte 1949, 439).

My claim is not that such anatomical allegorizing substantiates psychoanalytic criticism, but that Freudian readers have long been attracted to detective fiction just because the genre's structure and themes so often echo central psychoanalytic scenarios. What looks like Poe's eerie anticipation of psychoanalytic motifs may say as much about generic as about psychic structure. Certainly, the literary interest of Freud's case studies depends in no small part on an essentially cryptographic sense of power over the body. Despite Freud's frequent attempts to distance himself from writers of fiction, his early conception of psychoanalysis as "the task of making conscious the most hidden recesses of the mind" (Freud 1963a, 96), of rendering the body transparent to language, is driven by the same themes of cryptographic interiority at play in Poe's detective fiction. And Dupin's boast that "most men, in respect to himself, wore windows in their bosoms" (Poe 1984b, 401) is actually a more modest version of Freud's famous declaration in his study of Dora: "He that has eyes to see and ears to hear may convince himself that no mortal can keep a secret. If his lips are silent, he chatters with his finger-tips; betrayal oozes out of him at every pore" (Freud 1963a, 96).

Although critics have remarked on the embarrassing frequency with which detective stories draw on stock psychoanalytic imagery, no one has yet called attention to how thoroughly "Rue Morgue" seems to gloss the analytic process itself. Freud describes the "essence of the psychoanalytic situation" as follows:

> The analyst enters into an alliance with the ego of the patient to subdue certain uncontrolled parts of his id, i.e., to include them in a synthesis of the ego.... [If] the ego learns to adopt a defensive attitude towards its own id and to treat the instinctual demands of the latter like external dangers, this is at any rate partly because it understands that the satisfaction of instinct would lead to conflicts with the external world. (Under the influence of its upbringing, the child's ego accustoms itself to shift the scene of the battle from outside to inside and to master the *inner* danger before it becomes external.) (Freud 1963b, 253)

Freud's clinical observations would serve almost equally well to describe the sailor's visit to Dupin, with Dupin standing in for the analyst, the sailor for the analysand, and the orangutan as a figure for the remembered "primal scene." In *Dora*, Freud notes that "the patients' inability to give an ordered history of their life insofar as it coincides with the story of their illness is not merely characteristic of the neurosis," but is, in fact, a defining feature of mental illness; and Freud's essential test for recovery simply is the patient's newfound ability to narrate his or her life, to "remove all possible symptoms and to replace them by conscious thoughts" (Freud 1963a, 31, 32). In this case, the sailor must recount under duress the story of the crime, which is formally parallel to the dreams that provide the analytic material for Freud's case studies. His wish to hide his knowledge makes sense in terms of the plot, but it is less easy to explain away Dupin's insistence, at once solicitous and stern, that the sailor narrate what he knows. Dupin, one might say, enters into an alliance with the sailor in order that he might "subdue certain uncontrolled parts of his id," unmistakably represented by the ape. As a corollary, Dupin repeatedly insists that the sailor acknowledge the beast as his own: "Of course you are prepared to identify the property?" (Poe 1984b, 427), even as he declares that the sailor is both innocent and complicit: "You have nothing to conceal. You have no reason for concealment. On the other hand, you are bound by every principle of honor to confess all" (ibid., 428). Pressed to take a reward for ostensibly recovering the ape, Dupin continues the same theme: "You shall give me all the information in your power about these murders in the Rue Morgue" (ibid., 427).

Forced at gunpoint to answer, the sailor responds first by losing the ability to articulate ("The sailor's face flushed up, as if he were struggling with suffocation.... He spoke not a word" [Poe 1984b, 427]), and then by threatening compensatory violence ("He started to his feet and grasped his cudgel" [ibid.]), as the story of the ape homeopathically reproduces itself in the sailor's telling. The stress of confession threatens to produce a repetition of the original crime, but Dupin's mixture of firmness and kindness ("I perfectly well know that you are innocent of the atrocities in the Rue Morgue. It will not do, however, to deny that you are in some measure implicated in them" [ibid., 427]) permits him to redirect his symptomatic repetition into narrative—precisely the result of a successful analytic intervention predicted by Freud. The sailor explains how, having brought the ape from Borneo to Paris in order to sell it for profit, he returned one night to find that the orangutan had escaped into his bedroom,

> into which it had broken from a closet adjoining, where it had beef), as was thought, securely confined. Razor in hand, and fully lathered, it was sitting before a looking-glass, attempting the operation of shaving, in which it had no doubt previously watched its master through the key-hole of the closet. Terrified at the sight of so dangerous a weapon in the possession of an animal so ferocious, and so well able to use it, the man, for some moments, was at a loss what to do. He had been accustomed, however, to quiet the creature, even in its fiercest moods, by the use of a whip, and to this he now resorted. Upon sight of it, the Ourang-Outang sprang at once through the door of the chamber, down the stairs, and thence, through a window, unfortunately open, into the street. (Ibid., 428–29)

Having only heard up to this point about the animal's "intractable ferocity," this image of the orangutan is rather touching; even when the ape imitates "the motions of a barber" with the Mmes L'Espanaye, its purposes, we are told, are "probably pacific" (ibid., 430). Poe offers us a Darwinian revision of Freud, a primate scene in which the ape—still "in the closet," forced to peep through a keyhole—sees its master shaving, and tries to imitate him. Shaving codes the body as a part of culture, not nature; and as in David Humphreys's contemporary poem "The Monkey" (printed in Duyckinck and Duyckinck 1875, 1:392), the ape takes up the razor out of a wish to be human.[11] But without language, the developmental scenario implied by the ape's mimicry stalls: whatever its "imitative propensities," as a mute, the ape cannot readily make its intentions known. The ape's frustrated turn from gesture to violence reveals the abject inadequacy of mimesis in comparison with speech. Unable to manipulate abstract symbols, the ape takes out its rage on the flesh; and while the story's focus on injured mouths and throats may be an instance of displacement upward, it is also a direct attack on the organs of speech. The orangutan represents both Bonaparte's murderous infant, poised at the moment of discovering sexual difference, and a liminally human, highly evocative image of the body's resistance to signification. These elements are synthesized in a Lacanian revision of the primal scene as the entry into signification. Poe's use of the orangutan serves as his own myth of human origins, which condenses within itself both individual and evolutionary history, both linguistic and sexual desire.

Thanks to Dupin's narrative therapy, the sailor is afforded the opportunity to break the cycle of repetition through the type of analytic transference that, in Brooks's words, "succeeds in making the past and its scenarios of desire relive through signs with such vivid reality that the reconstructions it proposes achieve the *effect of* the real" (Brooks 1987, 13). Although it is meaningless to speak of curing a fictional character, this protoanalytic scene is one way in which Poe stages the reader's textual cathexis, though such a proleptic parody may suggest that, like "Rue Morgue" itself, the psychoanalyst's function is to manufacture a narrative rather than to reveal one. The sailor's mistake has been to assume that once he had succeeded in lodging the ape at his own residence, the danger that it posed was over. The sailor has yet to learn to "treat the instinctual demands of the [id] like external dangers." Hence, the captive ape escapes from the sailor, forcing him to face the violent consequences of its acting-out. The process of admitting his possession of the ape is a precondition for its taming, which requires that the sailor objectify and confront as an external danger ("no mean enemy") the fact of the bodily unconscious. The recapture of the erstwhile brute (a story Poe does not even bother to recount) represents the sailor's psychic reintegration. As Freud writes: "The struggle between physician and patient, between intellect and the forces of instinct, between recognition and the striving for discharge, is fought out almost entirely on the ground of transference-manifestations. This is the ground on which the victory must be won, the final expression of which is lasting recovery from the neurosis.... in the last resort no one can be slain *in absentia* or *in effigie*" (Freud 1963b, 114–15). By implication, literature might be said to stage *in effigie* just such ego-training sessions, teaching the reader "to shift the scene of the battle from outside to inside": from behaviors to an internalized encounter with the text.

Once the sailor confesses, and thereby owns up to his implication in the killings, the story is finished; the narrator has "scarcely anything to add," and hastily concludes by noting that the ape "was subsequently caught by the owner himself, who obtained for it a very large sum at the *Jardin des Plantes*. Le Bon was instantly released, upon our narration of the circumstances (with some comments from Dupin) at the *bureau* of the Prefect of Police" (Poe 1984b, 431). Since the real story of "Rue Morgue" concerns the production of uncanny effects in the reader, Poe has no qualms about violating the principles of narrative construction. Instead, the extreme brevity of the denouement, and the untidiness of the story's conclusion, remind us that Poe's characters are merely puppets, technical apparatuses deployed in the attempt to intensify our affective transference onto his tales. Although the allegorical reading sketched here could be elaborated further, the parallels between Freud's method in the case studies and Poe's narrative are clear. The elaborate sexual symbolism, the fetishization of analysis, the literalization of the "talking cure," and, above all, the story's peculiar staging of metaphor and metonymy are coordinated devices through which Poe enhances the reader's identification.

Thus far, the reader has had little incentive to identify with anyone except Dupin. But though Dupin's cryptographic power is specifically predicated on his linguistic prowess, the resolution of this case is not a matter of language alone. Instead, Dupin now finds himself confronting the tangible world, carefully measuring the "impression" made by the orangutan's fingers on Camille L'Espanaye's neck against the span and pattern of a human hand, only to find that the prints on the strangled woman are not even approximately the same ("'This' I said, 'is the mark of no human hand'" [ibid., 423]). Dupin continues his physical investigation: "Besides, the hair of a madman is not such as I now hold in my hand. I disentangled this little tuft from the rigidly clutched fingers of Madam L'Espanaye. Tell me what you can make of it: 'Dupin!' I said, completely unnerved, 'this hair is most unusual—this is no *human* hair'" (ibid.). Recall that in the opening paragraph of the story, the analyst is said to glory "in that moral activity which *disentangles*": just the word Dupin uses to describe the process of physically extracting his tuft of hair from the "rigidly clutched" hand of the corpse. For all the text's insistence on the separation between the pleasures of the strong man and those of the analyst, the solution of the Rue Morgue murders requires that Dupin make forceful, even violent, contact with the traces of the ape.

After producing his assembled physical evidence, Dupin asks the narrator: "What impression have I made upon your fancy?" repeating as a metaphor the word used to refer to the uncanny and inhuman marks left on the dead woman's neck. Prior to the moment in which Dupin histrionically reveals the orangutan as the culprit, the reader's body has been anesthetized by Dupin's disembodied analytics (an anesthetization also evident in Dupin, who in moments of excitement becomes "frigid and abstract," his eyes "vacant in expression" [ibid., 401, 415]). In the "creeping of the flesh" that follows (ibid., 423), the narrator's body identifies with the ape through Dupin's recreation of the crime, revealing that he, too, through his direct somatic response, is implicated in the narrative to which he listens. "A symptom," writes Lacan, is "a metaphor in which flesh or function is taken as a signifying element" (Lacan 1977, 166); and in the moment when the reader's skin shivers in sympathy with the narrator, we witness the overthrow of the metonymic order. In the shift to the metaphoric, in the symptomatic reproduction within the reader's body of a sensational response, the reader reveals his collaboration with the ape. Through the creation of this response, Poe circumvents Freud's complaint that in analysis "the patient hears what we say but it rouses no response in his mind" (Freud 1963b, 251). To rouse the mind, a text must also arouse the body: only through the symptomatic commitment of the reader's flesh can the text realize its transferential effects.

Appropriately, it is the knowledge of his own embodiment that permits Dupin to solve the mystery of the L'Espanayes' deaths. This is the implication of Dupin's final comments on the Prefect, in which he takes pains to emphasize the futility of the latter's "bodiless" wisdom: "In his wisdom is no *stamen*. It is all head and no body, like the pictures of the Goddess Laverna—or, at best, all head and shoulders, like a codfish. But he is a good creature after all. I like him especially for one master stroke of cant, by which he has attained his reputation for ingenuity. I mean the way he has '*de nier ce qui est, et d'expliquer ce qui n'est pas*'" (Poe 1984b, 431). Though figured as a "creature," it is just the Prefect's failure to negotiate between head and body that prevents him from imagining the animal nature of the killer. As a kind of walking bust, all head and shoulders, the Prefect, not Dupin, is an emblem for excessive rationality, unable to accommodate the ape's physical presence. By contrast, Dupin twice notes his admiration for the animal. "I almost envy you the possession of him," he admits to the sailor (Poe 1984b, 431); and we may suppose that Dupin longs for the animal's intense physicality, even as he revels in the physical effects, the "creeping of the flesh," he produces in his listeners. (Once more, Dupin appears as a stand-in for Poe, who also relies for his very bread and butter on the ability to conjure identification.) "Where is the ingenuity of unravelling a web which you yourself have woven for the express purpose of unravelling?" Poe asked of Cooke; we may now be able to answer that it lies in having in the meantime caught something in that web. In the present case, Dupin's greatest exertions are not to catch the monkey, but its owner, lured in by the text placed in the newspaper. Just so with the story's readers: drawn in by another piece of paper, by another thread or web, we find ourselves trapped within its self-dissolving structure, as any assumptions about the nature of analysis are undone by our own somatic performance.

As "The Murders in the Rue Morgue" concludes, the divergent senses of the word "stamen" crystallize its irreconcilable oppositions:

> "stamen, n.; pl. stamens rare stamina, [L., a warp in an upright loom, a thread; lit., that which stands up, from *stare*, to stand.] 1. a warp thread, especially in the ancient upright loom at which the weaver stood upright instead of sitting. [Obs.] 2. in botany, the male reproductive organ in flowers, formed principally of cellular tissue.[12]

Insofar as "stamen" refers to the male generative organ of a flower, it marks the (male) reader addressed by the text; call this the Freudian reading, in which to have a male body seems inseparable from complicity in the orangutan's gendered violence. But the first meaning, now obsolete, indicates the warp thread in a loom; and through familiar paths (loom, weaving, text), we arrive at the stamen as the narrative thread running throughout Poe's text. The story's overdetermined treatment of heads and bodies, words and things, analysis and its effects, implies the close association of the origins of narrative with the discovery of sexual difference, though it is impossible to tell which came first. Instead of reinforcing an evolutionary hierarchy that would separate us from our simian relations, the cryptographic narrative structure of "Rue Morgue" acts to remind us of our corporeal investment:

through the story's enacted rhetoric, the reader lives out the distance between the tale's opening metaphor and its closing one—between the simile comparing analysis and the strong man's pleasure, which safely separates its terms even as it joins them, and the metaphor of the stamen, which reveals the degree to which the reader, too, finds himself hopelessly entangled.

NOTES

1. It is a cliché of detective-fiction criticism that its most avid readers are professionals distinguished for their own analytic abilities—doctors, lawyers, and the like. W.H. Auden, one remembers, was a compulsive reader of detective fiction, as is failed Supreme Court nominee Judge Robert Bork, who consumes at least one a day.

2. The deception is accomplished by thrusting "a stiff piece of whalebone" down the throat of the corpse and doubling it over in the wine cask, so that it springs up when released. As for Mr. Shuttleworthy's impressive accusation, the narrator "confidently depended upon [his] ventriloquial abilities" (Poe 1984b, 742).

3. "It is not a situation *comprising* words that becomes repressed; the words are not dragged into repression by a situation. Rather, *the words themselves, expressing desire, are deemed to be generators of a situation that must be avoided and voided retroactively*" (Abraham and Torok 1986, 20). For hints of a cryptonymic reading of Poe's writing, see Riddel 1979.

4. *Webster's New Twentieth-Century Dictionary*, s.v. "analysis."

5. I use the male pronoun as a way of recognizing how extremely "The Murders in the Rue Morgue" genders its readers. While it would be profitable to investigate how the female reader locates herself in Poe's text, I am concerned here to elucidate the dominant assumptions of the genre, which begins with this story.

6. For a collection of eighteenth-century treatments of feral children, see Malson 1972, which includes Joan Itard's famous treatment of the Wild Boy of Aveyron. Shattuck 1980 offers a detailed but dull interpretation of Itard's work. The idea of a criminal orangutan was not original to Poe: Peithman records that Poe "very likely saw an article, 'New Mode of Thieving,' in the *Annual Register for 1834* ... which tells of an 'extraordinary burglary' in which a woman entering her bedroom is attacked by a 'Monkey (or a Ribbed-face Baboon) which threw her down, and placing his feet upon her breast, held her pinned firmly to the ground.'" The animal, it turns out, belonged to "itinerant showmen" from whom it had "been let loose for the sake of plundering" (Poe 1981a, 196–97).

7. Cuvier actually boasted about the superiority of his method to that of the detective: "This single track therefore tells the observer about the kind of teeth; the kind of jaws, the haunches, the shoulder, and the pelvis of the animal which has passed: it is more certain evidence than all of Zadig's clues" (Coleman 1964, 102). Voltaire's novel is typically cited as the source for the detective's method, in the inferential reasoning by which three brothers perfectly describe a horse they have not seen, relying only on the circumstantial traces that remained.

8. Foucault suggests the intellectual ties between Dupin and Cuvier by using a quotation from Schlegel: "the structure or comparative grammar of languages furnishes as certain a key of their genealogy as the study of comparative anatomy has done to the loftiest branch of natural science" (Foucault 1973, 280).

9. Sedgwick's emphasis on male homosocial desire initially seems like a promising

way of reading Poe's detective stories, which manifest many of the gendered conventions—including the doubling of criminal and detective, the detective's social and physical alienation, and the violence directed against female bodies—that have long characterized crime fiction. Yet Poe's homosocial pairs keep turning into repetitions of a single self (Dupin and the narrator, Dupin and Minister D—, D— and his imagined brother), without the triangulation of difference needed to set sexual desire in play. On the Gothic and male homosociality, see Sedgwick 1985, 83–117.

10. Reacting against this type of tropic determination, Geoffrey Hartman warns critics not to move too quickly from rhetorical analysis to narrative significance: "The detective story structure—strong beginnings and endings and a deceptively rich, counterfeit, 'excludable' middle—resembles almost too much that of symbol or trope. Yet the recent temptation of linguistic theorists to collapse narrative structure into this or that kind of metaphoricity becomes counterproductive if it remains blind to the writer's very struggle to outwit the epileptic Word" (Hartman 1975, 214). Hartman's caution is well taken, but the meaning of the detective story's rhetorical form lies primarily in its somatic effects on the reader, and not in its unsustainable claims to revelation.

11. Attempting to imitate its master, Humphreys's animal accidentally cuts its own throat (Poe 1981a, 197). Poe habitually associates hair, the sexualized body, and violence. The first thing discovered at the crime scene are "thick tresses—very thick tresses—of grey human hair ... torn out by the roots," "perhaps half a million of hairs at a time" (Poe 1984b, 422); and Marie Rogêt's jilted paramour identifies her body by stroking her arms to see if they have her characteristically luxuriant hair.

12. *Webster's New Twentieth-Century Dictionary*, s.v. "stamen."

SCOTT PEEPLES

Black and White and Re(a)d All Over:
The Narrative of Arthur Gordon Pym

WHY DID POE WRITE *PYM*?

Before leaving the *Southern Literary Messenger* near the end of 1836, Poe had begun his only novel, although that term seems inappropriate for the enigmatic *Narrative of Arthur Gordon Pym of Nantucket*. At once a mock nonfictional exploration narrative, adventure saga, bildungsroman, hoax, largely plagiarized travelogue, and spiritual allegory, *Pym* stands as one of the most elusive major texts of American literature.[1] Apparently Poe and T. W. White had planned to serialize the work in the *Messenger*, but only two installments appeared early in 1837; by that time Poe had moved to New York, where by May he had arranged for Harper and Brothers to publish Pym in book form. As Poe's first book of prose and his first book under the imprint of a major publisher, *Pym* represented a golden opportunity for the aspiring 29-year-old author. But the book did not fare well: although better distributed than his volumes of poetry, it met with poor sales and mixed reviews. Poe himself referred to *Pym* as a "silly book" the year after it was published (*Letters*, 1:130), which raises the question of why Poe, acutely aware of the literary market and determined to perfect his craft, would write a book that lacks the coherence he would insist on in his and others' short fiction, a book that either fails to meet or disregards readers' expectations (in his time or ours) in regard to narrative consistency and wholeness of plot.

From *Edgar Allan Poe Revisited*, edited by Nancy A. Walker. ©1998 by Twayne Publishers.

At the time, writing a book-length narrative must have seemed a necessary career decision to Poe, for it was probably not a labor of love. Although Poe had improved his prospects for a literary career by editing the *Messenger* for a year, he still could not interest publishers in his "Tales of the Folio Club." He had no steady job in New York, and, with the onset of the economic depression of 1837 (which began while Poe was probably still working on *Pym* and which delayed its publication by a year), his future as a professional writer must have seemed dim. While waiting for *Pym* to be published, he was sufficiently discouraged to write to a well-connected author, James Kirke Paulding, asking for help in obtaining a clerkship that would release him from "the miserable life of literary drudgery."[2] Such a gesture suggests that he might have undertaken *Pym* somewhat grudgingly and with a heightened cynicism toward the profession of authorship. In rejecting "Tales of the Folio Club," Harper and Brothers had advised Poe to "lower himself a little to the ordinary comprehension of the generality of readers" and explained that American readers preferred a "single and connected story [that] occupies the whole volume, or number of volumes, as the case may be" (Thomas and Jackson, 193). Although Poe could hardly afford to spend months on a single project (even established authors did not receive advances for books in the 1830s), he might have reasoned that only a popular novel could raise his status and earning power and was therefore worth the gamble.[3]

If Poe's aim was to appeal to a mass audience, a voyage to the South Pole provided ideal subject matter. The abundance of travel writing and sea lore in the 1830s—published as pamphlets and books and in weekly and monthly magazines—indicates the popularity of the mode he had chosen for his novel. In the wake of Jeremiah Reynolds's 1829 to 1830 polar expedition and his efforts in 1836 to persuade Congress to sponsor further exploration, Americans had become particularly interested in these uncharted regions. Poe imported facts, plot devices, and sometimes entire passages from Reynolds's published reports (which he reviewed in the same issue of the *Southern Literary Messenger* that included the first installment of *Pym*), as well as Benjamin Morrell's best-selling *Narrative of Four Voyages* (ghost-written by Samuel Woodworth) and dozens of other popular sea narratives.[4]

Poe, then, had legitimate reasons for choosing to write a sea-adventure tale culminating in a polar discovery. But given the novel's timeliness, along with Poe's virtuosity as fiction writer and his awareness of the public demand for "sensations," the question remains why he crafted *Pym* so that it frustrates readers' expectations more often than it fulfills them. One logical but unsatisfying answer is that Poe simply lacked a novelist's "vision" or sensibility, that he would soon champion the "single-effect" theory of the short story because he could not negotiate the multiple interlocking elements of plot or elaborate the depths of character necessary to produce a coherent novel. But regardless of Poe's ability to write a coherent novel, his mixed feelings toward the reading public might have prodded him to concoct a large-scale mystification, a novel that encourages and then subverts its readers' attempts to find meaning. I have already discussed Poe's interest in hoaxes and mystifications up to this point in his career, his desire to appeal to a mass audience while encoding inside jokes and erudite satire for the benefit of a highbrow audience; he might well have responded to the Harpers' practical advice by deliberately writing a novel with all the outward appearances of a best-selling potboiler but with a hole—a vortex, in fact— that would drain away coherence and meaning. If Poe had intended to create a mystification in the spirit of Von Jung, he half succeeded: on the one hand, the Harpers accepted *Pym*, and the book continues to baffle (and perhaps mystify) readers and critics to this day; on the other hand, the book did not gain Poe the literary celebrity or the money that he desperately needed.

Perhaps we should add to the list of reasons for *Pym* turning out as it did Poe's tendency to sabotage his best opportunities to attain professional stability. Biographers almost invariably attribute to Poe a personal "imp of the perverse," as he would later call it; writing against the principles of unity and verisimilitude that Poe and his contemporaries recognized as essential to the novel could be yet another instance of that impulse.[5] Toward the end of the book, in fact, Pym gives in to an overwhelming desire to annihilate himself by plunging off a steep cliff (only to be caught by his companion Dirk Peters): "For one moment my fingers clutched convulsively upon their hold, while, with the movement, the faintest possible idea of ultimate escape wandered, like a shadow, through my mind—in the next my whole soul was pervaded with *a longing to fall*; a desire, a yearning, a passion utterly uncontrollable" (*IV*, 198). Poe's ambiguous use of the word "escape" is worth noting, for while Pym and Peters are trying to escape death, either from starvation or discovery by the Tsalalians, "escape" in this context also suggests the escape *through* death from Pym's predicament, from the nearly constant suffering and terror he has experienced on his journey. Similarly, a frustrated Poe might have seen *Pym* as a means of escape from the life of literary drudgery, either attaining celebrity or committing professional suicide. But like Pym's leap into Peters's arms, Poe's novel-writing plunge provided him no escape.

While I have taken some license in reading Poe's predicament into Pym's plunge into the abyss, other instances of Poe writing himself into his novel are more specific and less speculative. As many critics have pointed out, "Arthur Gordon Pym" sounds somewhat like "Edgar Allan Poe," with the same number of syllables in each part of both names, the same ending consonants in the first and middle names, and the same initial consonant and number of letters in the last.[6] (As has also been noted, "Pym" is an anagram for "ymp," again suggesting impulse or the imp of the perverse.) Biographers and critics, notably Richard Wilbur and Burton R. Pollin, have called attention to several intriguing biographical echoes, particularly in the earlier chapters; for instance, Wilbur claims that the character of Augustus Barnard is based on Poe's boyhood friend Ebenezer Burling as well as his brother, William Henry Poe (Augustus dies on August 1, the date on which William Henry died in 1832).[7] In the first paragraph of chapter 1 Pym tells us that Augustus's father "has many relations, I am sure, in Edgarton" and also notes that his own grandfather speculated "in the stocks of the Edgarton New-Bank" (*IV*, 57): Poe uses the proximity of Edgartown, Massachusetts, to slip these self-references into Pym's and Augustus's genealogy. He also makes his own birthday, January 19, the date for a turning point late in the novel, the *Jane Guy* crew's fateful meeting with the Tsalalians. A few commentators have seen Poe's preoccupation with food and consumption throughout *Pym* in terms of his own marginal existence, reflecting perhaps the hunger Poe, Virginia, and Muddy experienced as Poe was writing the book, or, as Alexander Hammond claims, invoking a commonplace metaphor of food consumption for the public's purchase and reading of literature, their "consumption" of "the authorial self": "Poe was evidently scripting into the text figures for the threat he felt from the new marketplace in which he labored."[8] Considering the instances in the novel where humans are devoured (by sharks, birds, and even other humans), Poe's fear of his fate as an author in a modern consumer culture must have been unusually morbid as he composed *Pym*. Faint though they may be, the biographical echoes in *Pym* underscore how important this "silly book" must have seemed to its author, who correctly perceived it as a turning point in his career.

Going to Extremes

These instances of self-reference have reinforced many readers' contention that *Pym* should be read strictly on the level of hoax (like many eighteenth- and early-nineteenth-century sensational novels, the book is attributed to its narrator, not to Poe) or satire aimed at the conventions of sea-adventure narratives and popular novels. Against the claims of authenticity suggested by the title page, with its subtitle promising "details of a mutiny and atrocious butchery on board the American brig *Grampus*," the reference to the town of Edgarton can be read as a tip-off—or reminder—to astute readers that the journey they are about to take has been fabricated by Edgar Poe. More significant are the preface and the concluding note, which at once affirm and question the veracity of Pym's narrative. Like the detailed subtitle, the inclusion of an introduction signed by the fictional author was, by the 1830s, a fairly conventional authenticating device for novelists. But Poe makes the very issue of truth and believability the subject of *Pym*'s preface:

> One consideration which deterred me was, that, having kept no journal during a greater portion of the time in which I was absent, I feared I should not be able to write, from mere memory, a statement so minute and connected as to have the *appearance* of that truth it would really possess.... Another reason was, that the incidents to be narrated were of a nature so positively marvellous, that, unsupported as my assertions must necessarily be (except by the evidence of a single individual, and he a half-breed Indian), I could only hope for belief among my family, and those of my friends who have had reason, through life, to put faith in my veracity—the probability being that the public at large would regard what I should put forth as merely an impudent and ingenious fiction. (*IV*, 55)

Racked with anxiety over whether the people who are now reading the preface will believe the narrative, and having given those readers good reasons *not* to believe it, Pym explains that one Mr. Poe assured him that he could "trust to the shrewdness and common sense of the public" (*IV*, 55): Such an assertion, attributed to the master-cryptologist/parodist/hoaxer Poe, is ironic enough, but Poe adds the explanation that the narrative's "very uncouthness, if there were any, would give it all the better chance of being, received as truth" (*IV*, 55–56). As concerned as he is that readers will not believe his story, Pym still consents to allow Poe to "draw up in his own words, a narrative of the earlier portion of my adventures" and to publish it in the *Southern Literary Messenger* "*under the garb of fiction*" (*IV*, 56). Poe—now a character in his own fiction—is apparently confident enough that the "shrewd" public will believe Pym's story that he is willing to publish it *as* fiction—and according to Pym, Poe is right: "I thence concluded that the facts of my narrative would prove of such a nature as to carry with them sufficient evidence of their own authenticity, and that I had consequently little to fear on the score of popular incredulity" (*IV*, 56). Given the series of incredible adventures that make up most of the narrative, readers who return to the preface will recognize the thick sarcasm behind that statement. Poe engineered this series of reversals partly for a practical reason: to explain why the early chapters had appeared under his name in the *Southern Literary Messenger*. But in so doing, Poe and Pym proclaim the public's gullibility: if Pym's narrative were true, the best way to get the public to believe it would be to present it as fiction. Poe might well have thought he was letting "the few" in on a joke at the expense of "the many," but it is hard to imagine two distinct groups in this case: Poe insults all his readers and winks at us at the same time. Ostensibly stage setting for a hoax—one that, if reviews are any indication, fooled almost no one—the preface works more effectively as a satire on authenticating devices and readers' willingness to be taken in.

The concluding note, like the preface, pretends to authenticate the narrative while justifying an embarrassing feature of the text, in this case its abrupt, mysterious ending. But here, too, the explanation raises more questions than it answers. Adopting the persona of an editor, Poe opens the note with one of his trademark mystifications, claiming that fictional "facts" need not be given because they are already well known: "The circumstances connected with the late sudden and distressing death of Mr. Pym are already well known to the public through the medium of the daily press" (*IV*, 207). Whatever Pym experienced the moment after he confronted the great white figure, he did not die: the preface, as well as references to his surviving the journey within the narrative, has already established that Pym's manuscript was not found in a (very large) bottle. But are we to imagine that while the circumstances of Pym's death are well known, the circumstances of his earlier survival—whatever headline-making discovery awaited him beyond the white veil—remain *unknown*, 10 years after the fact? Pym's fatal "accident," occurring when the entire book had gone to press except those chapters explaining how he managed to escape an almost certain death, is suspiciously convenient, symptomatic of a writer who had run out of time, or perhaps ingenuity. (Even so, Poe lays the groundwork for a sequel by promising that either the remaining chapters or Dirk Peters will be found.) While covering his tracks, Poe calls the veracity of the entire narrative into question: the editor tells us that Poe will not finish Pym's account because he does not believe "the latter portions of the narration" (the two or three "lost" chapters, or the last published chapters? "the editor" does not say), and he sneeringly points out that the nature and meaning of the hieroglyphic writing, which baffled Pym, also "escaped the attention of Mr. Poe" (*IV*, 207). As J. Gerald Kennedy observes, "This successive discrediting ... compels us to ask why, in the last analysis, we ought to accept the editor's construction of 'truth' as decisive and definitive";[9] in devising a way to "anchor" the narrative in some kind of truth, Poe has ironically set it even further adrift.

If the suspicious preface and note were not enough, the narrative itself contains enough contradictions and factual errors to arouse suspicion. In his notes to the standard edition of *Pym*, Burton R. Pollin not only points out approximately 200 errors, ranging from nautical calculations to contradictions in *Pym*'s plot, but theorizes as to which errors are intentional on Poe's part and which are not. Regardless of Poe's intentions, however, to read such an error-laden text—assuming one notices the errors—is to be constantly reminded of its fictional nature, no matter how much nautical (and botanical and zoological) detail Poe includes to convince us that the story is "real." In chapter 5, for example, Pym tells us that his breaking a bottle while trapped in the hold of the *Grampus* had saved his life, because Augustus had given up his search and was about to return to the forecastle when he heard the noise. "Many years elapsed, however, before I was aware of this fact. A natural shame and regret for his weakness and indecision prevented Augustus from confiding to me at once what a more intimate and unreserved communion afterward induced him to reveal" (*IV*, 94). However, Augustus dies not many years but only a few weeks later, on the floating wreck of that same ship. Such errors may be attributed to Poe's writing intermittently and more quickly than usual, but in this case he seems to have gone out of his way to make the mistake, for why should Pym mention that Augustus waited years to tell him he had abandoned his search? For that matter, why should Augustus have been ashamed, for as Pym explains, "[H]e had every good reason to believe me dead ... and a world of danger would be encountered to no purpose by himself" if he did not return to the forecastle (*IV*, 95). The only purpose Augustus's delay of "many years" serves is to be contradicted eight chapters later.

Similarly, Pym points out that Augustus wrote his warning note to Pym in the hold ("*I have scrawled this with blood—your life depends upon lying close*") on "the back of a letter—a duplicate of the forged letter from Mr. Ross," which had bought Pym enough time away from his father to stow away on the *Grampus* (*IV*, 92). This detail serves some purpose, for readers might otherwise wonder how Augustus, a prisoner, would happen to have paper to write on (since he had to use a toothpick and his own blood for pen and ink). Furthermore, there is some irony in the fact that the note that saves Pym from dying in the ship's hold is written on the reverse of (a copy of) the note that got him there in the first place. But the revelation that there was writing on the reverse side of the blood-written note contradicts Pym's earlier assertion that the side of the paper he had first tried to read in the dark using phosphorous matches was "a dreary and unsatisfactory blank" (*IV*, 78). Again, Poe certainly could have forgotten while writing chapter 5 what he had written in chapter 2, but within a novel pervaded by confusion, contradiction, and deception, it is unsafe to assume such things; indeed, as David Ketterer notes in his comments on Pollin's painstaking editorial work, to try to distinguish between "planned absurdities" and "errors" in *Pym* leads one to a subjective interpretation rather than Poe's true intentions: "Pollin, no less than Pym, is ultimately pursuing a chimera, a shadow."[10] Throughout his narrative, Pym constantly seeks truth but finds either that his senses (or his friends, or his enemies) have deceived him or that he was simply unable to read (that is, gain information from) whatever is in front of him. Augustus's three-sided paper symbolizes Pym's *Narrative*: a warning to the reader on one side, a deliberate deception on the other, and on the impossible third side, "a dreary and unsatisfactory blank."[11]

Even readers who overlook such internal contradictions are likely to have a hard time suspending disbelief as Pym comes face to face with death repeatedly throughout his travels. The *Ariel* adventure in chapter 1 establishes the pattern for the rest of the novel: Two unconscious adolescents tossed from a demolished boat would stand a slim chance for survivals: even with the *Penguin*'s crew searching for them. Incredibly, Augustus is saved because Pym had tied him in an upright position to a portion of the boat that remained afloat; more incredibly, the sailors find Pym fastened to the *Penguin* by a timber-bolt that had pierced his neck. Both in the hold of the *Grampus* and on the wreck of the *Grampus* Pym nearly starves; he survives an attack by a mad dog and a battle with piratical mutineers; he comes within a splinter of being cannibalized; he and Peters survive the massacre on Tsalal only by being buried alive by a landslide and surviving *that*, and although last seen in a canoe heading into a cataract near the South Pole, Pym somehow makes it home to write his story. These nearly continuous hairbreadth escapes seem "too much," even for an adventure novel, but their very implausibility could be satiric, parodying through hyperbole the sensationalistic plots of exploration narratives, both fictional and nonfictional.

Indeed, Pym emphasizes his extreme peril with hyperbolic language, which he uses so often that it seems as if he had taken lessons, along with Psyche Zenobia, from Mr. Blackwood. He tells us, for instance, that his dreams in the hold of the *Grampus* were "of the most terrific description" (*IV*, 72). *Description* in this context means "nature" or "character," but the more common meaning of the word ("representation") also comes to mind: the "events" in *Pym* are not real events at all but mere *descriptions*, so Poe

(Pym) assails us with superlatives in a seemingly desperate effort to make those descriptions sufficiently intense. The next sentence, in fact, reads, "*Every* species of calamity and horror befell me" (my emphasis). Pym invokes superlatives so often that these examples could come from almost anywhere in the book: "Never while I live shall I forget the intense agony of terror I experienced at that moment" (*IV*, 60); "My head ached excessively; I fancied that I drew every breath with difficulty; and, in short, I was oppressed with a multitude of gloomy feelings" (*IV*, 71); "Had a thousand lives hung upon the movement of a limb or the utterance of a syllable, I could have neither stirred nor spoken" (*IV*, 72); "My sensations were those of extreme horror and dismay" (*IV*, 75); "I felt, I am sure, more than ten thousand times the agony of death itself" (*IV*, 83); "It was, indeed, hardly possible for us to be in a more pitiable condition" (*IV*, 115); "[E]very particle of that energy which had so long buoyed me up departed like feathers before the wind, leaving me a helpless prey to the most abject and pitiable terror" (*IV*, 134); "I *then* thought human nature could sustain nothing more of agony" (II; 149).

As if to flaunt the fact that his descriptions do not reflect actual events but rather the conceptions of Poe, Pym repeatedly insists that his ordeals are *beyond* conception or too fantastic for words to convey: "[I]t is nearly impossible to conceive" how the rescuers from the *Penguin* escaped destruction (*IV*, 63); in chapter 10 Pym's experiences are "of the most unconceived and unconceiveable character" (*IV*, 122); when Pym, Peters, and Augustus kill Parker for food, he explains, "Such things may be imagined, but words have no power to impress the mind with the exquisite horror of their reality" (*IV*, 135); elsewhere, "It is quite impossible to conceive our sufferings from thirst" (*IV*, 143); "Such weakness can scarcely be conceived" (*IV*, 145); the "agony and despair" Pym and Peters suffer while buried alive "cannot be adequately imagined by those who have never been in a similar situation," as they inspire "a degree of appalling awe and horror not to be tolerated—never to be conceived" (*IV*, 182); finally, "the extreme hazard" of their later escape from the cliff "can scarcely be conceived" (*IV*, 196). Although these oft-repeated assertions lose their force early in the novel, they insist that the author, if he has not *experienced* what other people cannot even imagine, has at least *created* what other people cannot even imagine. For Poe the hoax provides an ideal medium for demonstrating the creative power of the writer—to make the fantastic become "real" for readers. As in his poems and his Folio Club tales, he calls attention to that power, as if afraid the reader will not sufficiently appreciate it otherwise.

The consecutive episodes of extreme peril, then rescue or reprieve (usually followed by an explanation) create a narrative that reads like a series of *Blackwood* articles. Thus, despite the book's shortcomings as a novel, as Bruce Weiner argues, in writing *Pym* Poe perfected the "explained gothic" tale of effect: "Like his *Blackwood's* counterparts, *Pym* is rescued and restored to his senses so that he can tell his tale.... Establishing natural causes for the most delusive of Pym's sensations, the explanation counteracts the imaginative excesses evoked by the predicament."[12] Much of Poe's later short fiction hinges on explaining the perverse or the mysterious, although explanations are often left up to the reader, as is the case with the last chapter of *Pym*. As Weiner suggests, *Pym* may be best appreciated as a series of rehearsals for the "classic" tales Poe would write between 1838 and 1844.[13] Like many of those tales (to be discussed in chapters 4 and 5), and like Poe's burlesques of *Blackwood*, *Pym* should probably be read both literally as a sensational adventure narrative and as a parody of sensational adventure fiction. After all, parodies do not always set themselves apart from the genre at which their satire is directed; a parodist can demonstrate an appreciation for the formula or the work he of she is lampooning. Again, the two audiences Poe imagined are really one audience that can see the excesses of a particular style and still appreciate that style.

"We Were Destined to Be Most Happily Deceived"

So far I have described *Pym* as if it should not be taken seriously, except as a particularly intricate example of Poe's propensity for hoax and satire. But I have also tried to suggest that readers need to balance two sets of expectations when reading Poe: on the one hand, the expectations of literary satire, of a bantering relationship between author and reader, of a text whose real subject is other texts, and on the other hand, the expectation that the work has its own subject and its own themes that convey the author's perspective on the "real world" as well as the literary/publishing world. Such is the case with *Pym*, where the writerly deceptions that permeate the narrative reflect a worldview in which to be deceived is simply to be human. Patrick Quinn and Edward Davidson, two of the first critics to devote extended analysis to *Pym*, identify deception as its principal theme, a premise shared by numerous commentators.[14] "Schoolboys," Pym explains, "can accomplish wonders in the way of deception" (*IV*, 64), an assertion he demonstrates repeatedly in the early chapters: he covers up his wounds (incredibly enough) from the *Ariel* incident to fool his parents, forges a letter and impersonates a sailor to get on board the *Grampus*, and plays the role of Hartman Rogers's ghost to frighten the cook's party and help take over the ship. On a larger scale, Pym the writer builds deception into his narrative by chronicling repeated instances in which *he* is deceived, often in matters of life and death. David Ketterer, in *The Rationale of Deception in Poe*, terms the perils from which Pym is rescued "pseudocrises" or "red herrings," as Pym repeatedly explains after the fact why what appeared to be catastrophic proved to be benign if not lucky.[15] As Poe toys with his readers, then, God, fate, or mere chance toys with Pym.

The paradigm for the seemingly countless episodes of deception occurs in the hold of the *Grampus* in chapters 2 and 3. The wooden box in which Pym stows away has been so sumptuously provisioned by Augustus that Pym moves in "with feelings of higher satisfaction ... than any monarch ever experienced upon entering a new palace" (*IV*, 69), but he also describes it in terms that suggest nothing so much as a coffin: an "iron-bound box, such as is used sometimes for packing fine earthenware [a possible pun hinting that it will hold a corpse]. It was nearly four feet high, and full six long, but very narrow" (*IV*, 69). Indeed, it nearly becomes his coffin, as the mutiny on deck prevents Augustus from freeing him as planned, leaving Pym to wonder why he has been "thus entombed" (*IV*, 75). Even when Pym tries to find his way out, the "labyrinths of the hold" prevent him from getting his bearings. Yet, ironically, his entombment ultimately saves him, for had he found his way to the deck, he probably would have been killed. Pym's disorientation throughout this ordeal initiates him into the world of confusion and deception that he will inhabit for the rest of the novel. His food having spoiled during his first long sleep, Pym's delirium is heightened by hunger and liquor, which becomes his only sustenance. During his second sleep, he awakens from nightmares of suffocation, demons, and serpents to find "[t]he paws of some huge and real monster ... pressing heavily upon my bosom" (*IV*, 72). As the monster proves to be his faithful dog, Tiger, Pym is happy to have been deceived—until the dog goes mad and does in fact threaten Pym's life. And yet, by bringing Pym the note from Augustus (a note whose writing Pym cannot see, and whose message he can only partially read), Tiger helps save Pym's life as well. Given these reversals and double reversals, to say that nothing is as it seems in these chapters would be an understatement.[16] Drunk, famished, dropping in and out of consciousness, lost in a labyrinth of crates, and constantly in the dark, Pym's senses tell him nothing—at least nothing he can trust.[17]

By the middle of his narrative, several harrowing crises and pseudocrises later, Pym reflects on his changing perspective:

> Notwithstanding the perilous situation in which we were still
> placed, ignorant of our position, although certainly at a great

distance from land, without more food than would last us for a fortnight even with great rare, almost entirely without water, and floating about at the mercy of every wind and wave, on the merest wreck in the world, still the infinitely more terrible distresses and dangers from which we had so lately and so providentially been delivered caused us to regard what we now endured as but little more than an ordinary evil—so strictly comparative is either good or ill. (*IV*, 139)

Pym's sanguine outlook smacks of self-delusion, as J. Gerald Kennedy argues: "Pym's interpretation of past events as divinely ordained ... rationalizes unspeakable happenings.... His reckoning betrays an understandable need to construe the horrors that he undergoes as ordered and meaningful rather than random and senseless."[18] Readers, however, are less likely than Pym to see the hand of providence at work on his behalf. true, he keeps escaping, but only to endure the next atrocity. And, as Kennedy notes, by this point Pym has witnessed and participated in more than his share of horrors, among them cannibalizing Parker and encountering the Dutch brig littered with putrescent Corpses.[19]

Whereas in the hold of the *Grampus* Pym was relieved upon having his delusions clarified, in both these cases the reality is more horrifying than the misperception. In the case of Parker, the cannibalism proves to have been unnecessary: five days later, Pym remembers where he left an axe °that will enable the three survivors to break into the forecastle and obtain food. The meeting with the Dutch brig, which Pym describes in much more gruesome detail, suggests either the absence of providence or a God who mocks his victims. As the brig and the *Grampus* near each other, Pym believes his party is saved. He sees a sailor seemingly "encouraging us to have patience; nodding to us in a cheerful although rather odd way, and smiling constantly so as to display a set of the most brilliantly white teeth" (*IV*, 123). After "pour[ing] out our whole souls in shouts and thanksgiving to God for the complete, unexpected, and glorious deliverance that was so palpably at hand" (*IV*, 124), the castaways discover the true state of things: the sailor's motions, which they had seen as a sign of hope, are caused by a huge seagull on the dead man's back, eating away at his flesh. Perhaps in the wake of this episode, Pym comes to see God's providence in the fact that he and Peters, and at the time Parker and Augustus, are still alive, at least, but the image of the death ship could just as easily be seen as God's ironic answer to their prayers.[20]

If *Pym* is about the human need to "discover" meaning in a world where meaning is either hidden or nonexistent, Poe's abrupt; problematic ending epitomizes that theme (or perhaps we should say "anti-theme"). As Paul Rosenzweig points out, Pym's final words in the last published chapter constitute only one of three endings, since the book actually ends with the editor's note, which in turn alludes to another lost ending.[21] Even the ending of the editor's note has a deceptive ring to it: "*I have graven it within the hills, and my vengeance upon the dust within the rock*" only *sounds* biblical, and although it suggests some curse upon the Tsalalians, its meaning is unclear (*IV*, 208).[22] The first ending (chapter 25) also intimates more than it actually delivers, as Pym discovers some incredible phenomenon or vision that he and Peters are pulled toward at a "hideous, velocity" through milky waters: "And now we rushed into the embraces of the cataract, where a chasm threw itself open to receive us. But there arose is our pathway a shrouded human figure, very far larger in its proportions than any dweller among men. And the hue of the skin of the figure was of the perfect whiteness of the snow" (*IV*, 206). Read purely on the level of hoax, these sentences do nothing but taunt the reader with the hint of a profound revelation but no substance, and not enough evidence to draw a reasonable inference. Like the "never-to-be-imparted secret" of "Ms. Found in a Bottle;" the "truth" about the South Pole—is it, as Poe suggests in both "Ms." and *Pym*; a vortex, a passageway into a hollow earth?—is never revealed.[23] Read as the (anti-) conclusion of a novel about deception, the passage presents one final instance of the protagonist (and, through him; the reader) being mocked either: by his unreliable senses or by the natural world: Pym finds at the end of his journey a figure of pure whiteness, a blank, human in form but shrouded. Critics influenced by deconstruction have, in various ways, found the blank, human figure emblematic of the absence of stable meaning, whether textual or spiritual or both. John T. Irwin argues that the white figure is Pym's "unrecognized shadow," suggesting a link between Pym and readers of *Pym*: "[W]hen one finds one, absolutely certain meaning in a situation where the overdeterminedness of the text makes meaning essentially indeterminate, then the reader is likely not to recognize how much that single meaning is a function of self-projection."[24] For other deconstructionist readers (and those who emphasize hoax and satire in *Pym*) the white figure suggests the absence of transcendent meaning or "the body of the narrative" itself, reminding readers how much the novel is about reading and writing, emphasizing Pym's duplicity as a writer and his repeated "misreadings" of messages, appearances, and his own experience.[25]

Critics who find unity, coherence, and meaning in *Pym*, however, tend to regard the white figure as an archetypal symbol, a conclusion to a spiritual journey that has not been aimless after all. Marie Bonaparte, in her groundbreaking psychoanalytic reading of Poe's works, reads the final episode as a "return to the mother" (hence the milky water).[26] Richard Kopley, in a series of articles, has developed an argument for reading *Pym* as a kind of Christian allegory in which the great white figure turns out to be the masthead of the *Penguin* (the ship that rescued Augustus and Pym in the first chapter) and a symbol of Christ resurrected.[27] And Richard Wilbur, in his introduction to a 1973 edition of *Pym*, describes Pym's journey as a spiritual quest that ends with a new self-awareness: "[The figure represents] Anthropos, or the Primal Man, or the snow-white Ancient of Days (Daniel 7:9), or the 'one like unto the Son of Man' in Revelation 1:13, whose 'head and ... hairs were white like wool, as white as snow.' In other words, the figure stands for the coming reunion of the voyager's soul with God or—what is the same thing—with the divinity in himself."[28]

I have dwelt on various interpretations of the ending of *Pym* in order to demonstrate that this book invites, even begs for, analysis, coaxing readers with the promise of another level of meaning behind the hoaxical elements, or just "beyond the veil" of white water in the final scene; and yet, more than most literary texts, *Pym* frustrates any effort to draw firm conclusions and attracts a range of interpretations so wide as to suggest that *Pym*'s interpreters have themselves been taken in by a hoax. Of course, *Pym*'s commentators have long recognized that they, too, are part of the audience Poe wished to mystify, that—as the subtitle to J. Gerald Kennedy's study of the novel suggests—*Pym* is "an abyss of interpretation." But such self-consciousness of the potential absurdity or (to use a more Poe-esque word) perversity of trying to explain the unexplainable is no more likely to stop Poe's readers than it is to stop Pym from trying to understand and explain.

A BLACK-AND-WHITE WORLD

Readers of *Pym* who search for the meaning—or exact nature of the non-meaning—of the white figure must take into account the episode that precedes it, in which a tribe of dark-skinned "savages" massacres the *Jane Guy*'s Anglo explorers. In fact, the episode's emphasis on race and colonial encounter has attracted considerable attention and scholarly debate. From chapter 17 on, Poe emphasizes a black-and-white color scheme, with notable touches of red. As the *Jane Guy* cruises south, its crew discovers a bear with "perfectly white" wool and "blood red" eyes, and then a smaller mammal, whose hair, although straight, is also "perfectly white," with scarlet claws and teeth. The day after spotting that animal, Pym notices the sea becoming "extraordinarily dark" as the *Jane Guy* nears what turns out to be the island of Tsalal. There, virtually everything—landscape, people, tools—is dark or black. The Tsalalians' complexions are "jet black," they wear the skins of black animals, and the shelters of the more important tribesmen are made of black skin (*IV*, 168, 172–74). Pym observes a "black albatross," "black gannets," "blackfish," and "species of bittern, with jet black and grizzly plumage" (*IV*, 173, 174, 191); he explores pits and chasms of "black granite" (*IV*, 192). The inhabitants of Tsalal recoil or express horror at anything white: a handkerchief (*IV*, 168); "several very harmless objects" from the *Jane Guy* "such as the schooner's sails, an egg, an open book, or a pan of flour" (*IV*, 170); the white water and white birds that terrify Pym and Peters's hostage; and, of course, the "white" visitors themselves. In yet another example of Poe's inconsistency, Peters, previously identified as a "half-breed Indian," is "white" at the end of chapter 21 (*IV*, 185); in Pym's color scheme, Peters is now white because he is not black, but in fact no caucasian, especially after a long voyage, could accurately be described as "white." Appropriately, Pym's world—or, perhaps, his worldview—has become polarized as he nears the Antarctic, whiteness predominating everywhere but on this one dark island where the natives fear and loathe all things white.

Given the escalating sectional tensions over slavery in the 1830s, it is difficult, if not impossible, to dismiss this black-and-white world as anything less than an allegory of "natural" distinctions between the races. Throughout the decade, Southern states became much more aggressive in their defense of slavery, both practically and philosophically: they passed stricter laws regulating slaves' behavior and censored antislavery writings while defending their system with biblical references and pseudoscientific "evidence" of "black" inferiority. Nat Turner's 1831 rebellion in Southampton, Virginia, along with a growing abolitionist movement in the North, spread the sort of fear that led to this new militancy.

Poe's personal racism and support for slavery have posed a problem for many of his twentieth-century admirers. His "defenders" on race issues point out that he never incorporated *explicit* proslavery arguments into his fiction or poetry, as did many other antebellum Southern authors; relatively little of his fiction is even set in the southern United States; and only a handful of African-American characters appear in his work. But the scarcity of direct references to race and slavery does not justify overlooking the issues when they do appear in Poe's work.[29] Although the larger cultural preoccupation with race provides sufficient reason to read the Tsalal' episode in the context of Southern defenses of slavery, we can add to it the near certainty that Poe supported slavery.[30] He had established what literary reputation he had (by 1838) as the editor of a magazine that promoted not only Southern belles lettres but the "peculiar institutions" occasionally writing book reviews endorsing proslavery arguments; and whenever Poe did depict an African character in his work, he invoked demeaning racial stereotypes. But Poe does not play the Tsalalians for racist laughs as he does Jupiter in "The Gold Bug" and Pompey in "A Predicament"; on the contrary, the Tsalalian "savages" might be Poe's vision of how the "black race" would behave if not for the strict paternalistic control provided by slavery.

Two days before the *Jane Guy* encounters the Tsalalians, the crew spot "a singular ledge of rock ... projecting into the sea, and bearing a strong resemblance to corded bales of cotton" (*IV*, 165), an image that suggests a correspondence between the black tribe they will soon meet and the Africans who inhabit another "white world," where real bales of cotton are part of the landscape. As Sidney Kaplan notes, Pym describes the Tsalalians in terms that closely resemble a popular caricature of Africans: "[A]bout the ordinary stature of Europeans, but of a more muscular. and brawny frame," with "thick and long woolly hair," "thick and clumsy" lips, and childish mannerisms (*IV*, 168, 174).[31] The polar relatives of African slaves differ only by being more purely "black": they have "jet black" skin and black teeth (*IV*, 205). Poe's fictitious editor deciphers the characters suggested by the chasms as the Ethiopian verbal root, "to be shady" (*IV*, 207), and the inscription on the chasm wall as an Arabic-Egyptian cognate meaning "to be white—the region of the South" (*IV*, 208). Furthermore, Kaplan translates from Hebrew the name of the chief Too-wit, "to be dirty"; Klock-Klock, the name of the town, "to be black"; Tsalemon, the king of the archipelago, "to be shady"; and Tsalal itself, "to be dark."[32] Tsalal, then, is the home not just of a tribe of dark-skinned people but the home of blackness itself.

In Christian typology black is associated with Satan; moreover, Genesis establishes the snake as an animal form the devil is likely to take, and the Tsalalians "do not fear the 'formidable' serpents that cross their path [and] they pronounce the names of their land and king with a 'prolonged hissing sound.'"[33] Kaplan concludes that Tsalal is Hell;[34] at the least, it is a cursed land inhabited by what appear to be Hebrew-speaking descendants of Canaan, Noah's grandson who was punished when Ham, Canaan's father, saw the nakedness of his own father, Noah: "Cursed be Canaan! The lowest of slaves shall he be to his brothers" (Genesis 9:25). When Poe makes Hebrew the Tsalalian language, inscribes into the landscape hieroglyphic messages that put Pym in mind of "descriptions ... of those dreary regions marking the site of degraded Babylon" (*IV*, 198), and concludes *Pym* with a pseudobiblical curse ("I have graven it within the hills, and my vengeance upon the dust within the rock"), he invokes an audacious but well-circulated

Southern justification for slavery. Surrounded by the whiteness that torments them, perhaps even under the watchful gaze of the Great White Father, the Tsalalians seem "the most barbarous, subtle, and blood-thirsty wretches that ever contaminated the face of the globe," elsewhere described as "the most wicked, hypocritical, vindictive, blood-thirsty, and altogether fiendish race of men" (*IV*, 180, 201).[35]

Of course, that assessment of the Tsalalians, like everything else in the narrative, comes from the decidedly unreliable A. Gordon Pym. This observation does not "clear" Poe from responsibility for creating a racist fantasy, but it does point toward yet another interpretive wrinkle. Pym has misread appearances throughout his journey, and Poe provides considerable evidence to contradict him in this episode as well. Dana Nelson regards the encounter on Tsalal as an illustration of how colonizers misperceive indigenous peoples by assuming that "white is right."[36] In the tradition of European (and American) imperialism, the crew of the *Jane Guy* clearly intends to exploit the Tsalalians: "We established a regular market on shore, just under the guns of the schooner, where our barterings were carried on with every appearance of good faith, and a degree of order which their conduct at the village of *Klock-Klock* had not led us to expect from the savages" (*IV*, 177). Pym's reference to the "appearance of good faith" foreshadows the later massacre by the Tsalalians, but in the same statement he reveals that the *Jane Guy*'s crew conducts business not on good faith but "under the guns of our schooner." Furthermore, the high "degree of order" with which the Tsalalians trade should tip Pym off to their intelligence and organizational ability, but ethnocentrism and greed blind him to such a possibility.[37]

In chapters 19 and 20, Pym proudly expounds on the value of bêche-de-mer and the ease with which they can be obtained and processed by natives who apparently do not know their value on the world market. As Nelson points out, when the natives prove shrewd enough to coax the crew into a false sense of security and to engineer the landslide that buries their enemies, Pym "shift[s] his cognitive framework from 'ignorant' to 'treacherous' to explain the event."[38] But the ambush may be best seen not as Pym sees it but as a necessary preemptive strike: especially if these were not the first "white" men the Tsalalians had encountered, the natives knew that their way of life was being threatened and that they would be slaughtered in an open battle with men who were, as Pym puts it, "armed to the teeth" (*IV*, 180). When the crew first ventures onshore, Too-wit, the Tsalalian chief, tells them "there was no need of arms where all were brothers" (*IV*, 180). The explorers "took this in good part," assuming that

Too-wit is announcing the Tsalalians' peaceful intentions (*IV*, 180); in hindsight, Pym regards it as simple deception. But while Too-wit probably intends the remark to be misunderstood, his literal, truthful meaning is that the *Jane Guy's* crew have already shown, by brandishing weapons, that they do not come in peace.[39] Pym and his crewmates do not realize it, but at that point the battle has already begun.

Through Pym, Poe casts the Tsalal episode in ethnocentric terms, feeding his readers' racism, but at the same time he undermines that worldview, showing the fatal consequences of misreading the ethnic "other." Indeed, while no single concept can be said to unify *Pym*, Pym's misreading pervades a novel that is itself "unreadable"—that is, impossible to interpret without encountering contradictions and gaps of meaning. Why does Tsalal appear black and white to Pym? Few who have read his narrative would be comfortable with the answer "because that's how it really is," for nothing up to the Tsalal chapters has been as it seems to Pym. Perhaps Pym sees predominately in black and white in the last chapters because those colors are the easiest for reading. And yet, metaphorically, to "see everything as black or white" is to oversimplify and therefore to misunderstand, to settle for easy answers to complex questions. Here and throughout *Pym* Poe explores, in terms of reading and misreading, the difficulty of interpreting the world; in this case readers of *Pym* are literally looking at the black-and-white world of the printed page as they vicariously experience the black-and-white world of Tsalal and the region to the south. The traces of red on Tsalal may suggest the bloodthirstiness of the natives, but they also suggest a pun on which a famous children's riddle is based: What's black and white and re(a)d all over? "A newspaper" is the typical answer. But Tsalal, as seen by Pym, is also black and white and read all over, for the writer of the editorial note and generations of critics have "read" the hieroglyphic messages—"to be shady" (or dark) and "to be white"—that baffled Pym and "escaped the attention of Mr. Poe" (*IV*, 207). Finally, like newspapers, books (such as *The Narrative of Arthur Gordon Pym*) also fit the black-and-white-and-read description, again suggesting a correspondence between Pym's failed attempts to read the physical world and his readers' futile attempts to interpret his narrative.

In *An Anthropologist on Mars*, neurologist Oliver Sacks describes "the case of the color-blind artist," who, after a car accident, suddenly saw only in black and white, losing all awareness and memory of color. For several days, he also suffered from alexia, a sudden loss of the ability to read.[40] The two phenomena are medically and, as applied to *Pym*, thematically linked. Although Pym does not literally suffer from these neurological symptoms, his limited perception "creates" a monochromatic world that *seems* easy to read but is actually easy to misread. While Poe does not lead us to any clear conclusion or theme with *Pym*, he does, perhaps inadvertently, expose a paradox of the human predicament. Whether classifying people by race, trusting our senses—or other texts—for information, or seeking the one true meaning behind Poe's only novel, our desire to understand and explain blinds us, because explanations are always incomplete. As we interpret our experience ever more aggressively, we risk narrowing our vision and reducing our own stories, our own world, to black and white.

NOTES

1. Even *Pym*'s status as a "major text" is rather slippery: critical attention has come to it relatively recently (it was virtually ignored until the 1950s) and its "classic" status would still likely be challenged even by many Poe specialists.

2. Silverman, *Edgar A. Poe*, 132.

3. For information on the conditions under which Poe wrote *Pym* and substantiated theories regarding distinct phases of composition, see Joseph V. Ridgely, "The Growth of the Text," in *IV*, 29–36.

4. Burton R. Pollin traces similarities of style and other details to 36 sea narratives that Poe could have found compiled in five anthologies in his note on the text in *IV*, 37–47. *Pym* (the last chapters especially) should also be read in light of contemporary interest in ancient Egypt and hieroglyphics: see John T. Irwin, *American Hieroglyphics: The Symbol of the Egyptian Hieroglyphics in the American Renaissance* (New Haven, Conn.: Yale University Press, 1980), 43–235. Joseph J. Moldenhauer argues that Poe's use of picture-writing on Tsalal was influenced by contemporary publications concerning the "Picture Rock" near Dighton, Massachusetts, in "*Pym*, the Dighton Rock, and the Matter of Vinland," in *Poe's Pym: Critical Explorations*, ed. Richard Kopley (Durham, N.C.: Duke University Press, 1992), 75–94.

5. See Bruce I. Weiner, "Novels, Tales, and Problems of Form in *The Narrative of Arthur Gordon Pym*," in *Poe's Pym: Critical Explorations*, ed. Richard Kopley (Durham, N.C.: Duke University Press, 1992), 44–56, for more on Poe's (and his contemporaries) awareness of the novel's conventions.

6. See, for instance, Richard Wilbur, introduction to *The Narrative of Arthur Gordon Pym* by Edgar Allan Poe (Boston: Godine, 1973); reprinted in *Responses: Prose Pieces 1953–1976* (New York: Harcourt Brace Jovanovich, 1976), 195.

7. Wilbur, introduction, 195; Burton R. Pollin, "Poe's Life Reflected in the Sources of *Pym*," in *Poe's Pym: Critical Explorations*, ed. Richard Kopley (Durham, N.C.: Duke University Press, 1992), 93–103.

8. Alexander Hammond, "Consumption, Exchange, and the Literary Marketplace: From Folio Club Tales to *Pym*," in *Poe's Pym: Critical Explorations*, ed. Richard Kopley (Durham, N.C.: Duke University Press, 1992), 165. See also Silverman, *Edgar A. Poe*, 136–37; and Wilbur, introduction, 213.

9. J. Gerald Kennedy, *The Narrative of Arthur Gordon Pym and the Abyss of Interpretation* (New York: Twayne, 1995), 78; see also Paul Rosenzweig, "'Dust within the Rock': The Phantasm of Meaning in *The Narrative of Arthur Gordon Pym*," *Studies in the Novel* 14 (1982): 137–51.

10. David Ketterer, "Tracing Shadows: *Pym* Criticism 1980–1990, with Bibliography: A Checklist of *Pym* Criticism," in *Poe's Pym: Critical Explorations*, ed. Richard Kopley (Durham, N.C.: Duke University Press, 1992), 237.

11. See Ketterer, *Rationale*, 134. See also Kennedy's discussion of inconsistencies in the *Grampus* chapters in *Narrative*, 45–51. Several critics have focused on the importance of the mysterious note as trope for unreadability or the displacement of meaning from writing: see, for instance, Irwin, *American Hieroglyphics*, 43–235; John Carlos Rowe, *Through the Custom House: Nineteenth-Century American Fiction and Modern Theory* (Baltimore and London: Johns Hopkins University Press, 1982), 91–110; J. Gerald Kennedy, *Poe*, 145–76; and Michael J. S. Williams, *A World of Words: Language and Displacement in the Fiction of Edgar Allan Poe* (Durham, N.C.: Duke University Press, 1988), 125–27.

12. Weiner, "Novels," 50. As Weiner points out, those "natural causes" in *Pym* sometimes prove as frightening as any flight of imagination, as is the case with Augustus's death (53).

13. Ibid., 56.

14. Patrick F. Quinn, *The French Face of Edgar Poe* (Carbondale: Southern Illinois University Press, 1957).

15. Ketterer, *Rationale*, 127.

16. See Rosenzweig, "'Dust within the Rock,'" 141; and Kennedy, *Narrative*, 42.

17. Joseph J. Moldenhauer ("Imagination and Perversity in *The Narrative of Arthur Gordon Pym*," *Texas Studies in Literature and Language* 13 [1971]: 267–80) and J. Gerald Kennedy (*Narrative*) maintain that the *Grampus* symbolizes Pym's mind or consciousness, and that the hold of the ship suggests the irrational or subconscious part of the mind.

18. Kennedy, *Narrative*, 49.

19. Ibid.

20. Ibid., 47–51.

21. Rosenzweig, "'Dust within the Rock,'" 138.

22. Ibid., 149. See also Kennedy, *Narrative*, 79; and Sidney Kaplan, who concludes that "there was in the Bible no prophecy of black damnation clear enough for [Poe's] needs, and he therefore wrote his own" (introduction to *The Narrative of Arthur Gordon Pym* by Edgar Allan Poe [New York: Hill and Wang, 1960]: xxiii).

23. Poe was almost certainly familiar with John Cleves Symmes's theory that the earth was hollow, with openings at the poles. An 1820 novel entitled *Symzonia: A Voyage of Discovery by Adam Seaborn* (a pseudonym, possibly for Symmes) described a utopia located within the South Pole, inhabited by purely white people (Kaplan, introduction, xiii). Rudy Rucker's 1992 novel *The Hollow Earth* (New York: Avon) utilizes this theory and features Poe as a character.

24. John T. Irwin, "The Quincuncial Network of Poe's *Pym*," in *Poe's Pym: Critical Explorations*, ed. Richard Kopley (Durham, N.C.: Duke University Press, 1992), 187.

25. See Kennedy, Poe, 172. See also Jean Ricardou, "The Singular Character of the Water," trans. Frank Towne, *Poe Studies* 9 (1976): 1–6; Rowe, *Through the Custom House*; Irwin, *American Hieroglyphics*; and Dennis Pahl, *Architects of the Abyss: The Indeterminate Fictions of Poe, Hawthorne, and Melville* (Columbia: University of Missouri Press, 1989).

26. Marie Bonaparte, *The Life and Works of Edgar Allan Poe: A Psychoanalytic Interpretation*, trans. John Rodker (London: Imago, 1949), 341.

27. Richard Kopley, "The Secret of *Arthur Gordon Pym*. The Text and the Source,"

Studies in American Fiction 8 (1980): 203–18; "The Hidden Journey of Arthur Gordon Pym," in *Studies in the American Renaissance 1982*, ed. Joel Myerson (Boston: Twayne, 1982), 29–51; "The '*Very* Profound Undercurrent' of *Arthur Gordon Pym*," in *Studies in the American Renaissance 1987*, ed. Joel Myerson (Charlottesville: University Press of Virginia, 1987), 143–75.

28. Wilbur, introduction, 213.

29. John Carlos Rowe ("Poe, Antebellum Slavery, and Modern Criticism," in *Poe's Pym: Critical Explorations*, ed. Richard Kopley [Durham, N.C.: Duke University Press, 1992], 117–38] and Joan Dayan ("Amorous Bondage: Poe, Ladies, and Slaves," *American Literature* 66 [1994]: 239–73) argue that race is a key issue throughout Poe's work and that Poe scholars traditionally have ignored or denied its importance. The Poe Studies Association made "Poe and Race" the topic of one of its panels at the American Literature Association conference in 1996.

30. Considerable controversy has surrounded the authorship of a review in the *Southern Literary Messenger* in 1836, bearing the title "Slavery" and discussing proslavery books by James Kirke Paulding and William Drayton. Bernard Rosenthal ("Poe, Slavery, and the *Southern Literary Messenger*: A Reexamination," *Poe Studies* 7 [1974]: 29–38) and others contend that Poe probably wrote this unequivocal endorsement of slavery based on the supposed inferiority of blacks. J.V. Ridgely ("The Authorship of the 'Paulding-Drayton Review,'" *PSA Newsletter* 20 (1992): 1–3, 6) supports, with persuasive evidence, the claim made by William Doyle Hull II ("A Canon of the Critical Works of Edgar Allan Poe with a Study of Poe as Editor and Reviewer," Ph.D. diss., University of Virginia, 1941) that the review was written by Judge Beverly Tucker. But the fact remains, as Rowe points out, that Poe admired proslavery spokesmen such as Tucker and Thomas R. Dew and edited a magazine that promoted their ideas ("Poe, Antebellum Slavery," 119–20). In his forthcoming book *Edgar Allan Poe and the Masses*, Terence Whalen devotes a chapter to Poe's views on race, slavery, and literary nationalism. Whalen agrees that Tucker wrote the Paulding-Drayton review."

31. Kaplan, introduction, xvii. For more on Poe's use of racist caricature and the proslavery defense in the Tsalal episode, see Sam Worley, "*The Narrative of Arthur Gordon Pym* and the Ideology of Slavery," *ESQ* 40 (1994): 219–50.

32. Ibid. "Too-wit" is also a likely pun on "to wit" and "two-wit," the latter, as Kennedy points out, suggesting the character's "two-faced" nature (*Narrative*, 289). Pollin questions Kaplan's translation of Klock-Klock, and points out the possibility that "the spelling is intended to make an ironic point about a village outside of time" (*IV*, 322). Tsalemon also puns on "Solomon."

33. Kaplan, introduction, xix.

34. Ibid.

35. Ibid., xix–xxi.

36. Dana D. Nelson, *The Word in Black and White: Reading "Race" in American Literature, 1638–1867* (New York and Oxford: Oxford University Press, 1992), 90–108.

37. Ibid., 98–99.

38. Ibid., 99.

39. Ibid., 99–100.

40. Oliver Sacks, *An Anthropologist on Mars: Seven Paradoxical Tales* (New York: Knopf, 1995), 3–42.

HARRIET HUSTIS

"Reading Encrypted But Persistent": The Gothic of Reading and Poe's "The Fall of the House of Usher"

Trickery, hoaxes, hieroglyphs, and ciphers: few writers have foregrounded such mechanisms of duplicity in their fiction as did Edgar Allan Poe. This is perhaps why the status of Poe's texts within the American literary canon has been so fiercely contested and debated. As many critics have noted, it is precisely the prevalence of such motifs of ambiguity and linguistic, hermeneutic, and ontological uncertainty that have led to the resurrection and revaluation of texts such as "The Purloined Letter" and "The Raven." And yet Poe's status was never in question within the framework of the French tradition, for example; Poe was always more famous and his works better appreciated in Europe than in the United States. Debates about the place of Poe's texts within the canon are always "American" debates, since elsewhere the point is strangely moot.

Interestingly, whereas French theorists such as Lacan and Derrida readily take *to* Poe's texts, American critics often assume a more cautionary stance and warily reflect on the fact that Poe's writings have a tendency to take their readers in. Shoshana Felman highlights this "insidious" influence with respect to Poe's poetry:

> The case of Poe in literary history could in fact be accounted for
> as one of the most extreme and complex cases of "the anxiety of

From *Studies in American Fiction* 27, no. 1 (Spring 1999). ©1999 by Northeastern University influence," of the anxiety unwittingly provoked by the "influence" irresistibly emanating from this poetry. What is unique, however, about Poe's influence, as about the "magic" of his verse, is the extent to which its action is unaccountably insidious, exceeding the control, the will, and the awareness of those who are subjected to it.[1]

Felman's statement echoes early criticism of Poe's "The Fall of the House of Usher," which often focuses on the reliability of the narrator—in particular, whether he contracts Roderick Usher's hysterical phobophobia and whether he, like the critic, perceives Usher's submerged incestuous desire for Madeline. Felman's description of the "action" *of* Poe's text is curiously similar to the "action" that occurs within Poe's text: the influence to which the narrator and Roderick Usher are subjected is also "unaccountably insidious, exceeding [their] control, [their] will, and [their] influence."

More recent criticism has moved away from an exclusive focus on close readings of Poe's life and work in order to explore Poe's discursive position within American culture of his time. Nevertheless, analyses that explore Poe's situation with respect to emerging "lowbrow" culture (such as Jonathan Elmer's *Reading at the Social Limit*) and/or the "seriousness" of his literary endeavors (i.e., his desire to earn a place as a creator of "highbrow" literature despite his use of "lowbrow" literary strategies and motifs) demonstrate a similar preoccupation with whether or not the reader should be taken in by Poe's stories—the shift has merely been to questions of *how*, exactly. In the introduction to their collection *The American Face of Edgar Allan Poe* Shawn Rosenheim and Stephen Rachman thus identify a need "to recognize that Poe's most extravagant literary maneuvers were usually based in the specific cultural and political climate of antebellum America."[2] This desire to reconnect Poe with the American literary tradition or simply to reassert the existence of that connection, since according to Rosenheim and Rachman, it was always there but disavowed by both parties[3] exists alongside recognition that for so long Poe's texts were read as highlighting the insufficiencies of any attempt to fix a subject's location in time or space.[4] Previously, Poe was seen as decidedly "un-American" because his stories did not seem to reflect "Americanness" *à la* Hawthorne or Melville; now he is regarded as decidedly American precisely because he presumably *chose* not to reflect the "American" literary flavor of a Melville or a Hawthorne. The very qualities that previously disqualified Poe from a place within the American literary canon now assure him of that place, and previously anxious detraction has become determined reclamation.

And yet the parameters of this new trend toward (albeit lukewarm) critical acceptance of Poe, as Joseph Kronick recognizes, are by no means necessarily motivated by an innocent desire to do justice to an oft-castigated "genius." In the wake of literary scholarship's move away from the textually-oriented practices of New Criticism and formalism toward the critic- or interpretation-oriented practices of deconstruction and poststructuralism, Poe's texts "naturally" begin to seem more palatable to the critic predisposed to regard him/herself as a clever interpreter of literature:

> Poe's love of cryptography, literary hoaxes, and puzzles opens his texts to pyrotechnical displays of interpretive skills, for Poe remains a writer who draws many of his readers not because they like or admire him but because his texts are so malleable for the close interpreter ... This transformation of Poe's works into texts, to borrow Roland Barthes's distinction, has produced readings striking not only for their theoretical insights but also for their avoidance of those issues that have plagued Poe criticism: the uncertainty of his intentions and his so-called execrable style.[5]

Kronick recalls an earlier warning issued by Allen Tate: "All readers of Poe, of the work or of the life, and the rare reader of both, are peculiarly liable to the vanity of discovery" (qtd. on 217). Such qualifications are designed to remind the critic of Poe's shortcomings—as if there can be, or, more insidiously, *should* be no "pure" pleasure derived from reading Poe, no Poe scholarship that is without its misgivings about his true literary worth. In "On Reading Poetry: Reflections on the Limits and Possibilities of Psychoanalytical Approaches," Shoshana Felman highlights one of the most interesting paradoxes of Poe scholarship, the fact of its sheer bulk coupled with its overwhelmingly negative value-judgments:

> Curiously enough, while Poe's worldwide importance and effective influence is beyond question, critics nonetheless continue to protest and to proclaim, as loudly as they can, that Poe is *un*important, that Poe is *not* a major poet ...
>
> Poe's detractors seem to be unaware, however, of the paradox that underlies their enterprise: it is by no means clear why anyone should take the trouble to write—at length—about a writer of no importance. (123)

Felman summarizes and deflects the paradox of Poe scholarship succinctly: "The fact that it so much matters to proclaim that Poe *does not matter* is but evidence of the extent to which Poe's poetry is, in effect, a *poetry that matters*" (122).

Nevertheless, this tendency in much of Poe scholarship to qualify (at best) and condemn (at worst) has had a crippling effect on interpretations of Poe's texts, as in essays like Kronick's "Edgar Allan Poe: The Error of Reading and the Reading of Error." Kronick relies on a contrast between surface/superficiality and depth/significance but simultaneously suggests that critics who focus on either are engaged in a misreading of Poe's texts, that the "depth" or interpretive significance with which Poe's texts are endowed by critics is as misapplied as those critiques which focus on the mere surface superficialities of Poe's works.

Kronick's apparent conclusion, however, that interpretation of Poe's texts highlights the function of interpretation as erroneous illusion[6] is not all that different from the critical assessments of Poe's work that have appeared all along. Thus earlier debates about the reliability of the narrator of "The Fall of the House of Usher," for example, began by assuming that we (as readers and as critics) don't want, or, more importantly, don't *like* to be deceived, and that if the narrator is tricked by Usher into believing what Usher believes, then he might well trick us. In claiming that "error opens up the identity of language and thought to the radical difference between signifier and signified" (223), Kronick is only calling attention to the "space" of trickery, if you will, the "gap" of error opened by reading. The more complex question, however, raised by "The Fall of the House of Usher" is what happens to reading once this gap (or, in its earliest manifestation, this "fissure") becomes apparent and begins to widen. Furthermore, critics of Poe need to consider the possibility that it is precisely the presence of this space of trickery embedded within Poe's texts that has led to such debate over the status of Poe's work within the canon; the gap of error opened by reading has consistently served to destabilize Poe's position within the "house" of American literature.

But if, as Jonathan Elmer suggests, Poe's texts represent a kind of literary embodiment of the Barnumesque object and "what Barnum sells, by means of his objects, is interpretation and the satisfactions to be had from such interpretation,"[7] then there is no way to enjoy Poe's texts, as a critic, without putting oneself on the slippery slope, without entering the very space of trickery. As Charles May suggests, "Poe believes that if we do not allow ourselves to be tricked, we will not learn."[8] As Elmer emphasizes,

Barnum's successes—Poe's as well, in his fictional hoaxes—
depend less on a massive duping of his public than on the
mobilization of a dynamic in which deception and enlightenment
operate together as inextricable complements. (187)

This mobilized "dynamic" is precisely the activity of reading and, in
particular, characterizes the way in which the reader is "activated" by Poe's
text.[9] This essay will explore this dynamic of readerly activation in "The Fall
of the House of Usher." While "Usher" is one of Poe's most often
interpreted works, it has traditionally been subject to predominantly
conventional, thematic readings (discussions of the reliability of the narrator,
the role of doubling, and/or the motif of incest). Alongside "The Raven,"[10]
"Usher" represents one of the most prominent (and least explored)
foregroundings of the very space of trickery, the gap of error that constitutes
reading and that is illusively filled by interpretation, in all of Poe's work.

In general, the function of the reader in "The Fall of the House of
Usher" has been subsumed under discussions of the role of the writer or of
writing in both this particular tale and in Poe's work in general. Analyses that
highlight Poe's "writerly" motivations in "Usher" consistently remove the
reader to a safe distance from which the reader is presumably able to look
with condescension upon Poe's text. For example, in "Playful 'Germanism'
in 'The Fall of the House of Usher': The Storyteller's Art," Benjamin
Franklin Fisher argues that Poe's text embodies the influence of gothicism
and Germanism on the literature of the day by incorporating numerous
standard gothic motifs which it then parodies.[11] Because Poe's purpose is
parodic, Fisher believes that an interpretive distance is maintained between
the gullible narrator and the more sensible reader; while the narrator and
Roderick Usher are depicted as readers of gothic run amuck, the reader of
"The Fall of the House of Usher" is presumed safe from such confusion.
According to Fisher, the reader's awareness of the gothic, "Germanic" folly
of Roderick and the narrator measures the hermeneutic, aesthetic, and
psychic distance between these fictional figures and the reader:

> ... the teller of the tale could not be more appropriate. By means
> of this figure, Poe burlesques the quenchless sensibility of those
> virtuous, high-minded, sexless arty types in Gothicism, whose
> curiosity always outruns their rationality in prompting them to
> actions and emotions altogether rash, daring, or ridiculous in the
> face of what readers readily size up as horrors. (360)

Poe's "burlesque" of the figure of the narrator would thus seem to serve a purpose like that of the epigraph to "The Facts of the Case of M. Valdemar," as described by Jonathan Elmer: "An entire world is pointed to in this opening, a world of garbled accounts, confused and disbelieving people, which readers are silently invited to imagine as separate from themselves" (181). But is the silent invitation sincere? And similarly, if we are asked to laugh at the "burlesque" that is the narrator's and Roderick Usher's gothicism, to "readily size up as horrors" the text that is "The Fall of the House of Usher," whom, ultimately, are we laughing at and what exactly are we "sizing up"? If Poe is indeed highlighting, via parody, the conventions of the gothic text (and Fisher's evidence on this score is quite convincing), what is the significance of such an undertaking? It would seem that Poe is interested in creating more than just a bizarre story or incisive parody—his dual critique and enactment of the gothic in "The Fall of the House of Usher" represent an exploration of the very nature of gothic textuality itself and its effects (both aesthetic and psychic) on the reader.

As Garrett Stewart observes in his work on the role of the conscripted reader in nineteenth-century British fiction,[12] the foregrounding of the writer's function and of the text-as-written is necessarily accompanied by a foregrounding of the reader and of the text-as-read:

> When classic novels own to their very execution as writing, they also foreground their prosecution as read. Novels about the production of textuality tend to entail a metanarrative of reading concerned with reading's own nervous perversity, its surrogate pleasure and pain, its psychosomatic risks rather than institutional stability, less its humanist reach or stretch than its parasitic grasp. (347)

Analysis of Poe's writing, his "production of textuality," needs to be accompanied by analysis of this "metanarrative of reading"—particularly since Stewart's characterization of the qualities of reading explored by such a metanarrative incorporates so many terms applicable to Roderick Usher's own personality ("nervous perversity," "surrogate pleasure and pain," "psychosomatic risks," "parasitic grasp"). Is it possible to read Roderick Usher as a kind of figurative embodiment of what Stewart labels a "gothic of reading"? If so, what are we to make of the fact that Poe inserts such a metanarrative of reading in a tale not about textual production, but rather (textual) collapse?

Briefly, Stewart argues that gothic texts (like those of Wilde, du Maurier, Stevenson and Stoker)

> generate, not a terror of the text, but a carefully controlled gothic of reading, a reflexive disturbance in the circuit of reception which bothers without quite spoiling narrative pleasure, exposing it as participatory, collusive, and two-faced, enticing because in part predatory, feeding off the psychic shock—the depicted horror of characters inside the plot—with which it rushes to identify. (344)

In effect the gothic text mirrors the reader. Furthermore, it is precisely this mirroring that creates the effect of, the reader's response to, the gothic text. The reader is thus both implicated in and co-conspirator with the gothic plot: "Hystericized like the narrative agents by plot's whiplash surprises and escalating suspense, the unnerved reader fulfills in his own person the narrative aesthetic" (Stewart, 344).

Poe embodies this co-conspiracy between reader and text in the opening pages of "Usher" by notifying the reader of how the narrator came to be on the scene in the first place, namely, through an implicit summons conveyed by letter:

> A letter, however, had lately reached me ... —a letter from him— which, in its wildly importunate nature, had admitted of no other than a personal reply. The MS. gave evidence of nervous agitation.... It was the manner in which all this, and much more, was said—it was the apparent heart that went with his request— which allowed me no room for hesitation; and I accordingly obeyed forthwith what I still considered a very singular summons.[13]

The narrator admits himself to be "hystericized" and "unnerved" by Roderick's letter and yet he appears equally powerless to resist, not its contents, but its "manner." The gothic of reading generated by the "manner" of a gothic text is never traceable to a particular source. Instead, its "participatory," "collusive" and "predatory" force "feeds off" a "psychic shock" that, like Roderick and Madeline Usher's twin illnesses, has no discernible origin. Like Roderick Usher's fear of fear, the gothic of reading poses no danger "except in its absolute effect—in terror" (222).

The accumulated effects of a gothic of reading nevertheless enable a text like Poe's "Usher" to become "activated," to take on a life of its own. This activation is not unlike the narrator's admission that "the consciousness of the rapid increase of my superstition ... served mainly to accelerate the increase itself" (218). Even more appropriately, this activation of a gothic of reading is analogous to Roderick's *idée fixe*: the "sentience of all vegetable things" (228). The narrator nervously dismisses Usher's belief that "the conditions of the sentience had been here ... fulfilled in the method of collocation of these stones" (228), but Poe's text suggests that the "conditions of the sentience" of a gothic text are activated by no less lifeless entities: not stones, but words and letters. And just as for Roderick "the evidence of the sentience—was to be seen, he said ... in the gradual yet certain condensation of an atmosphere of their own about the waters and the walls" (228), the "evidence of the existence" of a gothic of reading can be seen in the "atmosphere" inanimate words and letters create when "the reflexive disturbance in the circuit of reception" is made manifest.

It is ultimately the collusion between text and reader that creates the gothic; the reading of the gothic text effectively activates the text as gothic. In Stewart's words, "it gradually dawns on you that *all this is your doing* as well as the author's—and not only your doing, but a figurative rendition of it: of an immanent and activating interest heated, derivative, vicarious, now schizoid, now parasitic, even a little vampiric" (343–44). In the figure of Roderick Usher, Poe not only embodies but duplicates and then re-duplicates this kind of gothic activation. Thus it is when Roderick is listening to the narrator's reading of "The Mad Trist of Sir Launcelot Canning" that "The Fall of the House of Usher" is activated as a gothic text; the representation of the effects of a gothic reading on Roderick Usher as a reader activates the gothic of reading within the reader of Roderick Usher. Poe's representation of gothic activation relies on duality and mirroring—with a difference.

According to Stewart, gothic texts differ radically from works such as Jane Austen's *Northanger Abbey* and *Persuasion* that valorize the act of reading and "heroize" the reader:

> What Austen's novels bring out is an ingrained generic reciprocation of consciousness and conscience, or in a word, the coming to *know better* ... The reader is thereby tacitly heroized through the demonstration of energies cognate with those harder won by the characters, the ability to stay with it, attend closely, adjust judgements, see them through—in short, to persevere without illusion, curious but not credulous, everywhere on alert. (106)

In Stewart's characterization of the implied reader in Austen's novels we can see the mold into which critics have tried to fit the narrator of Poe's "Usher." When critics look at "Usher" what they *want* to see reflected is this "heroic" reader, preferably embodied in the figure of the narrator, providing a neat (and implicitly instructive) contrast with Roderick Usher's "wrong" reading, his hysterical, gothic sensibilities. Thus discussions of the narrator's reliability center, whether implicitly or explicitly, on the status of the narrator's consciousness and conscience; the question is precisely whether the narrator "comes to know better" than Roderick Usher. As Stewart recognizes, however, such progress is premised upon a certain degree of moral, cognitive, hermeneutic, and psychic staying power. That the narrator is a figure for the reader is apparent in the opening sentence: "During the whole of a dull, dark, and soundless day in the autumn of the year ... I had been passing alone, on horseback, through a singularly dreary tract of country." Several points highlight this passage as a scene of reading, and the narrator as more than a simple storyteller relating a finished sequence of events. The first word emphasizes the notion of duration and process, key elements of reading. Likewise, the narrator envisions himself as "passing alone ... through a dreary tract"—an image which can easily connote travel or reading (or both). Particularly striking is the word "soundless": a "dull" and "dark" day can easily be imagined, but a "soundless" one? After all, when is an entire day without sound? Only when it is textual; that is, when it is read.

Unlike the "heroic" reader, however, instead of "persevering without illusion, curious but not credulous, everywhere on alert," the narrator immediately exposes his propensity for affective impression.

> I know not how it was—but, with the first glimpse of the building, a sense of insufferable gloom pervaded my spirit. I say insufferable; for the feeling was unrelieved by any of that half-pleasurable, because poetic, sentiment, with which the mind usually receives even the sternest natural images of the desolate or terrible. (216)

While it may initially appear that the narrator is simply "attending closely," it quickly becomes apparent that the effect of the house is all the narrator's doing: he activates its gothicism in and of himself by reading into it "an iciness, a sinking, a sickening of the heart—an unredeemed dreariness of thought which *no goading of the imagination could torture* into aught of the sublime" (216, emphasis added). Further evidence of the narrator's participatory reading of the scene posed by Usher (both the house and the man) appears throughout the text: thus he "collapses" the character of the house into the character of the man through his consideration of "the very remarkable fact" that "the entire family lay in the direct line of descent":

> It was this deficiency, *I considered*, while running over in thought the perfect keeping of the character of the premises with the accredited character of the people, and *while speculating* upon the possible influence which the one, in the long lapse of centuries, *might have exercised* on the other—it was this deficiency, *perhaps*, of collateral issue ... which had, at length, so identified the two as to merge the original title of the estate in the quaint and equivocal appellation of the "House of Usher"—an appellation *which seemed* to include, in the minds of the peasantry who used it, both the family and the family mansion. (218, emphasis added)

The narrator's repetition of the statement "it was this deficiency" and its repeated qualification with "I considered," "might have exercised," "seemed," and "perhaps" suggest that this conflation of house and family is primarily his interpretation, possibly superimposed on the always unrepresented "minds of the peasantry" and strangely reflected in Roderick Usher's belief in "the sentience of all vegetable things." Similarly, the narrator later admits "I had *so worked upon my imagination as really to believe* that about the whole mansion and domain there hung an atmosphere peculiar to themselves and their immediate vicinity" (219, emphasis added). This "working upon," "goading," and "torturing" of his own sensibilities marks the narrator as quite different from the alert, persevering, "heroic" narrator implied in Austen's novels.

Although critics have often debated whether, in the course of "Usher," the narrator contracts Roderick Usher's brand of paranoid susceptibility, the opening pages suggest that the narrator already has it; his immediate reaction to the house indicates the presence of "an immanent and activating interest heated, derivative, vicarious, now schizoid, now parasitic, even a little vampiric"—he overtly seeks to "goad" his imagination and to "torture" his image of the house of Usher, if possible, into something "sublime." While critics have wanted the narrator, the figure who opens "Usher," to possess the qualities attributed by Stewart to the "heroic" reader, Poe's text seems to suggest that an inclination toward a "gothic of reading" is a preexisting condition of his narrator. And yet, if the narrator embodies a reader already predisposed toward the gothic, how can we evaluate his reliability as the narrator of a tale designed for readers predisposed toward the gothic?

This duplication is rendered increasingly complex by the fact that the narrator is not only "figuring" the reader, he is also (and simultaneously) "ushering" in "Usher." The narrator is "usher" for the text of "The Fall of the House of Usher" and a reflection (in his status as reader activated by the gothic) of *both* Roderick Usher and the reader of "Usher." Although he does not reflect the "heroic" reader so desired by critics, the narrator's gesture of looking into the tarn is, ironically, a mirror image of the critical desire to "rearrange" a text to suit an interpretive predisposition:

> I reined my horse to the precipitous brink of a black and lurid tarn that lay in unruffled lustre by the dwelling, and gazed down—but with a shudder even more thrilling than before— upon the remodeled and inverted images of the gray sedge, and the ghastly tree-stems, and the vacant and eyelike windows. (217)

The narrator's "shudder even more thrilling than before" is explicitly provoked by his attempt to "read" the house differently—it is as if he attempts to hold his interpretation up to a mirror:

> It was possible, *I reflected*, that a mere different arrangement of the particulars of the scene, of the details of the picture, would be sufficient to modify, or perhaps to annihilate its capacity for sorrowful impression. (217, emphasis added)

The ironic phrase "I reflected" is both subtle and revealing: the narrator holds his interpretive response up to a mirror, only to see his response (his "I")[14] reflected. It is as if a reader (or critic) began reading a text only to be presented with the image of a reader (or critic) reading that very text.[15]

Garrett Stewart describes the impact of such an inscripted scene of reading on the reader:

> The text has become a phenomenal world. Suddenly one of the subjects that people this world is described poised over a book. You thus see in your mind's eye a character engaged upon an act of obliviousness and withdrawal which is effected through means other than an immediate engagement with the space and time to which you have been introduced. (17)

Such another space and time frames the narrator's attempt to read the house of Usher, which creates "The [Fall of the] House of Usher" that is to be read.

An interesting example of this kind of sudden exposure of fictionality occurs in "Usher" when the narrator tries to "shake off" the effects of the "atmosphere" of Usher. This moment occurs immediately after the narrator has admitted to the increase of his superstition through his awareness that his superstitions have increased and that he has "so worked upon [his] imagination as really to believe" in this "atmosphere": "Shaking off from my spirit what *must* have been a dream, I scanned more narrowly the real aspect of the building" (219). By indicating that he will "now" (when?) "scan more narrowly *the real aspect of the building*," the narrator effectively calls our attention to the existence of an alternative space constructed by his own reading of Usher. We have been reading "The Fall of the House of Usher" only to here be confronted with the fact that the narrator has not been narrating "the house of Usher" so much as *reading it himself.*

Significantly, it is in the conclusion of the paragraph that begins this report on "the real aspect of the building" that the narrator vaguely mentions the infamous "barely perceptible fissure":

> ... the fabric gave little token of instability. Perhaps the eye of a scrutinizing observer might have discovered a barely perceptible fissure, which, extending from the roof of the building in front, made its way down the wall in a zigzag direction, until it became lost in the sullen waters of the tarn. (219)

The narrator's presentation of this all-important fissure is striking: why does he claim that it is a mark which "perhaps" "might have [been] discovered" by "the eye of a scrutinizing observer"? More importantly, why does he do so at precisely that point when he claims to be "narrowly detailing" for the reader "the real aspect of the building"?

Ultimately, Poe's fissure marks a textual space which, as Stewart argues, represents more than *mise en abyme.* A space he characterizes as the "transacted gap between reader and read" has been exposed, and a "regression with a difference" created. This "regression" can become like a hall of mirrors in which characters are infinitely "dropped away" from their readers in order to exist otherwise and to inhabit a psychic space located elsewhere:

> When the realist scene of reading brings before you characters lost to the world of the narrative, they are dropped away into

another *mise en scène* than the one to which you have been granted mental access. Your sense of visualizing such characters in their milieu is thus at odds with their being elsewhere caught up, their now reinhabited psychic space having nothing to do with the immediately narrated work it has previously served to confirm and interiorize. (17–18)

Poe's representation of the fissure—as "perhaps" part of the text of the house of Usher, or "perhaps" a figment of the narrator's (retrospective) interpretation, or "perhaps" a mark only discernible to "the eye of a scrutinizing observer"—creates such an "other" space, a gap which the text does not allow the reader "to confirm and interiorize."

Furthermore, Stewart argues that once this "transacted gap between reader and read" has been exposed or, in the case of Poe's text, glimpsed (possibly), no amount of reading can smooth over the rupture:

Your denied access to the precise contour or texture of that intermission—even if the inlaid text is "read into evidence," quoted whole or in part, within the enclosing narrative in order to engage your own subjective response—has to do with the nature of reading as an *invisible* activity within a visible (or in fiction, visualized) posture of attention.... At the level of textual processing, then, the narrated activity of reading provides not a strict *mise en abyme* of reception but a regression with a difference. (17)

Poe dramatizes two crucial scenes of this "regression with a difference" in "The Fall of the House of Usher." The first occurs when Roderick Usher tells the narrator the story of his condition and of his sister's imminent death, a narrative that clearly forms an "inlaid text" within the overall structure of Poe's tale. At the conclusion of Roderick's summarized narrative, Madeline Usher emerges as if invoked by the story itself:

While he spoke, the lady Madeline ... passed slowly through a remote portion of the apartment, and, without having noticed my presence, disappeared. I regarded her with an utter astonishment not unmingled with dread—and yet I found it impossible to account for such feelings. A sensation of stupor oppressed me, as my eye followed her retreating steps. (223)

Like the fissure, Madeline Usher's fleeting presence at this textual moment marks the "gap between reader and read." She exists in a textual space invoked by "The Fall of the House of Usher" only to be revealed as existing elsewhere. The collusion between reader and text (whether represented by the narrator and Roderick Usher's narrative or the reader and "The Fall of the House of Usher") that creates the gothic of reading is thus overtly dramatized here.

Roderick Usher's premature burial of his sister thus becomes a clever narrative representation of the way in which she (like the "barely perceptible fissure" that also marked the space opened by a gothic of reading) is "encrypted" throughout the text. Garrett Stewart remarks upon a trend in nineteenth-century British novels toward

> all manner of vicarious, voyeuristic, mesmeric, and vampiric phenomena in which psychic usurpation, somatic doubling, or perversely gendered otherness doubles for the aesthetic distance—and transacted gap—between reader and read. And so it goes—unsaid: reading encrypted but persistent, made immanent in its own pantomimes of itself. (18–19)

The degree of "persistence" that characterizes gothic reading in "The Fall of the House of Usher" becomes apparent in one of the most famous and striking scenes of "psychic usurpation, somatic doubling, and perversely gendered otherness" in all of Poe (or, for that matter, in all of American literature): the scene in which the narrator and Roderick Usher read "The Mad Trist of Sir Launcelot Canning." Significantly, the narrator's description of his own state of mind on the evening of the reading marks one of the most striking "regressions with a difference" in the entire story: mentally, psychically, and emotionally, he is a reflection of Roderick Usher:

> I struggled to reason off the nervousness which had dominion over me. I endeavored to believe that much, if not all of what I felt, was *due to the bewildering influence of the gloomy furniture of the room ...* But my efforts were fruitless. An irrepressible tremor gradually pervaded my frame; and, at length, there sat upon my heart *an incubus of utterly causeless alarm ...* Overpowered by an intense sentiment of horror, *unaccountable yet unendurable*, I threw on my clothes with haste ... and endeavored to arouse myself from the *pitiable condition* into which I had fallen. (232, emphasis added)

The narrator thus shares all of Roderick Usher's physical and psychological symptoms; he is a mirror image of Usher and yet he is not Roderick Usher. This motif of reflected difference is emphasized by "their" reading. While the narrator sees their activities as unifying and essentially similar, "I will read, and you shall listen;—and so we will pass away this terrible night together" (233), the two characters embody different kinds of readers by evincing different reading "activities": one reads aloud, one "listens." Thus, the gothic text of "The Mad Trist" undergoes a dual reception (one active and "immediate," the other passive and "deferred")—not including, of course, its third reading, as a Poe text, by the reader of Poe's text.

Ultimately, the two characters "activate" a gothic of reading (both within and outside of the text—with the help of the reader of "The Fall of the House of Usher," of course) by reading a gothic text together. Unlike the "inlaid text" of Madeline Usher's illness and impending death, however, "The Mad Trist of Sir Launcelot Canning" is "read into evidence" in the text. Such a strategy would seem designed to ensure that the reader's response to this scene of gothic reading (his/her gothic of reading) in "The Fall of the House of Usher" is synonymous with the narrator and Roderick Usher's gothic reading (and the representation of *their* gothic of reading). Once again, the mirror is held up to the reader: the activity of reading has been made visible. Nevertheless, as Stewart suggests, the result is *not* "a strict *mise en abyme* of reception," although the synchronicity of read text ("The Mad Trist") with read text ("Usher") might seem to suggest such a possibility. Despite the fact that the narrator first hears "the very cracking and ripping sound which Sir Launcelot had so particularly described" (234), then "a low and apparently distant, but harsh, protracted, and most unusual screaming or grating sound—the exact counterpart of what my fancy had already conjured up" (235), and finally "a distinct, hollow, metallic, and clangorous, yet apparently muffled reverberation" that sounds exactly "as if a shield of brass had indeed, at the moment, fallen heavily upon a floor of silver" (236), Poe's text once again testifies to the resurgence of that "aesthetic distance and transacted gap—between reader and read." Even when the text read and the effect created are presumably synchronized, the fissure appears and immediately begins to widen. First, the reading is interrupted by the insertion of Roderick Usher back into the text: the reader, much as in the scene in which the narrator abruptly shifted to a description of the "real aspect" of the house of Usher, is reminded that s/he has been watching characters who have been "caught up" "elsewhere," "their now reinhabited psychic space having nothing to do with the immediately narrated work it has previously served to confirm and interiorize."

Secondly, this awareness of an/other "psychic space" is again marked by the entrance of Madeline Usher. Roderick's sister is the quintessential embodiment of the notion of "reading encrypted but persistent"; she literally brings down the house:

> As if in the superhuman energy of his utterance there had been found the potency of a spell—the huge antique panels to which the speaker had pointed, threw slowly back, upon the instant, their ponderous and ebony jaws. It was the work of the rushing gust—but then without those doors there *did* stand the lofty and enshrouded figure of the lady Madeline of Usher. (237)

As in her previous appearance, Madeline appears on cue, as if textually invoked; indeed, as a figure for the gothic of reading, the "reflexive disturbance in the circuit of reception," she *is* textually invoked. The "energy" of Roderick's "utterance" seems to open doors and call her forth with "the potency of a spell"—much as his previous description of her illness and impending death seemed to do. In a gesture similar to his earlier turn to a description of "the real aspect of the building," the narrator offers an explanation for the opened doors ("It was the work of the rushing gust"), but just as he could not previously erase the elusive (and potentially illusive) presence of the fissure, so too he must admit "without those doors there did stand the lofty and enshrouded figure of the lady Madeline of Usher." Gothic textuality and the dynamic it generates between reader and text cannot be explained away or situated firmly within the realm of the fictive "real," that is, the space of narrative interiorized and assimilated by the reader. A gothic of reading, as "The Fall of the House of Usher" demonstrates, opens a textual space elsewhere by calling attention to precisely that gap between reader and text which cannot be read away. Like Madeline Usher, the gothic of reading may be encrypted but it will persist, revealing itself at the moment when the gothic text becomes most gothic, precisely because it is this gap, doubly figured in "Usher" as a "barely perceptible" fissure and an encrypted revenant, that makes the text gothic.

It is possible to see the gothic of reading as a text's revenge upon its critics—such a perspective may offer one way of explaining the anxious and contradictory relationship between Poe's texts, their critics, and the American literary tradition. Poe's works haunt literary critics because they remain, in large part, unassimilable and inexplicable as "literature," and particularly as "American" literature. And yet, as many critics have acknowledged, their effects cannot be denied (even if they are often dismissed as inappropriate). Poe's "The Fall of the House of Usher" calls attention to the narrative space it occupies *as* gothic text in order to question those parameters and the means by which critics arrive at such dimensions. Instead of safe havens and reliable narrators, Poe gives his readers and critics a house of mirrors; the resulting dynamic of interpretive uncertainty makes up his texts.

NOTES

1. Shoshana Felman, "On Reading Poetry: Reflections on the Limits and Possibilities of Psychoanalytical Approaches," in Joseph H. Smith, ed., *Psychiatry and the Humanities*, Vol. 4: The Literary Freud: Mechanisms of Defense and the Poetic Will (New Haven: Yale Univ. Press, 1980), 122.

2. Shawn Rosenheim and Stephen Rachman, eds., *The American Face of Edgar Allan Poe* (Baltimore: The Johns Hopkins Univ. Press, 1995), x–xi.

3. Thus Rosenheim and Rachman suggest that Poe and American cultural criticism were always well aware of one another: "critical dismissal of Poe has followed from Poe's own seeming disengagement with American culture, as if Poe and his critics had silently agreed to turn their backs on one another.... That Poe could appear at once 'out of step' with his own day and culture and yet intimately bound to it is evident even from writings of his own period" (x).

4. As Rosenheim and Rachman acknowledge, "Anyone who would locate Poe's writing within a cultural context must confront the way his work tends to advertise itself as ethereal and otherworldly, or avowedly timeless, or preoccupied with aesthetic, cognitive, and linguistic categories of psychopathological conditions" (xi).

5. Joseph G. Kronick, "Edgar Allan Poe: The Error of Reading and the Reading of Error," in Jefferson Humphries, ed., *Southern Literature and Literary Theory* (Athens: The Univ. of Georgia Press, 1990), 208.

6. Thus Kronick argues, "We discover in Poe's texts and their scenes of misreading that error makes interpretation possible" (209).

7. Jonathan Elmer, *Reading at the Social Limit: Affect, Mass Culture, and Edgar Allan Poe* (Stanford: Stanford Univ. Press, 1995), 184.

8. Charles E. May, *Edgar Allan Poe: A Study of the Short Fiction* (Boston: Twayne Publishers, 1991), 28.

9. Again, Felman notices this "Poe-etic" drive with respect to the influence of Poe's poetry on the production of literary scholarship: "regardless of the value-judgement it may pass on Poe, this impressive bulk of Poe scholarship, the very quantity of the critical literature to which Poe's poetry has given rise, is itself an indication of its effective poetic power, of the strength with which it drives the reader to an action, compels him to a reading act" (124). She argues, "The question of what makes poetry lies, indeed, not so much in what it was that made Poe write, but in what it is that makes us read him and that ceaselessly drives so many people to write about him" (129).

10. Elmer's discussion of "The Raven" in Chapter Four of *Reading at the Social Limit* offers an interesting counterpoint and dynamic with my own reading of "Usher" and has, quite obviously, influenced my own interpretation.

11. Benjamin Franklin Fisher IV, "Playful 'Germanism' in 'The Fall of the House of Usher,'" in G.R. Thompson and Virgil L. Lokke, eds., *Ruined Eden of the Present: Hawthorne, Melville, and Poe, Critical Essays in Honor of Darrel Abel* (West Lafayette: Purdue Univ. Press 1981), 359–60.

12. Garrett Stewart, *Dear Reader: The Conscripted Audience in Nineteenth-Century British Fiction* (Baltimore: The Johns Hopkins Univ. Press, 1996). Stewart argues that nineteenth-century British novels "conscript" the "responses" of their readership by writing their readings into and along with their texts: "As members of an audience, your private reading—along with that of every other reader—is actually convoked and restaged, put in service to the text. Either as an identifying notation or as a narrative event, this reading in of your reading—or of you reading—is what I mean by the notion of a conscripted response. Implicated by apostrophe or by proxy, by address or by dramatized scenes of reading, you are deliberately drafted by the texts, written with. In the closed circuit of conscripted response, your input is a predigested function of the text's output—digested in advance by rhetorical mention or by narrative episode" (8).

13. Edgar Allan Poe, "The Fall of the House of Usher," in *Great Short Works of Edgar Allan Poe*, ed. G. R. Thompson (New York: Harper and Row Publishers, 1970), 216–38. Hereafter cited parenthetically.

14. Significantly, we learn little about the narrator in the course of the story; his characterization is primarily limited to his aesthetic and hermeneutic responses or interpretations of other characters, their behavior, and their environment.

15. The "shudder" produced is precisely that of Freud's concept of "unheimlich" or "the uncanny": the familiar has been radically defamiliarized.

LELAND S. PERSON

Poe's Philosophy of Amalgamation: Reading Racism in the Tales

ABBREVIATIONS

Throughout the present volume, references to works by Edgar Allan Poe are provided parenthetically in the text of each selection.

CW   *Collected Writings of Edgar Allan Poe.* Ed. Burton R. Pollin and Joseph V. Ridgely. 5 vols. New York: Gordian Press, 1985–97.

    Vol. 1: *The Imaginary Voyages.* Boston: Twayne, 1981; New York: Gordian Press, 1994.

    Vol. 2: *The Brevities.* New York: Gordian Press, 1985.

    Vol. 3: *Writings in the Broadway Journal, Nonfictional Prose.* Part 1, The Text. New York: Gordian Press, 1986.

    Vol. 4: *Writings in the Broadway Journal, Nonfictional Prose.* Part 2, The Annotations. New York: Gordian Press, 1986.

    Vol. 5: *Writings in the Southern Literary Messenger, Nonfictional Prose.* New York: Gordian Press, 1997.

Essays   *Essays and Reviews.* Ed. G.R. Thompson. New York: Library of America, 1984.

From *Romancing the Shadow: Poe and Race*, edited by J. Gerald Kennedy and Liliane Weissberg. ©2001 by Oxford University Press.

Letters   *The Letters of Edgar Allan Poe.* Ed. John Ward Ostrom. 2 vols.
           1948. New York: Gordian Press, 1966.

Mabbott   *The Collected Works of Edgar Allan Poe.* Ed. Thomas Ollive,
           Maureen C. Mabbott. 3 vols. Cambridge, Mass.: Belknap
           Press of Harvard University Press, 1969–78.
           Vol. 1: *Poems.*
           Vol. 2: *Tales and Sketches, 1831–1842.*
           Vol. 3: *Tales and Sketches, 1843–1849.*

Works   *The Complete Works of Edgar Allan Poe.* Ed. James A. Harrison. 17
           vols. New York: Kelmscott Society, 1902.

Emphasizing the "horror, and thick gloom, and a black sweltering desert of ebony," as well as the "southward" drift of his ship, the narrator of Poe's early story "Ms. Found in a Bottle" (1833) discovers "black stupendous seas" swelling above him and then a gigantic ship, whose "huge hull" is a "deep dingy black," bearing down upon him (Mabbott, 2:139, 140). When he is hurled from his own ship to the other, he quickly secretes himself in the hold because, he says, "I was unwilling to trust myself with a race of people who had offered, to the cursory glance I had taken, so many points of vague novelty, doubt, and apprehension" (Mabbott, 2:141). As he becomes convinced that his new, "terrible," ship is doomed, he finds himself on deck, "unwittingly" daubing with a black tar brush upon the "edges of a neatly-folded studding-sail." When it is unfurled, he reports, the black-on-white message he has unwittingly written reads "DISCOVERY" (Mabbott, 2:142).

Toni Morrison has recently challenged American literary scholars to discover a racial presence even in texts from which race seems absent. "Explicit or implicit," argues Morrison, "the Africanist presence informs in compelling and inescapable ways the texture of American literature. It is a dark and abiding presence, there for the literary imagination as both a visible and an invisible mediating force. Even, and especially, when American texts are not 'about' Africanist presences or characters or narrative or idiom, the shadow hovers in implication, in sign, in line of demarcation" (*Playing in the Dark*, 46–47).[1] Poe scholars such as John Carlos Rowe and Sam Worley have analyzed race and racism in *The Narrative of Arthur Gordon Pym*; both have situated that text within its antebellum cultural and political context. Louis Rubin and Joan Dayan have gone furthest in reading race in other works that do not seem to be "about" race. Dayan in particular brilliantly decodes some of the tales, including "Ligeia," to disclose what Morrison calls an Africanist presence. In this chapter I want to go further still in reading several of Poe's tales within a discursive context of race and race differences. Specifically, I want to create a conversation between Poe's short fiction and its historical and cultural context to determine (if not overdetermine) the function rather than simply the presence of race and racism. Color and race differences fascinated eighteenth- and nineteenth-century Americans, and I think Poe inscribes such fascination in those tales such as "Ligeia," "The Murders in the Rue Morgue," and "The Black Cat," that feature black and white exchanges and triangulated, arguably racial relationships. I want to trace an evolutionary line, in fact, through those three tales to "Hop-Frog" (1849), Poe's last tale and his most obvious drama of racism and racial revenge. In short, I want to explore the white imagination Poe represents in selected tales and to discover the significance, to return to the narrator of "Ms. Found in a Bottle," of black and white color coding.

Evidence has accumulated over the years to indicate that, regardless of whether he wrote the infamous Paulding-Drayton review for the *Southern Literary Messenger* in 1836, Poe sympathized with proslavery rhetoric. Bernard Rosenthal effectively made that case even without relying on the Paulding-Drayton text. Poe himself, of course, hardly engraved invitations to his readers to recognize the racial significance of his tales. Like the buried corpses in "The Cask of Amontillado," "The Tell-Tale Heart," and "The Black Cat," race lurks behind walls and screens in Poe's writing. Part of the challenge of recovering racial signifiers from Poe's fiction, in fact, is trying to coordinate racial content with other features of his writing that seem to discourage the discovery of racial or any other particular cultural meaning. David Reynolds and John Carlos Rowe address this issue from very different perspectives. Both resituate Poe's writing within its cultural context, but both argue that aspects of Poe's fictional project work against each other. In Reynolds's view, Poe tried to exploit the market for sensational fiction even as he censured its excesses; the complex aesthetic surface of his fiction distanced it from the rich undercurrent of event. The result is a kind of double-headed fiction, characterized by "apolitical irrationalism" that becomes "simultaneously a full enactment of the popular Subversive imagination and a careful containment of it" (230). Poe's first-person narrators in particular, Reynolds asserts, provide a "firm device for controlling the sensational" (237). Rowe unequivocally considers Poe a "proslavery Southerner" (117), but he points out that the deconstructive tendencies of Poe's writing (or at least poststructuralist analyses of it) have the ironic effect of "complementing" Poe's "racist strategy of literary production" (118) by realizing precisely what Poe himself had hoped: "the substitution of an immaterial world for the threatening world of material history" (121). The challenge I wish to pose for myself in this chapter, then, is coordinating Poe's racial content (however indirectly signified) with both his playful, deconstructive impulse and his exploitation of first-person psychological romance. Indeed, I want to argue, first-person psychological romance in the Gothic or sensational mode represented an ideal vehicle for representing and destabilizing the psychological constructs of white male racism.[2]

VITILIGO AND THE SLIPPERY SLOPE OF RACISM

As numerous scholars have established, color immediately became the primary criterion for instituting racial differences and a racial hierarchy in American culture. For obvious reasons, including amalgamation, color simultaneously became a slippery marker of difference. Virginia authorities tried to police miscegenation from the beginning, severely punishing miscegenators as early as 1630 and prohibiting it by law in 1662 (Williamson, 7, 8). But in 1785 Virginia defined a Negro as a person with a black parent or grandparent, thus defining as "white" any person with less than one-fourth black "blood" (Williamson, 13). Williamson claims, in fact, that this legal definition "became a sore upon the social body of Virginia and remained such for half a century"—leading, among other things, to cases of "passing," as some "blacks" "rushed to claim the privileges of whiteness" (14). It was not until after Poe's death, during the 1850 census, that mulattoes were counted as a separate category of people. In that year, the census listed 406,000 people as mulatto out of a Negro population of 3,639,000 (11.2 percent) and a total U.S. population of over 22 million; 80,000 mulattoes were counted in Virginia (Williamson 24, 25).

In *Notes on the State of Virginia* (1787), Thomas Jefferson describes an "anomaly of nature"—albino "blacks," including a

> negro man within my own knowledge, born black, and of black parents; on whose chin, when a boy, a white spot appeared. This continued to increase till he became a man, by which time it had extended over his chin, lips, one cheek, the under jaw and neck on that side. It is of the Albino white, without any mixture of red, and has for several years been stationary. He is robust and healthy, and the change of colour was not accompanied with any sensible disease, either general or topical. (71)

Jefferson reveals his fascination not only with color but also with vitiligo, or spontaneous color changes in the skin.[3] He disassociates color and racial identity, and he curtails the "plot" of this brief story before a total eclipse of blackness can occur that might make racial identification more difficult. "The first difference which strikes us is that of colour," Jefferson announces. "Whether the black of the negro resides in the reticular membrane between the skin and scarf-skin, or in the scarf-skin itself; whether it proceeds from the colour of the blood, the colour of the bile, or from that of some other secretion, the difference is fixed in nature, and is as real as if its seat and cause were better known to us" (138). Jefferson's treatment of color and race exemplifies the quasi-scientific discourse of racial differences of the eighteenth and nineteenth centuries, especially the desire to "fix" racial differences "in nature" and to affix them to color. Whether inherent or acquired and regardless of its source, Jefferson suggests, color represents the "first difference"—constituting a kind of optical essentialism. At the same time, Jefferson does not rest easy behind the lines of difference. "I tremble for my country," he admits, "when I reflect that God is just: that his justice cannot sleep for ever: that considering numbers, nature and natural means only, a revolution of the wheel of fortune, *an exchange of situations*, is among possible events: that it may become probable by supernatural interference!" (163; emphasis added).[4] Jefferson was hardly alone in trembling with fear as well as fascination at the prospect of color change, "revolution," and an "exchange of situation." Even a cursory study of American popular culture reveals numerous examples of color and racial "anomalies of nature."

Eighteenth- and nineteenth-century American fascination with color and color differences underwrote public exhibition and spectacle, especially of cases that tested racial differences. P.T. Barnum displayed a "leopard child" in his American Museum, as well as two albino Negro girls, "Pure White, with White Wool and Pink Eyes," beside their black mother and baby sister (Saxon, 101). Charles Willson Peale was so fascinated by his discovery (on his honeymoon) of a mulatto slave in Somerset County, Maryland, whose skin had changed color from dark brown to "paper-white," that he painted the portrait of James, a "White Negro," and hung it in his Philadelphia museum (Sellers, 53). Peale believed that "the Negro lacked only an equal advantage of education," that "only ignorance and skin color set the race apart" (Sellers, 53), so the social and political potential of vitiligo intrigued him. Whitening might eliminate race and race-based inequalities, or so Barnum certainly thought. M.R. Werner notes that in August 1850 a "negro came to New York who claimed to have discovered a weed that would turn negroes white." Barnum exhibited him at his American Museum and "hailed" him and his magic weed as the "solution of the slavery problem, contending in his advertisements that if all the negroes could be turned white the problem of slavery would disappear with their color" (Werner, 204).[5] Such erasure of racial difference figures prominently in the most famous case of vitiligo in late-eighteenth-century America.

Ira Berlin notes that freedom created some unusual opportunities for former slaves; in the late eighteenth century the South was "invaded by black vaudevillians," including Henry Moss, a "Negro turned White as Snow" (62). Moss traveled to Philadelphia in 1796, advertised himself as "A Great Curiosity," and charged an admission fee of "one Quarter of a Dollar each person," using the money he earned to purchase his freedom (Stanton, 6).[6] Fascinated with Henry Moss, who had fought in the Revolution as a member of the Continental Army (Stanton, 6), Samuel Stanhope Smith, professor of moral philosophy at the College of New Jersey, used him to underwrite a different "revolution" and to substantiate his claim that color differences were superficial—the effect of climate and other environmental conditions (Stanton, 5).[7] Smith's account of Moss's entrepreneurial hoax in his celebrated *Essay on the Causes of the Variety of Complexion and Figure in the Human Species* is worth quoting in full:

> Henry Moss, a negro in the state of Maryland, began, upwards of twenty years ago to undergo a change in the colour of his skin, from a deep black, to a clear and healthy white. The change commenced about the abdomen, and gradually extended over different parts of the body, till, at the end of seven years, the period at which I saw him, the white had already overspread the greater portion of his skin. It had nothing of the appearance of a sickly or albino hue, as if it had been the effect of disease. He was a vigorous and active man; and had never suffered any disease either at the commencement, or during the progress of the change. The white complexion did not advance by regularly spreading from a single center over the whole surface. But soon after it made its first appearance on the abdomen, it began to shew itself on various parts of the body, nearly at the same time, whence it gradually *encroached* in different directions on the original colour till, at length, the black was left only here and there in spots of various sizes, and shapes. These spots were largest and most frequent, where the body, from the nakedness of the parts or the raggedness of his clothing, was most exposed to the rays of the sun. This extraordinary change did not proceed by

gradually and equably diluting the intensity of the shades of black colour over the whole person at once; but the original black, reduced to spots, when I saw it, by the *encroachments* of the white, *resembled dark clouds insensibly melting away at their edges*. The back of his hands, and his face, retained a larger proportion of the black than other parts of his body; of these, however, the greater portion was changed. And *the white colour had extended itself to a considerable distance* under the hair. Wherever this took place, the woolly substance entirely disappeared, and a fine, straight hair, of silky softness succeeded in its room. (58; emphasis added)

This narrative description, in which amalgamation is already emplotted as an encroaching color change, stands ready-made for romance and already resembles one of Poe's narratives in its scientific detail and acute observation: Smith's metaphors colonize the black body, allegorizing and nationalizing Henry Moss as a kind of black—then white—Uncle Sam. Registering the hope or fear that amalgamation would spread—spreading with it the erasure of color and racial difference—Smith creates a kind of "cradle" of amalgamation in Moss's abdomen, even though he promulgates a polygenetic rather than single-origin theory of vitiligo. Although Smith comments that he lost track of Moss, who "removed into the State of Virginia," he concludes Moss's story very differently from the way Thomas Jefferson abridged his tale of vitiligo—with the information, provided "by respectable authority," that the "whitening process was soon afterwards completed, and that, in his appearance, he could not be distinguished from a native Anglo-American" (59). As William Stanton observes, Smith argued for the unity of the human species, monogenesis rather than polygenesis (despite the polygenetic coloration he described on Henry Moss), and he wished to "explain away the many differences that defined the races" (5). In this brief "plot," it seems to me, he uncannily illustrates a philosophy of amalgamation that anticipates Poe's. Accelerating the multigenerational process of "reversion," Smith inscribes the possibility that the color and racial foundation of (political) difference would become indistinguishable and disappear from an individual black body, which thereby offers a physical site for a potentially national phenomenon—a thoroughly amalgamated society in which racial differences can no longer be grounded in color.

In making color the primary sign of race differences (and "blood" the primary source of color), Americans created more problems than they solved. Dayan points out that the "law of reversion" in the South and the Caribbean "certified the futility in trying to remove blackness, even the least molecules of black blood, by successive alliances with whites." In fact, the "concept of blackness had to be reinforced, made absolute and unchangeable against the prima facie evidence of fading color, and the strategy was to call this idea *blood*" ("Amorous Bondage," 201–2). Poe seems acutely aware of this law of reversion in stories such as "Ligeia" and "The Black Cat," but he pushes the logic of color and color (inter)-change to the breaking point— deconstructing color as a reliable signifier of racial difference and refusing to ground racial differences stably in differences of appearance. Dana Nelson observes that *The Narrative of Arthur Gordon Pym* "reveals the general failure of Pym and his colonial epistemology to represent Otherness as 'radical,' to inscribe a stable opposition between 'black' and 'white' as well as between 'art' and 'nature' which would support colonial knowledge" (101).[8] Certainly "Ligeia" offers an object lesson in such instability, as dark and light change positions in a hallucinatory montage that calls their difference into question.

It will strike many readers as a leap of logic to connect Poe's obvious color coding in a story such as "Ligeia" with nineteenth-century race relations. As Winthrop Jordan reminds us, however, "Blackness had become so thoroughly entangled with the basest status in American society that at least by the beginning of the eighteenth century it was almost indecipherably coded into American language and literature." It is easy to understand the racial drama of *Othello*, Jordan concludes; it is "less easy to comprehend the cryptogram of a great white whale" (*White over Black*, 258). In other words, chiaroscuro color coding was so deeply ingrained in the American imagination that its particular reference to race could be repressed. My argument in this chapter, therefore, does not depend on the allegorical claim that Ligeia or the orangutan or the black cat is a black person but on the view that those characters and especially their functions within their respective stories can support racially relevant readings. Louis Rubin suggests dismissing the "notion of conscious intention or one-for-one allegorical relationships" in a search for connections between Poe and race or slavery in favor of examining Poe's writing for suggestive imagery and dramatic situations (177). Sam Worley has cogently situated *The Narrative of Arthur Gordon Pym* within the context of increasingly strident pro- and antislavery rhetoric of the late 1830s. He also notes the repressive climate in which Poe wrote—reflected most significantly in the passage of a radically suppressive censorship statute by the Virginia legislature in 1836 (238).[9] To write about race from anything but a proslavery perspective would have been extremely precarious after 1836, when Poe of course began to write his most famous tales. Poe may not have written plantation romances or directly engaged issues of slavery and racial difference in his tales, but he understood the symbolic value of color, and he clearly embedded dramas of color in his psychological romances. The dynamic function of racially encoded signs within Poe's texts resonates within a context of racial discourse and must have resonated at some level for nineteenth-century readers. In the process, I think, Poe ingeniously represented the workings of white racist psychology.

POE'S TOPSY-TURVY TALES

In analyzing the confluence of race and gender, abolitionism and feminism, Shirley Samuels and Karen Sánchez-Eppler both note the popularity of topsy-turvy dolls in nineteenth-century America. As Sánchez-Eppler explains, the "topsy-turvy doll is two dolls in one: when the long skirts of the elegant white girl are flipped over her head, where her feet should be there grins instead the stereotyped image of a wide-eyed pickaninny." "Always either one color or the other," she goes on, "the topsy-turvy doll enacts the binary structure of difference, emblematizing a nation governed by the logical dualism of segregation" and standing "as a cultural sign of the ways in which antebellum America conjoined racial issues with sexual ones" (133). I think it can be argued, especially in "Ligeia," that Poe has literalized and narrativized the topsy-turvy doll, inscribing a topsy-turvy plot that turns on the optical illusion of exchange and displacement the doll so efficiently enacts. The "hideous drama of revivification" (Mabbott, 2:328) in "Ligeia," moreover, can be reinterpreted in the context of antebellum fascination with color and color changes as a drama of amalgamation—of color and racial confusion. This is not to say that Ligeia herself is really "black," but the "unspeakable horrors" that arise "from the region of the ebony bed" (Mabbott, 2:238) do make her, in Dayan's terms, the "site for a crisis of racial identity" ("Amorous Bondage," 200).[10] With her ivory skin and raven hair Ligeia is already an amalgamated figure, the narrator's "amalgamate," and as a figure of extraordinary learning she poses a problem for the narrator similar to the one Phillis Wheatley posed for Jefferson.[11]

Dayan ingeniously suggests that the "three or four large drops of a brilliant and ruby colored fluid" that fall into Rowena's cup toward the end of the story (Mabbott, 2:325) can be read as blood, "the sign by which the spectral presence of race becomes incarnate as an ineradicable stain" ("Amorous Bondage," 201). Jefferson had noted that, when freed, the African American would be "removed beyond the reach of mixture" (*Notes*, 143), but in "Ligeia" the "contamination"—or poisoning of the white female body with dark "blood" issues forth in a nightmarish amalgamation: not a subtle case of vitiligo but the exchange of light woman for dark, the total eclipse of whiteness by blackness—a massive "encroachment" (to recall Smith's term) by "huge masses of long and dishevelled hair ... *blacker than the wings of the midnight*" and "the full, and the black, and the wild eyes—of my lost love— of the lady—of the LADY LIGEIA" (Mabbott, 2:330).[12]

Although Louis Rubin claims that C. Auguste Dupin's discovery that an orangutan committed the brutal murders in "The Murders in the Rue Morgue" (1841) renders them "literally meaningless"—"there is no motive, no crime, no villain, but only helpless victims" (142)—appreciating the racial connections in this tale restores a particular cultural meaning to the murders. Winthrop Jordan discusses the persistent linkage of African Americans and apes, especially orangutans, as well as the common belief that apes assaulted and even mated with women (*White over Black*, 31).[13] Dayan cites colonial historian Edward Long's *History of Jamaica* and his assertion that the orangutan "has in form a much nearer resemblance to the Negro race, than the latter bear to white men" ("Romance and Race," 103) to emphasize the necessary dehumanization of blacks on which white racism depends. Given the racist link between apes and blacks, the murders of two women in "The Murders in the Rue Morgue" ingeniously test the conceptual lines between species and between races. Offering a "glimpse," in Harry Levin's terms, of an "old Southern bugbear: the fear of exposing a mother or a sister to the suspected brutality of a darker race" (141), the murders seem rooted in white racist fears of black uprisings—especially as those uprisings would register on the bodies of white women.[14] Furthermore, in depicting "something *excessively outré*—something altogether irreconcilable with our common notions of human action, even when we suppose the actors the most depraved of men" (Mabbott, 2:5 57)—Poe seems not only to restore the lines of difference he had blurred in "Ligeia" but also to inscribe the common rationalization of species difference that often buttressed white racism.[15] In his verbal sketch of the murderer, Dupin combines "the ideas of an agility astounding, a strength superhuman, a ferocity brutal, a butchery without motive, a *grotesquerie* in horror absolutely alien from humanity, and a voice foreign in tone to the ears of men of many nations, and devoid of all distinct or intelligible syllabification" (Mabbott, 2:558). Indeed, only by interpreting the barbarity as the work not of a "madman" (the narrator's guess) but of a different species can Dupin solve the crime. At the same time, he and the narrator test the structures of difference in the white imagination. For example, Dupin makes a facsimile drawing of the marks found on Mademoiselle L'Espanaye's throat; he invites the narrator to place his fingers "in the respective impressions" and then try to wrap the drawing around a "billet" of wood approximately the size of the woman's neck (Mabbott,

2:559). This ironic reenactment places the narrator in the murderer's position while it exempts him from occupying that position. He concludes that this "is the mark of no human hand" (Mabbott, 2:559) even as he tries out and thus humanizes the subject position of the murderer.

"The Murders in the Rue Morgue," in fact, turns on the paradox that, to solve the crime, the detective, the narrator, and reader must identify with and thus humanize even the most "*excessively outré*" act of butchery—if only to attribute the crime to some "other" being. Furthermore, Poe clearly demonstrates that the orangutan's act represents a learned behavior. It has simply imitated its sailor-owner, who discovered it one day, razor in hand, "sitting before a looking-glass, attempting the operation of shaving, in which it had no doubt previously watched its master through the key-hole of the closet" (Mabbott, 2:565). When the sailor attempts to quiet the creature "by the use of a whip" (Mabbott, 2:565), it flees, only to end up in the Rue Morgue and in the bedroom of Madame L'Espanaye and her daughter. "As the sailor looked in, the gigantic animal had seized Madame L'Espanaye by the hair (which was loose, as she had been combing it), and was flourishing the razor about her face, in imitation of the motions of a barber" (Mabbott, 2:566). Nearly severing the woman's head from her body with "one determined sweep of its muscular arm," "flashing fire from its eyes," and then embedding its "fearful talons" in the daughter's throat, the orangutan happens to notice its master in the window. Indeed, its "wandering and wild glances fell at this moment upon the head of the bed, over which the face of its master, rigid with horror, was just discernible" (Mabbott, 2:567). This reciprocal gaze of owner and animal across the bed (and sexuality) of white womanhood—triangulates desire and violence in a possessive, murderous relationship between master and slave that becomes displaced upon the body of the white woman. Without necessarily adopting the Oedipal model that Joel Kovel employs in his analysis of white racism, we can still observe another instance of Poe's purposeful triangulation.[16] Unlike the triangle in "Ligeia," however, in which the male narrator found himself positioned between women, the narrator (as well as the sailor) in "The Murders in the Rue Morgue" finds himself witnessing racially encoded, male-on-female violence. Male power and the male gaze are between men, Poe suggests, until their inherent violence issues forth in a psycho-logic of violent murder. Ostensibly a spectator at this scene of inhuman, unmotivated violence, the sailor is ultimately revealed to be the source of violence—the orangutan only the agent he has set in motion. Jefferson had noted:

> The whole commerce between master and slave is a perpetual exercise of the most boisterous passions, the most unremitting despotism on the one part, and degrading submissions on the other. Our children see this, and learn to imitate it; for man is an imitative animal. This quality is the germ of all education in him. From the cradle to the grave he is learning to do what he sees others do. If a parent could find no motive either in his philanthropy or his self-love, for restraining the intemperance of passion towards his slave, it should always be a sufficient one that his child is present. But generally it is not sufficient. The parent storms, the child looks on, catches the lineaments of wrath, puts on the same airs in the circle of smaller slaves, gives loose to his worst of passions, and thus nursed, educated, and daily exercised in tyranny, cannot but be stamped by it with odious peculiarities. The man must be a prodigy who can retain his manners and morals undepraved by such circumstances. (*Notes on the State of Virginia*, 162)

Poe goes one obvious step further, tracing the roots of white racist fears to white racist behavior—to the unwitting education of slaves, through the "use of a whip," in the possession and murder of women. Under the gaze of its master, Poe notes, "the fury of the beast, *who no doubt bore still in mind the dreaded whip*, was instantly converted into fear" (Mabbott, 2:567; emphasis added), and the animal sets about trying to conceal the two women's dead bodies. In that action, as Poe's readers will recognize, the orangutan acts humanly and rationally—at least as humanly as the murderer—narrators of such tales as "The Tell-Tale Heart," "The Black Cat," and "The Cask of Amontillado."

Also featuring an intimate relationship between man and beast, "The Black Cat" challenges readers to discover "the Africanist presence" even as it obscures racial connections. "Supporters of slavery struggled to explain why slaves were running away (besides the obvious explanation)," notes Robert V. Guthrie, and in an 1851 article one nineteenth-century physician, Samuel Cartwright, diagnosed such "unnatural" behavior as a mental disorder called *drapetomania*, "which he said was common to Blacks *and to cats*" (Guthrie, 116; emphasis added). Without suggesting that the cat in Poe's tale "The Black Cat" *is* a surrogate black *person*, it is fair to note the similarity between the narrator's attitude toward the cat and the attitudes of many slaveholders. Like Melville's Amasa Delano, who takes to "negroes, not philanthropically, but genially, just as other men to Newfoundland dogs" (*Piazza Tales*, 84), the narrator appreciates the "unselfish and self-sacrificing love of a brute" whom he also admires as a "remarkably large and beautiful animal, entirely black, and sagacious to an astonishing degree" (Mabbott, 3:850).[17] Initially, Pluto acts like a faithful house cat. He "attended me wherever I went about the house," the narrator comments. "It was even with difficulty that I could prevent him from following me through the streets" (Mabbott, 3:851). Like Cartwright's "drapetomaniacs," however, Poe's black cat finally offends his master by avoiding his presence and then biting his hand (Mabbott, 3:851). Whether or not they performed a racially allegorical reading of the tale, nineteenth-century readers would have recognized and perhaps identified with the psychology of power that Poe dramatizes in this gruesome incident. Lesley Ginsberg in fact considers "The Black Cat" a Gothic reenactment of Nat Turner's 1831 revolt. If the South was "haunted by Turner," she suggests, the gothic exaggerations of the narrator's drama with a dark animal whom he owns allows his story to be read as the nightmarish return of the South's inescapable repressions" (117). Influenced though it is by alcoholism, the narrator's enjoyment of absolute power over the black cat mirrors the absolute power of slave ownership. Indulging himself in the capricious violence that power enables, the narrator even "deliberately" cuts one of the cat's eyes "from the socket" after the animal bites his hand (Mabbott, 3:851). Although the wound heals, the cat does not forgive his master. He flees "in extreme terror," in fact, whenever the narrator approaches (Mabbott, 3:852). In effect, the narrator has created a "drapetomaniac."

"The Black Cat" represents one of Poe's best treatments of what he calls the "spirit of PERVERSENESS" (Mabbott, 3:852), but I think that spirit has a more particular reference. Without reducing the tale to a racial allegory, we can appreciate its analogical relevance to the "perverseness" of the master–slave relationship, especially when the narrator's self-confessed perverseness leads him to lynch the black cat by hanging it "in cool blood" from the limb of a tree (Mabbott, 3:852). While Poe stresses the ethical dimensions of this murderous act by defining perverseness as the "unfathomable longing of the soul *to vex itself*" and by ascribing the narrator's motives to his desire to commit a sin (Mabbott, 3:852), it is difficult to miss the cultural and political cross-references: the psychology of a white supremacy that recoils upon itself as the most intense fear and guilt. Even without consciously making the connection, readers are effectively forced in this first-person narrative to identify with a psychology of power (over women and beautiful black animals) that undergirds white male racism. At the same time, Poe destabilizes that psychology by reversing the lines of power he has established and, for the rest of the story, effectively placing his narrator in the slave's position—a "revolution" in the wheel of fortune and an "exchange of situation" that turns, as it had in "Ligeia," on a change in color.

In North Carolina, Winthrop Jordan notes, a "tradition was inaugurated at the turn of the century when lynching parties burned a Negro for rape and castrated a slave for remarking that he was going to have some white woman" (*White over Black*, 473). Poe's narrator first mutilates the black cat before hanging it, but he notes afterward (and after his house has burned down) that the cat's image has been transcribed on his chamber wall. "I approached and saw, as if graven in *bas relief* upon the white surface, the figure of a gigantic *cat*," he reveals. "The impression was given with an accuracy truly marvelous. There was a rope about the animal's neck" (Mabbott, 3:853). Deftly putting the reader's attention at the mercy of the narrator's "impression," Poe emphasizes the "white surface" and the inscriptive power of the black presence—a truly perverse testament to paranoid violence, rationalized as vigilante justice. This black-on-white inscription becomes reversed in the second part of the tale, however, as the black body of a second cat forms the surface on which Poe inscribes white writing.

In this topsy-turvy tale, I want to argue, Poe examines the effects of such murderous white racism (reinscribed logically in the racist mind as cruelty to animals). Like Smith's narrative of Henry Moss, Poe's narrative of murder and revenge—as well as the seemingly extraordinary *individual* psychology that seems to be the tale's focus—can be generalized to the nation at large. "For months," the narrator confesses, "I could not rid myself of the phantasm of the cat" (Mabbott, 3:853). When a second, almost identical black cat appears and quickly becomes a "great favorite" with his wife, he feels "unutterable loathing" (Mabbott, 3:854). Despite its uncanny resemblance to Pluto, the second cat is not the ghost of the first; for Pluto "had not a white hair upon any portion of his body; but this cat had a large, although indefinite splotch of white, covering nearly the whole region of the breast" (Mabbott, 3:854). Like the "white spot" Thomas Jefferson described, this splotch of white, which "constituted the sole visible difference" between the two cats (Mabbott, 3:855), resonates loudly within the context of color-coded race differences. Surely nineteenth-century readers would have felt the similarity to popular instances of vitiligo, if not directly to someone like Henry Moss. The might also have suspected amalgamation, racial crossbreeding that, by initiating the "whitening" process, portends the erasure of visible color differences. Instead of simply spreading over the cat's body as in most cases of vitiligo, the white spot on the cat's breast grows more distinct, ultimately forming the "image of a hideous—of a ghastly thing—of the GALLOWS!" (Mabbott, 3:855). Attributing a kind of intentionality to this white mark, Poe ironically thematizes the progress of vitiligo not as a sign of racial "encroachment" or erasure but as a sign of white racial guilt and black revenge. "And now was I wretched beyond the wretchedness of mere Humanity," the narrator confesses (Mabbott, 3:855), and his situation—his exchange of situation—anticipates Benito Cereno's in its reversal of fortune. Used to enjoying absolute power over his "domestic pets," he now finds himself at the mercy of a "brute beast" and thus struggling to maintain the absolute species difference on which his authority depends. "And *a brute beast*," he says incredulously, "whose fellow I had contemptuously destroyed—*a brute beast* to work out for *me*—for me a man, fashioned in the image of the High God—so much of insufferable wo!" (Mabbott, 3:855–56). Like the dehumanizing language of difference in "The Murders in the Rue Morgue," the narrator's disbelief reflects at least analogically the race-based logic of white racism in which African Americans figure as some lesser species—not human at all—and white Americans can deify themselves as "fashioned in the image of the High God."

Poe adroitly complicates the narrator's arguable master–slave relationship with the black cat, further, by triangulating it, much as he had in "The Murders in the Rue Morgue," through the body of the white woman. In the climax of the tale, after all, when the narrator exasperatedly tries to kill the cat with an ax, only to have the blow "arrested" by his wife, he buries the ax in her brain instead (Mabbott, 3:856). Employing the same "logic" as the orangutan in "The Murders in the Rue Morgue," he then attempts to bury the evidence of the murder by walling his wife up in the cellar—only to have her location revealed by the screams "half of horror and half of triumph," of the cat he has inadvertently walled up with her (Mabbott, 3:859). Poe's topsy-turvy plot of racial "exchange" ends up toppling the narrator.

In an even more gruesome scene of black revenge, Poe's last published tale, "Hop-Frog" (1849), depends on a racially charged exchange of positions and features another topsy-turvy plot that imbrutes and punishes the "master" race. More like the ingenious Babo in "Benito Cereno" than like the orangutan or black cat, Hop-Frog carefully crafts a counterplot to reveal and then revenge himself upon white racists who have abused and insulted both him and his female friend Trippetta. Hop-Frog stages a topsy-turvy scene in which the king and his seven counselors come to occupy the positions of servants, or slaves. Given Hop-Frog's ingenious decision to dress the king and his ministers as orangutans and the common nineteenth-century association of orangutans with African Americans, the racial dimensions of this revenge plot become obvious. Hop-Frog himself need not be construed as a black man. His "otherness" resides primarily in his dwarfism, a condition he shares with such nonwhite characters in Poe's fiction as Dirk Peters in *The Narrative of Arthur Gordon Pym* and the three-foot-tall Pompey in "How to Write a Blackwood Article" (1838).[18] Characterized by "prodigious muscular power" and "wonderful dexterity" that makes him resemble a squirrel or a "small monkey" (Mabbott, 3:1346), Hop-Frog also shows little tolerance for alcohol, which quickly excites him "almost to madness" (Mabbott, 3:1347). The "work of vengeance" (Mabbott, 3:1354), moreover, obviously plays into, even as it plays with, white racial fears. Twice, for example, Poe emphasizes that women become especially frightened by orangutans (Mabbott, 3:1350, 1352). In tarring the king and his ministers and covering them with flax, chaining them together, hanging them en masse from the ceiling, and then burning them to a "fetid, blackened, hideous, and indistinguishable mass" (Mabbott, 3:1354), Hop-Frog clearly marks this performance of a lynching with color and racial signifiers.[19] As it had in "The Black Cat," black revenge inscribes itself on the white body in an ironic reversal of vitiligo—white bodies turning black. As Dayan puts it, the "epidemic curse—the fatality of being black or blackened—has been visited on the master race" ("Romance and Race," 104). As in "Ligeia," "The Murders in the Rue Morgue," and "The Black Cat," furthermore, Poe uses the white female body as a medium for vengeful racial exchange. The deaths of Rowena, Madame L'Espanaye and her daughter, and the narrator's wife and the insult to Trippetta provoke black-on-white vengeance that violently subverts color categories in the white racist imagination. Although the orangutan masquerade has its origins in Hop-Frog's native culture, he converts that country "frolic" to vengeful purpose only after the king insults Trippetta. "I cannot tell what was the association of idea," he tells the king, "but *just after* your majesty had struck the girl and thrown wine in her face ... there came into my mind a capital diversion—one of my own country frolics—often enacted among us, at our masquerades" (Mabbott, 3:1349–50). Like Melville's Babo or the orangutan in "The Murders in the Rue Morgue," Hop-Frog learns violence from his master.

WHITE RACISM AND BLACK REVENGE

Regarding a similarly violent murder in *The Narrative of Arthur Gordon Pym*, John Carlos Rowe connects the demonic black cook's serial braining of the sailors he throws overboard to Nat Turner's gory use of a broadax to murder his master and the master's wife during his "Southampton Insurrection"

("Poe, Antebellum Slavery," 127–28). "Hop-Frog," like "Ligeia," "The Murders in the Rue Morgue," and "The Black Cat," seems to act out nightmarish fantasies of slave revolt and black-on-white vengeance, but the traces of racial and racist discourses that I have discovered in these selected tales make it difficult to conclude that Poe was simply a "proslavery Southerner," as Rowe suggests ("Poe, Antebellum Slavery," 117). Without speculating on Poe's intentions, I think these tales reveal complicated patterns of racism and antiracist sympathy, a recognition on Poe's part that racial signifiers are inherently unstable, while racism and racist efforts to ascribe fixed racial identities lead inevitably to revenge.

In light of contemporaneous interest in vitiligo, "white Negroes," and topsy-turvy dolls, Poe's color symbolism in "Ligeia" gains a complex significance. Ligeia's rebellion, her displacement of the fair Rowena (if only in the narrator's imagination), plays to fears of amalgamation, black insurrection, and (in Jefferson's phrase) an "exchange" of racial "situations," but the ending of the tale also suggests the impossibility of suppressing or repressing blackness, however "disheveled" the "masses" of black hair may be. The racially encoded murders in "The Murders in the Rue Morgue" play obviously upon the same fears of uncontrollable black violence, but by locating the source of violence in *white* behavior, Poe refuses to maintain the popular Southern boundary between white civility and black barbarism. Poe works an obvious "exchange of situation" in "The Black Cat," and he uses vitiligo and the black body on which it appears to inscribe a provocative symbol (the gallows) of white-on-black violence that the rest of the tale bears out—a nightmarish vision or uncontrollable *white* violence visited upon black male and white female bodies alike. Only the posthumous alliance of black "cat" and white woman, on top of whose body the narrator has effectively installed the black male body, can bring the white male murderer to justice. "Hop-Frog" radically reverses the spontaneous whitening associated with vitiligo, as well as the strategic imbrutement associated with white racism, as if the "masses" of disheveled black hair Poe had described at the end of "Ligeia" have become a blackened "mass" of formerly white orangutans. Leaving the kingdom with the (presumably black) woman he has saved from white assault, Hop-Frog leaves a mass of morally (and genetically) blackened white folksy perverse fulfillment of amalgamated nightmare.

Recognizing an "Africanist presence" in Poe's tales means reading race and racism in deeply encoded symbolism that obviously signifies on many other levels. Critics such as Louis Rubin, John Carlos Rowe, and especially Joan Dayan have certainly begun the process of resituating Poe's writing in the material conditions of its production, including nineteenth-century discourses of slavery, race, and racism. The tales I have discussed, it seems to me, reflect more than scattered traces of racial discourse. They cohere around particular images, ideas, and patterns—around what I have called a philosophy of amalgamation particularly and representatively situated in white male psychology. In representing race within the subject position most readily available to him, however, Poe did not transparently inscribe white racist ideology. Coordinating embedded (it is tempting to say repressed) racial discourse with first-person narratives of psychopathology, Poe inevitably represented the fault fines of racist psychology. Dana Nelson argues that *The Narrative of Arthur Gordon Pym*, while a "racist text" on one level, also "counters racist colonial ideology and the racialist scientific knowledge structure" (92), and I think the same can be said for "Ligeia," "The Black Cat," "The Murders in the Rue Morgue," and "Hop-Frog." Deconstructions of black essentialism, these four tales also posit the revenge of blackness as a critical fascination of white psychology. Poe's philosophy of amalgamation turns on a psychology of white male racism, but it turns out to produce a perverse, topsy-turvy reversal of racial differences—a nightmare of amalgamation, reversed racism, and ironic vigilante justice.

NOTES

1. Henry Louis Gates Jr. adds that the "themes of black and white, common to the bipolar moment in which the slave narratives and the plantation novel oscillate, inform the very structuring principles of the great gothic works of Hawthorne, Melville, and Poe" (50–51).

2. David Leverenz makes a related point when he argues that "Poe inhabits and undermines gentry fictions of mastery, not least by exposing the gentleman as a fiction." Poe "constructs, then deconstructs," the private lives of gentlemen, Leverenz says, "by transgressing the great social divide between public displays of mastery and an inwardness felt as alien to oneself. Arabesques of public leisure become grotesque enslavements to obsessions" (212).

3. For additional accounts of "white negroes" during the seventeenth, eighteenth, and nineteenth centuries, see Winthrop Jordan's *White over Black*, 249–52. Jordan points out that ethnocentrism and the widespread belief that blacks were utterly different militated against anyone's connecting white Negroes and albino Europeans as products of a "single physiological peculiarity" (252).

4. Louis Rubin cites this passage for its relevance to "The Fall of the House of Usher"—as if it forecast Roderick Usher's enslavement to terror and the collapse of the Southern slaveholding aristocracy as figured in the fall of the house (159–60).

5. According to William M. Ramsey, Melville based one of the confidence man's disguises on Barnum's hoax: John Ringman, the "man with the weed." Eric Lott discusses Barnum's racial exhibits and his penchant for performing in blackface (76–77). According

to Lott, such "instances of imaginary racial transmutation literalize one train of thought responsible for the minstrel show. They are less articulations of difference than speculations about it. They imagine race to be mutable; very briefly they throw off the burden of its construction, blurring the line between self and other, white workingman and black" (77).

6. William Stanton quotes the following advertisement:

> There is a black man at present at MR. LEECH'S Tavern, the sign of the BLACK HORSE, in Market-Street, who was born entirely black, and remained so for thirty-eight years, after which his natural colour began to rub off, which has continued till his body has become as white and as fair as any white person, except some small parts, which are changing very fast; his face attains more to the natural colour than any other part; his wool also is coming off his head, legs and arms, and in its place is growing straight hair, similar to that of a white person. The sight is really worthy of the attention of the curious, and opens a wide field of amusement for the philosophic genius. (*The Leopard's Spots*, 6)

7. As George M. Fredrickson points out, however, this environmentalist philosophy, which was "characteristic of Enlightenment thinking about human differences," was beginning to erode by 1810, paving the way in the middle of the 1800s for essentialist "scientific" studies of racial differences and inferiority: "For its full growth intellectual and ideological racism required a body of 'scientific' and cultural thought which would give credence to the notion that the blacks were, for unalterable reasons of race, morally and intellectually inferior to whites, and, more importantly, it required a historical context which would make such an ideology seem necessary for the effective defense of Negro slavery or other forms of white supremacy" (2).

8. Sam Worley makes a similar point in arguing that Poe's use of the proslavery argument toward the Tsalalians "exceeds the apologists' case in ways that bring the contradictions of proslavery to the forefront" (235).

9. "Given the intensity of the ideological struggle," Worley comments, "the suggestion that *Pym* bears marks of the debate seems not so unlikely as the suggestion that it somehow might have escaped such concerns" (223). The case for inevitable inscription is harder to make for tales like "Ligeia" and "The Black Cat," but Worley's point offers a valuable starting premise.

10. Dayan anatomizes Ligeia's character, noting her wildness and passion, her lack of paternal name, her eyes (in the narrator's words) "far larger than the ordinary eyes of our own race" (Mabbott, 2:313), in order to claim that she suggests a "racial heritage that would indeed be suspect." Even Ligeia's ivory skin "links her further to women of color," because the "epistemology of whiteness" depended "for its effect on the detection of blackness" ("Amorous Bondage," 201).

11. Jefferson had famously noted that "[r]eligion indeed has produced a Phyllis Whately [sic]; but it could not produce a poet. The compositions published under her name are below the dignity of criticism." Jefferson used Wheatley to exemplify his claim that he could never "find that a black had uttered a thought above the level of plain narration; never see even an elementary trait of painting or sculpture" (*Notes on the State of Virginia*, ed. Peden, 146).

12. In her study of nineteenth-century Circassian beauties, Linda Frost notes that all the women whose pictures she found had one thing in common: their "huge, bushy hair" (257). Even though Circassian women epitomized whiteness and Victorian womanhood, she concludes, their bushy hair "would have resonated for contemporary audiences with images of African and tribal women circulating in the culture" (259).

13. Jordan emphasizes the "sexual link between Negroes and apes" that enabled Englishmen to express "their feelings that Negroes were a lewd, lascivious, and wanton people" (*White over Black*, 32).

14. Louis Rubin argues that the "fear of servile revolt must have played a role in the highly active imagination of an impressionable youth growing up in Richmond" (162), where Gabriel Prosser's insurrection had occurred in 1800. Rubin also notes that the "shock waves" of Nat Turner's revolt in 1831 reached Poe's home in Baltimore "very quickly," amplified by Thomas Gray's publication of Turner's "confessions," including its "lurid account of women and children being hacked to death in their beds" (163).

15. George Fredrickson notes that by the middle of the 1830s proslavery spokesmen increasingly made the case for the "unambiguous concept of inherent Negro inferiority" (46), and Winthrop Jordan points out that, even though rational science insisted that "the Negro belonged to the species of man," the notion of species difference stayed alive. One of the most crucial components of this "irrational logic," Jordan says, was the myth of Negro–ape "connection" (*White over Black*, 236).

16. Analyzing the "basically sexualized nature of racist psychology" (67), Kovel argues that only the theory of the Oedipus complex—"enlarged into a cultural apparatus that defines and binds real roles even as it apportions fantasies amongst the players of these roles—will account for this variety of phenomena." Racist psychology thereby becomes largely a white male psychology. "Black man, white man, black woman, white woman— each realizes some aspect of the oedipal situation" (from the white male point of view). The black man, for example, represents both father and son "in their destructive aspects"; the "Southern white male simultaneously resolves both sides of the conflict by keeping the black man submissive, and by castrating him when submission fails" (71). Similarly, white male psychology projects radically different qualities (icelike purity, excessive sexuality) on white and black women, respectively, while fears of black male rape of white women act out unconscious fantasies those stereotypes were consciously designed to repress.

17. Without analyzing the tale, Dayan compares the relationship between the black cat and the narrator to that between slave and master. Poe wrote the tale, she suggests, "to demonstrate how destructive is the illusion of mastery" ("Amorous Bondage," 192).

18. After Psyche Zenobia has punished Pompey for stumbling into her by tearing out large clumps of his hair, Pompey gets his revenge when Psyche Zenobia finds herself pinned down by the hand of the belfry clock. "I screamed to Pompey for aid," she notes, "but he said that I had hurt his feelings by calling him 'an ignorant old squint eye'" (Mabbott, 2:253).

19. Poe works a similar reversal using apes in "The System of Doctor Tarr and Professor Fether" (1844), one of his most transparently racial tales, as Louis Rubin has perceptively shown. Having been displaced and locked up by the inmates (after being tarred and feathered), the former keepers of the lunatic asylum burst forth at the end of the tale; they appear as a "perfect army" of "Chimpanzees, Ourang-Outangs, or big black baboons of the Cape of Good Hope" (Mabbott, 3:1021).

DOROTHEA E. VON MÜCKE

Ligeia: "Her Large and Luminous Orbs"

LIGEIA: "HER LARGE AND LUMINOUS ORBS"

Poe's "Ligeia" has been read as a philosophical tale about the nature and limits of the mind, the human body, thought, and the will (Dayan); as a satirical take on the contrast between German idealism and English Romanticism (Griffith); and as a tale that exemplifies Poe's famous dictum from "The Philosophy of Composition" (1846) that "the death ... of a beautiful woman is, unquestionably, the most poetical topic in the world,"[18] be it in terms of a psychoanalytical dimension (Bronfen) or resonance with sentimental mass culture (Elmer).[19] In my analysis, I pay particular attention to the poetological dimension of "Ligeia," to the manner in which this text can be discussed not only as a fantastic tale but also as a reflection on the production of the fantastic, in view of the hallucinatory sensualities of print culture.[20]

The generic nature of "Ligeia" is not immediately obvious. Long, descriptive passages as well as the narrator's reflection on his mnemonic and linguistic limitations punctuate, interrupt, and fragment the narration. Two separate plots—one about the narrator's remembrance of his first wife (Ligeia) and her death; the other about his second wife (Rowena), her death, and the return of Ligeia—raise the question as to what would provide the connection, the unity for the piece of writing. The title, though, immediately suggests that Ligeia somehow constitutes this unifying element. But what or who is Ligeia: a text, a word, a name, a woman, a ghost, a spirit, an image or an idea, something material or immaterial, a medium or a message? The word *Ligeia* serves as both the title of a text and the name of a woman. However, this name does not come from a mortal woman but from a dryad, a tree nymph in Virgil's *Georgics*. Although the Greek etymology of the word suggests the medium of sound, a loud call, Poe's story quickly shifts from an imaginary aurality to a visual register: a shift that is motivated by the silence of print culture.

If we bear in mind the multiple options of who or what Ligeia might be and still approach this text as a narrative, we see in its plot not merely the telling of some past event but also the narrator's presence as a writer who attempts to conjure up the presence of his lost beloved in the act of writing. "Ligeia" then comes to stand for embodiment of the medium of writing, that element by which this particular text and shaped artifact achieves its coherence; she is the mediating instance by which writing becomes transparent; the spiritual guide, the muse, the beloved woman who turns a piece of writing into an effortless reading, and finally into a metaphor for the imaginary materiality of the signifier.

Before the actual narrative commences, the first person narrator calls Ligeia in a manner that resembles the traditional invocation of the muse:

> Ligeia! Ligeia! Buried in studies of a nature more than all else adapted to deaden impressions of the outward world, it is by that sweet word alone—by Ligeia—that I bring before mine eyes in fancy the image of her who is no more. And now, while I write, a recollection flashes upon me that I have *never known* the paternal name of her who was my friend and my betrothed, and who became the partner of my studies, and finally the wife of my bosom. Was it a playful charge on the part of my Ligeia? or was it a test of my strength of affection, that I should institute no inquiries upon this point? or was it rather a caprice of my own— a wildly romantic offering on the shrine of the most passionate devotion? I but indistinctly recall the fact itself—what wonder that I have utterly forgotten the circumstances which originated or attended it? And, indeed, if ever that spirit which is entitled *Romance*—if ever she, the wan and the misty-winged *Ashtophet* of idolatrous Egypt, presided, as they tell, over marriages ill-omened, then most surely she presided over mine.[21]

The "sweet word" Ligeia is opposed to the deadening surroundings, the sensory deprivations of the scholar. Not her voice but her name is sweet; the narrator evokes the sweet sound by calling her name. The story commences with an elegiac tone, with the narrator's narcissistic enjoyment of his lament. It is notable that her name is not a signifier that would partake of the symbolic order; indeed, it is opposed to the realm of writing qua law and name of the father. She stands for a kind of love that isolates lovers from all social context and consideration. Likening the radical exclusivity and absolute nature of this passion to the sin of idolatry, the narrator offers a further gloss on Ligeia's function for him. Not the representation of a divinity but an idol, the full presence of the divinity in the material object, she comes to stand for the identity between signifier and signified. Ligeia is introduced as an object that can be entirely possessed and worshipped. She is not a speaking subject, not a signifier for other subjects.

This object that is supposedly fully present and possessable, however, is a lost object. The writer/scholar has to struggle to evoke her presence, a struggle that seems particularly hard since he has no context for her, and hence has very little to narrate. He calls this isolated idol her "person," and this is the only thing the narrator can attempt to remember and describe. With this switch from her name to her person, the narrator leaves the initial aural register in favor of a visual one. From then on, his primary concern becomes evocation of sights: first the appearance of his beloved Ligeia, then the contrasting features of his second wife, and finally the scenario of his second wife's death and Ligeia's return in the bridal chamber of the old English abbey.

The purpose of these descriptions is to make an existentially absent object present to the narrator's mental sight, to give shape to her imaginary presence. To the extent that he attempts to depict her extraordinary beauty, the narrator is both dependent on and limited by his own language, which draws on the traditional blazon with its conventionalized catalogue of beauties. Initially, the description of Ligeia recalls some elements of an antique statue—for instance, the marble luster of her hand and her tall slender stature. However, to the extent that he wants to evoke the unique beauty of her person, he can only say what she is not: not a dead artifact, nor just one example in a series of such artifacts.

> Yet her features were not of that regular mould which we have been falsely taught to worship in the classical labors of the heathen. "There is no exquisite beauty," says Bacon, Lord Verulam, speaking truly of all the forms and *genera* of beauty,

"without some *strangeness* in the proportion." Yet, although I saw
that the features of Ligeia were not of a classic regularity—
although I perceived that her loveliness was indeed "exquisite,"
and felt that there was much of "strangeness" pervading it, yet I
have tried in vain to detect the irregularity and to trace home my
own perception of "the strange." I examined the contour of the
lofty and pale forehead—it was faultless—how cold indeed that
word when applied to a majesty so divine!—the skin rivalling the
purest ivory, the commanding extent and repose, the gentle
prominence of the regions above the temples.... I scrutinized the
formation of the chin—and, here, too, I found the gentleness of
breadth, the softness and the majesty, the fullness and the
spirituality, of the Greek—the contour which the god Apollo
revealed but in a dream, to Cleomenes, the son of the Athenian.
(250)

Although he expects to find a "strange" feature that might allow him to pin
down the element that marks her departure from classical regularity, he can
single out nothing. Informed by an enthusiasm reminiscent of Winckelmann
or Herder for the beauties of Greek antiquity, the narrator avoids turning her
into a dead artifact by emphasizing the spirituality of her beauty, not in terms
of concrete features but by evoking aspects of her form in their immateriality,
not as made or shaped but as a purely mental process, a process of formation
and divinely inspired revelation.

When in a second step the narrator attempts to locate Ligeia's
strangeness, and the beauty and singularity in her eyes, he departs from
classicist aesthetics but encounters another limit to his powers of description.
First, he hastens to point out that, once it comes to the eyes, classicist models
of beauty have nothing to say. But then he also realizes that the strangeness
of Ligeia's eyes is not a physical, optical feature.

The "strangeness," however, which I found in the eyes, was of a
nature distinct from the formation, or the color, or the brilliance
of the features, and must, after all, be referred to the *expression*.
Ah, word of no meaning! behind whose vast latitude of mere
sound we intrench our ignorance of so much of the spiritual. The
expression of the eyes of Ligeia! How for long hours have I
pondered upon it! How have I, through the whole of a
midsummer night, struggled to fathom it! What was it—that
something more profound than the well of Democritus which lay

far within the pupils of my beloved? What *was* it? I was possessed
with a passion to discover. Those eyes! (251–52)

The narrator leaves the regime of description, dependent upon classicist
notions of beauty as well as a textual model of representation, as he turns to
Ligeia's ineffable, unique, individualizing feature: "the expression of her
eyes." The expression of a person's eyes traditionally stands for the person's
alterity, individuality, and psychic interiority. Yet the narrator does not switch
from the representational paradigm to an expressive paradigm of language;
he chooses not to turn Ligeia's uniqueness into a hermeneutic issue of the
specificity of her interiority, or a psychological depth that can be expressed.
Nevertheless, the narrator insists on his inability to name or comprehend
this unique feature by pointing out that the term *expression* is an empty
signifier, a mere sound. Note that the narrator does not articulate his
separation from her as his distance or lack of understanding of her person,
but in terms of his being confronted with the opacity of language. Indeed, it
is in this passage that Ligeia assumes the position of the medium; that her
eyes stand for the virtual materiality of the signifier.

The expression of Ligeia's eyes becomes not something that can be
represented, described, understood, or consciously remembered. It becomes
the object of a spiritual quest and the subject matter of a story. As long as the
narrator remains within the regime of description, the absent Ligeia must be
represented by analogy to a dead object or artifact. With the shift of focus to
the expression of her eyes, however, Ligeia's person, her mortal corporeality,
and her relationship to temporal change emerge. It is here that a narrative
program begins to take shape as the writer is faced with his blockage, his lack
of access to the expression of her eyes. The agenda has been altered with
respect to the first attempts at invoking Ligeia's presence. Before, the
narrator tried to conjure up her looks, her ideational presence, through a
description of her physical appearance. Now, he approaches her person
through an opaque expression, a meaningless phrase, "the expression of her
eyes." By means of foregrounding the enigmatic expression, the opaque,
undecipherable phrase, he evokes the desire for transparency and insight.
The object of desire is no longer just the appearance of the absent beloved as
a concrete embodied woman. Rather, he longs for the kind of effect her
presence would have on his confrontation with the materiality of writing.

The object of the writer/narrator's quest now is no longer just his lost
beloved but the kind of knowledge and insight that he was able to gain in her
presence: "we often find ourselves *upon the very verge* of remembrance,
without being able, in the end, to remember. And thus how frequently, in my

intense scrutiny of Ligeia's eyes, have I felt approaching the full knowledge of their expression—felt it approaching—yet not quite be mine—and so at length entirely depart! And (strange, oh strangest mystery of all!) I found, in the commonest objects of the universe, a circle of analogies to that expression" (252). The narrator ceases to grasp for the meaning of the single enigmatic term and instead searches for the "many existences in the material world" that might awaken in him a sentiment analogous to the one aroused by "her large and luminous orbs" (ibid.). By moving from "the expression of her eyes," which he had glossed as an unintelligible term to "her large and luminous orbs," that is, by shifting away from the register of hermeneutics and unintelligibility to the physics of luminosity, to her eyes as physical objects that emit light, the narrator has situated Ligeia between a meaningless, illegible signifier and an embodiment of light—*the* medium of transparency.

Although he cannot represent, define, or analyze the uniqueness of the expression of Ligeia's eyes, he can inventory a paradigmatic set of phenomena that have given him a similar sentiment: The narrator modifies the object of his quest and also changes from a metaphorical procedure to a metonymical one, from the attempt to invoke the hidden signified by way of the right comparison to an attempt at invoking it through a string of similarly mysterious expressions:

> I recognized it, let me repeat, sometimes in the survey of a rapidly-growing vine—in the contemplation of a moth, a butterfly, a chrysalis, a stream of running water. I have felt it in the ocean; in the falling of a meteor. I have felt it in the glances of unusually aged people. And there are one or two stars in heaven.... I have been filled with it by certain sounds from stringed instruments, and not unfrequently by passages from books. Among innumerable other instances, I well remember something in a volume of Joseph Glanvill, which (perhaps from its quaintness—who shall say?) never failed to inspire me with the sentiment; "And the will therein lieth, which dieth not. Who knoweth the mysteries of the will, with its vigor? For God is but a great will pervading all things by nature of its intentness. Man doth not yield him to the angels, nor unto death utterly, save only through the weakness of his feeble will." (252–53)

The first set of examples, especially the series of the moth, the butterfly, and the chrysalis, suggests that he is concerned with metamorphosis, with a natural force that induces a radical change and still preserves some kind of identity that is not bound up with material decay or the shape of a particular body. A second set of examples involves human artifacts or expressions. In particular, the "glances of unusually aged people" and the citation from Glanvill suggest that the narrator senses some mysterious force of being able to overcome the finality of death: "Length of years, and subsequent reflection, have enabled me to trace, indeed, some remote connection between this passage in the English moralist and a portion of the character of Ligeia. An *intensity* in thought, action, or speech, was possibly, in her, a result, or at least an index, of that gigantic volition which, during our long intercourse, failed to give other and more immediate evidence of its existence" (253). Thus, beginning with the musings on the expression of her eyes, Ligeia's mysterious beauty also becomes an index "of that gigantic volition," of a mysterious natural force or cosmic connection that only appears in her approach to death. Throughout the first part, Ligeia's status has been shifted back and forth between some kind of signifier (a name, a meaningless expression, an index) and an affectively highly charged lost object and elusive, transcendent signified (the beloved, the muse, the spiritual guide, a cosmic force or idea).

The narration of the first part of "Ligeia" focuses on the writer's experience of her death. Her waning health and vitality is not integrated, nor connected to any external events; rather, it is exclusively portrayed, in view of her medial function, in the narrator's relationship to transcendentalist knowledge. Whereas her approaching death appears as the return of the opacity of the medium of writing, her state of health is depicted as her magical power to make unreadable texts transparent to him. "With how vast a triumph—with how vivid a delight—with how much of all that is ethereal in hope—did I *feel*, as she bent over me in studies but little sought—but less known—that delicious vista by slow degrees expanding before me, down whose long, gorgeous, and all untrodden path, I might at length pass onward to the goal of a wisdom too divinely precious not to be forbidden!" (254). Her medial function, which consists in enabling him to gain access to a "higher," "transcendent," or "spiritual" sight, is described in terms of the literalization and concretization of her role for him, captured in the metaphorical expression that she was able to *illuminate occult passages for him*. The light of her eyes makes him see through a textual passage onto an untrodden path to knowledge.

However, the status of this "vista" is more complex, for the expanded concretized image is overdetermined and calls up disparate traditional images of the woman as both seductress and spiritual guide. First, there is the schema of the spiritual quest and the likening of Ligeia's role to that of Dante's Beatrice. Yet, by the enigmatic claim that these vistas of divine knowledge are "too precious" and hence forbidden, the dark Lady Ligeia is dissociated from Beatrice and the positively coded spiritual guide. Likewise, with respect to the neo-Platonic version of spiritual sight as the ultimate insight into the last truths, a tradition suggested also through the Glanvill quotation, the vision of Truth and Beauty is dissociated from the Good. Finally, there is the concrete media-historical image that associates Ligeia with the print medium. Her eyes can turn a page of a book into a window that opens up a view into a new world, into an "untrodden" landscape. This image of the page that opens up onto a "delicious vista by slow degrees expanding before me" was typical of the Renaissance celebration of its new media technologies: linear perspective and the printing press.[22] Ligeia comes to stand for an illuminating presence behind the print medium. The writer remembers how in her presence he was an inspired reader who could access esoteric, transcendentalist insights or a spiritual vision almost immediately, without having to decipher what he was reading.

Ligeia's fatal illness, as her eyes begin to show less of their radiant luster, is described in terms of the emergence of writing's opacity. Instead of the look through the page onto the landscape of the mind, the narrator focuses on the look of the letters on the opaque page: "Without Ligeia I was but as a child groping benighted. Her presence, her readings alone, rendered vividly luminous the many mysteries of the transcendentalism in which we were immersed. Wanting the radiant lustre of her eyes, letters, lambent and golden, grew duller than Saturnian lead. And now those eyes shone less and less frequently upon the pages over which I pored. Ligeia grew ill" (254). In the previous image of reading, writing was rendered transparent to a quasi-immediate mental sight of the signified; now the image of reading focuses on the imaginary materiality of the signifier, the changing look of the letters: from golden brilliance to dull lead. When the narrator adds the adjective *Saturnian* to the "weighty" opacity and materiality of the lead, he evokes the traditional emblematics of melancholia: dull, brooding, lead, and Saturn. As Ligeia's vitality diminishes, the print medium loses its transparency. Her waning powers seem to transport the narrator backward into an earlier phase of the history of media technology. In contrast to print technology's tendency to render writing invisible, here we witness the waning of the realm of "illuminated" manuscripts with lambent, golden letters.

POE'S ARABESQUE, OR DEATH BY DRAPERY

The first part of "Ligeia" elaborates the imaginary materiality of the signifier in view of the ideal of transparency. The narrator invokes Ligeia's person by staging the effects of her vanishing. He narrates her death, the extinction of her luminous orbs, as his own repositioning toward the print medium. By contrast, the second part of "Ligeia" is dominated by images of the opacity of writing. Whereas the first part began with an attempt to describe the beautiful beloved woman, the second part commences with an elaborate description of the "unforgettable" bridal chamber, which the narrator furnished as he was grieving for Ligeia and in which he received his second wife, Rowena. This exuberantly luxurious interior space takes the place of the hallucinated presence of the beloved woman:

> I gave way, with a child-like perversity, and perchance with a faint hope of alleviating my sorrows, to a display of more than regal magnificence within.—For such follies, even in childhood, I had imbibed a taste and now they came back to me as if in the dotage of grief. Alas, I feel how much even of incipient madness might have been discovered in the gorgeous and fantastic draperies, in the solemn carvings of Egypt, in the wild cornices and furniture, in the Bedlam patterns of the carpets of tufted gold! I had become a bounden slave in the trammels of opium, and my labors and orders had taken a coloring from my dreams. But these absurdities I must not pause to detail. Let me speak only of that one chamber, ever accursed, whither, in a moment of mental alienation, I led from the altar as my bride—as the successor of the unforgotten Ligeia—the fair-haired and blue-eyed Lady Rowena Trevanion, of Tremaine.
>
> There is no individual portion of the architecture and decoration of that bridal chamber which is not now visibly before me. Where were the souls of the haughty family of the bride, when, through thirst of gold, they permitted to pass the threshold of an apartment so bedecked, a maiden and a daughter so beloved? I have said that I minutely remember the details of the chamber—yet I am sadly forgetful on topics of deep moment— and here there was no system, no keeping in the fantastic display, to take hold upon the memory. (258–59)

Clearly the interior of his abbey in England is the materialization of a phantasmatic scenario. The narrator associates this interior space with an entire list of mental abnormalities: a childhood perversity, institutionalized madness, melancholia with a vague hope of overcoming the grief, and finally the dreams of an opium addict. In this passage the interior of the abbey becomes indistinguishable from his psychic interiority; or does it actually take its place? In the vocabulary of clinical psychology, dissociation would describe the narrator's abdication of responsibility for his actions and his externalized, distanced view of the irresponsible family members of his bride who let their daughter marry somebody who was so clearly mad and potentially dangerous. The narrator, however, describes this phenomenon not in the clinical terms of dissociation but in terms of his observer position in relation to the external organization of memory. His exotic collections and strange decorations prevent controllable retrieval of information. He has only the detailed visual memory of the individual objects, no sustained memory of his actions, thoughts, or reflections that would force him to take responsibility for the fate of his second wife. The narrator's agency, memory, and consciousness have been handed over to the furniture and decorations. Indeed, as mad or fantastic as it might sound, it is the decoration of the bridal chamber that ultimately kills Rowena and reanimates Ligeia.

The window of the bridal chamber is the source of an unnatural, distorted, and distorting light: "an immense sheet of unbroken glass from Venice—a single plane, and tinted of a leaden hue, so that the rays of either the sun or moon, passing through it, fell with a ghastly lustre on the objects within. Over the upper portion of this huge window, extended the trellice-work of an aged vine, which clambered up the massy walls of the turret" (259). This "trellice-work of an aged vine" replaces what otherwise—without the lead tint—could be a view into the open landscape. In part one, the narrator listed a "rapidly growing vine" among those "material existences" that evoked for him a feeling analogous to the expression of Ligeia's eyes. Now a slightly different vine will also, by the end of the narrative, evoke the actual vision of Ligeia's eyes. Instead of the vine's rapid growth, there is the combined image of the constructed, segmented elements of the trellis, which distributes the growth across the plane. The lead-tinted window resembles the opaque surface of a sheet of paper, or a page in a book that is decorated by an ornamental vine. By distributing the vine over this surface, the trellis draws attention to the vine's ornamental aspect. Indeed the trellis analyzes the ornament by isolating repeatable, serially combinable, geometrically constructed elements of serpentine lines and leaves. This analytical intervention transforms the organic entity into an image of mechanical reproducibility.

The vine on the trellis serves as an image of the type of reproduction that informs print technology's usage of movable letters, that involves breaking up the serpentine line of handwriting into the isolated, combinable letters on the printed page. In this function, the image of the vine from Poe's text verbally picks up the pictorial tradition of that ornament that became known as the arabesque. Beginning with Albrecht Dürer and his thematization of print technology, the arabesque—situated at the threshold between the linearity of the two-dimensional composition of an image and the three-dimensional perspectival illusion of space—has been used to illustrate the imaginary materiality of the signifier.[23] In this sense, the arabesque is in an exact contrast to the complementary image of the open vista or view through the window, which quite frequently on the title page of a book was used to thematize transparency, that is, the imaginary immateriality of the signifier.[24]

There are further cues that Poe's text traces this function of the arabesque as an image that illustrates the imaginary materiality of the signifier. Immediately after the description of the window follows a description of the internal source of light: "From out the most central recess of this melancholic vaulting, depended, by a single chain of gold with long links, a huge censer of the same metal, Saracenic in pattern, and with many perforations so contrived that there writhed in and out of them, as if endued with a serpent vitality, a continual succession of parti-colored fires" (259–60). Both the Saracenic pattern and the "serpent vitality" invoke the aesthetics of the arabesque. Whereas outside, on the lead-tinted window, there is the dark arabesque of the vine, inside the bridal chamber there is the golden arabesque of the burning censer. The colors, gold and metal, recall the image of the lambent, golden letters that the narrator remembers from the phase of Ligeia's declining vitality, that phase of their relationship when she was about to leave him in her function as his spiritual guide, when she was no longer going to illuminate dark passages for him and open up his reading to new vistas and insights. Then, in the first part of "Ligeia," the narrator's imminent loss of immediate transcendentalist insight was captured by reference to a different, older technology of writing that invoked manuscript culture, with its golden letters turning into a dull Saturnian lead. Consequently, the arabesque as illustration of the virtual materiality of the signifier appears at the threshold of new media technologies, such as the transition from the culture of the illuminated manuscript to the new print technology of standardized, movable letters.

The narrator, however, also includes in his use of the arabesque its better-known, more familiar sense of referring to an orientalizing ornament that aestheticizes an enigmatic writing. The two senses—aesthetization of an enigmatic writing and ornamental illustration of the virtual materiality of the signifier at the threshold between seeing and reading, deciphering and interpreting, signifier and signified—are clearly related. The narrator's melancholia for his idolatrous love is translated into nostalgia for the culture of illuminated manuscripts, for the sensuous, external, ornamental features of an unknown Arabic script. To these traditional uses of the arabesque, which stem primarily from the pictorial tradition of art history, Poe's text adds a specifically literary aspect, one that is most centrally related to the transition from description to narration in this specific text and to the poetics of the fantastic tale:

> The lofty walls, gigantic in height—even unproportionably so— were hung from summit to foot, in vast folds, with a heavy and massive-looking tapestry of a material which was found alike as a carpet on the floor, as a covering for the ottomans and the ebony bed, as a canopy for the bed, and as the gorgeous volutes of the curtains which partially shaded the window. The material was the richest cloth of gold. It was spotted all over, at irregular intervals, with arabesque figures, about a foot in diameter, and wrought upon the cloth in patterns of the most jetty black. But these figures partook of the true character of the arabesque only when regarded from a single point of view. By a contrivance now common, and indeed traceable to a very remote period of antiquity, they were made changeable in aspect. To one entering the room, they bore the appearance of simple monstrosities; but upon a farther advance, this appearance gradually departed; and step by step, as the visitor moved his station in the chamber, he saw himself surrounded by an endless succession of the ghastly forms which belong to the superstition of the Norman, or arise in the guilty slumbers of the monk. The phantasmagoric effect was vastly heightened by the artificial introduction of a strong continual current of wind behind the draperies—giving a hideous and uneasy animation to the whole. (260–61)

When the narrator refers to "the true character of the arabesque" he seems to mean the ornamental use of an aestheticized mysterious linearity that resembles writing. To this traditional use of the arabesque, the drapery in the bridal chamber adds another aspect when the lines turn into changing shapes and forms in relation to the changing position of the observer. To a certain extent, one might argue that the draped bridal chamber can also be compared with a printed page: the ubiquitous and uniform use of the heavy tapestry, covering most of the interior space and furniture, would have the effect of removing the perspectival aspect of the room and the plasticity of individual pieces of furniture. Individual forms and shapes that would have their own colors, textures, and position in space are covered over, hidden under one bicolor, gold-and-black surface. In addition, the narrator emphasizes the thick, heavy, voluptuous fabrics of the tapestry and the curtains appealing to the senses of touch and feeling in all of their opacity. In contrast to the printed page, however, the observer is not faced with a uniform, plane surface of inscription bearing distinct characters but rather is enveloped or surrounded with an entirely disorienting environment in which the distinction between figure and ground vanishes. What emerges in this description stands in stark contrast to the richly detailed surface textures of the painters of the Northern Renaissance as well as to the classical and neoclassical understanding of drapery as a means of making the idealized human body, in all of its plasticity, perfectly transparent. Indeed, the description of the bridal chamber is anything but a vision of visual plenitude and bliss of the kind Gautier's fantastic tales would evoke. And, as opposed to Gautier's fantasy of visual plenitude in "The Dead Leman," Poe's phantasmagoria does not take its cues from the medium of painting but from the decorative genre of the arabesque, a genre that is associated with all kinds of technology of serial reproduction, especially with print technology.

Poe's text establishes an intimate link between the print medium and the fantastic. However, as was already indicated, the draped bridal chamber does not resemble just any printed page. Additional features need to be added to the printed text to make it oscillate, to produce the effect of a "hideous animation." Besides the hidden mechanism by which a stream of air moves the drapes in such a way that they give rise to fantastic shapes and figures to match superstition and guilty, obscene dreams, there is also a crazed, unstable observer/narrator. In other words, the unstable observer/narrator position--which is the defining feature of the fantastic tale—is linked to a mechanism that moves the opaque decorative fabric of the text such that the linear ornaments seem to acquire a soul or life of their own. Thus the supernatural intrusion of the fantastic tale is explained in terms of an optical illusion that arises exactly at the threshold of the imaginary materiality of writing. The climax and closure of the actual narrative, the narrative about Rowena's death, the watch at her corpse, and Ligeia's return can then be characterized as the actual emplotment of this hideous animation and as an illustration of the generic mechanists that has been outlined in terms of its media-technological conditions.

"Hideous Animation"

Immediately after the description of the drapery, the narrator talks about the first two months of his marriage to Rowena. During the first month, he takes pleasure in frightening his bride with his moodiness, his hatred for her, and his ardent love and yearning for Ligeia, "the beloved, the august, the beautiful, the entombed" (261), for whom he calls aloud at all hours. The only function left to Rowena is as the painfully tortured observer. During the second month of their marriage, she falls ill, briefly recovers, and then relapses into a fatal illness characterized by nervous irritation and excitability: "She spoke again, and now more frequently and pertinaciously, of the sounds—of the slight sounds—and of the unusual motions among the tapestries, to which she had formerly alluded" (262). Whereas the narrator knows all about the hidden mechanism by which the tapestry moves and thus creates the illusion of animation, he observes how his new wife is mortally terrified by it. The narrator does nothing to console or remove her from the terrors of the bridal chamber. When she is about to faint with fright, he merely hurries across the room to fetch a goblet of wine for her. Nor does he trust and act upon his own perceptions of an "invisible object" that he felt passing him, of a "faint, indefinite shadow of angelic aspect—such as might be fancied for the shadow of a shade," "a gentle footfall upon the carpet," and finally "three or four large drops of a brilliant and ruby colored fluid" which fell "within the goblet, as if from some invisible spring" (263). Although the narrator attributes these perceptions to his opium dreams, he nevertheless has to admit that immediately after Rowena drinks "a rapid change for the worse took place ... on the third subsequent night, the hands of her menials prepared her for the tomb, and on the fourth, I sat alone, with her shrouded body, in that fantastic chamber which had received her as my bride" (264).

The last formulation of this passage sharply articulates the result of Rowena's sojourn in the obscenely decorated room not in terms of her death nor his loss of her but in terms of a new scenario, one in which the bride is received and integrated into the fantastic chamber, in which she, like the draped furniture, has become part of this entire environment by way of her shrouded body—or in which her shrouded body, like the arabesque figures of the drapery, can give rise to superstition, guilty dreams and a hideous animation. For the narrator, the watch at Rowena's body becomes an occasion to think with utter intensity and passion "of that unutterable woe with which I had regarded *her* thus enshrouded. The night waned; and still, with a bosom full of bitter thoughts of the one only and supremely beloved, I remained gazing upon the body of Rowena" (264). Within the uniformity of the arabesque, ornamental bridal chamber (the perfect externalization of the imaginary materiality of the signifier), the shrouded body of Rowena presents the narrator/observer with one definite shape and site, the female corpse that is not covered by the ornamental drapery but merely by a shroud. The white shroud becomes a screen that allows him to hallucinate another body, the one of his beloved Ligeia, who stands for the imaginary immateriality of the signifier, the medial woman who can render writing transparent.

Within the constellation of this new scenario, a grotesque narrative program is played through, not just once but repeatedly, which lends to the whole action an even more horrifying, mechanical, automatic, and compulsive aspect: the narrator hears some faint noise, some sigh, watches the shrouded body intently, finally discovers a bit of color, some blood beginning to circulate along "the sunken veins of the eyelids." Horrified, awed and mortified, the narrator summons all of his energy, obeying some sense of duty that compels him "to call back the spirit still hovering," only to realize that his efforts are in vain, that he has in front of him nothing but a repulsive, clammy, and stiff corpse. Thereupon "I fell back with a shudder upon the couch from which I had been so startlingly aroused, and again gave myself up to passionate waking visions of Ligeia" (265).

In spite of the strong contrast between the body coming back to life and the increasingly disgusting, shriveled dead flesh, both the dead and the waking or reanimated body are dreadful to the narrator. Whereas the body trying to come back to life fills him with terror and mortifies him, the recently dead body is at the same time an object of sheer disgust and even indifference, to the extent that it does not require his attention and intervention but allows him to dream of Ligeia, to give himself up to "passionate waking visions of Ligeia." Thus the main contrast is not between the living body and the dead one, but between Rowena's body as capable of physically living and dying and Ligeia as the object of a mental sight and a purely mental passion. Yet, especially as the repetition of this narrative program makes clear, the two poles, Rowena's shrouded body and the mental vision of Ligeia, are intimately related. Only when Rowena is dead and the narrator is at her watch can he fully indulge in his recollections of Ligeia and project his "waking vision of Ligeia" onto the shrouded body. But the intensity of his passionate desire seems to be also the force that interrupts it, that brings Rowena's body back to life, such that he has to abandon his vision of Ligeia and engage his attention in the repeated, futile attempts at reanimation of a disgusting, horrifying corpse.

The last section of "Ligeia," about Rowena's wake and the narrator's passionate waking visions of Ligeia, draws its fantastic narrative program from an alternation between the two senses of *wake*, the watch kept at the side of a corpse and waking or awaking as rousing from sleep. The narrative moves back and forth between the narrator's horrified attempt to reanimate Rowena's corpse and his passionate vision of his beloved Ligeia. However, this narrative does not reach the conclusion desired by the narrator; Ligeia's illuminating presence never does return. Instead, the corpse suddenly gets up, shows itself in its full, tall stature; and as the shroud falls from its head, Ligeia's black hair and eyes become visible. It is when Ligeia's eyes return the narrator's gaze that the narrative has reached its abrupt end. In part one the expression of Ligeia's eyes was not merely an undefinable signifier; it was what guided the narrator's quest, his metonymical association of quotations, observations, perceptions—what reminded him of the secret of her individuality and her beauty, her particular intensity and willpower. In the last phrase of part two, her black eyes are merely physical marks that identify the walking, reanimated shrouded corpse as Ligeia's rather than Rowena's body. In this very last instance, Ligeia's black eyes do not stand out in terms of their ineffable expression but have become purely physical markers, like a scar or deformity that identifies the body of a particular individual.

By introducing the thematic complex of the arabesque, Poe's text is an extremely insightful commentary on the kind of fantastic tale that focuses on the fantasy of sensuous bliss without a body. "Ligeia" is built around the narrator's account of two distinctly different sets of encounters with an enigmatic signifier. In the first, the shape of Ligeia's eyes has an illuminating function and holds out the promise of access to a transcendent signified, which the story foregrounds as the vista into the valley, a concretization of a traditional image for the imaginary immateriality of the signifier. For the second set, the narrator's imagined illuminating presence of the beloved's gaze is replaced by his abandonment in an environment of the arabesque, of enigmatic and opaque writing, which cancels all transcendentalist prospects as well as the observer's memory and ability to distinguish what is within himself from what lies outside. The way out of this arabesque immanence appears to be through the shrouded corpse of his second wife. It is the one element in the bridal chamber that is not part of the disorienting, illegible ornamental writing; instead it becomes a screen, an occasion to hallucinate the absent beloved. But once Ligeia actually returns and takes possession of Rowena's corpse, her eyes are no longer large and luminous orbs; now they are merely indices of her physical identity and corporeal presence, which put an end to reading and signification. Her eyes are no longer an expression but merely black markers, like two dots. Full stop. The end.

Hoffmann's tale of the visionary hermit Serapion articulates a desire for escape into a realm of sensual and spiritual delights beyond the limitations of the mortal human body: a desire for the end of desire. Yet the programmatic status of this tale is problematic to the extent that Serapion's madness is characterized as the emphatic denial of all forms of mediation of the order of writing and sexuality. None of his supposedly wonderful tales are given, and indeed, any tale told by an unequivocal madman could not achieve the dimension proper to the fantastic tale. The stories of Councillor Krespel, Gautier's "The Dead Leman," or Poe's "Ligeia," by contrast, engage with the fantasy of an escape into the sensual delights beyond the limits of the mortal body. They address precisely those obstacles and limits of mortality, sexuality, the symbolic order, and the various aspects of mediation and media technologies that Serapion, in his madness, denies.

What makes these texts into fantastic narratives is the manner in which they make use of the personification of the medium—the figure of the medial woman suspended between life and death—as an extraordinary means of access to an aesthetic experience that is more than mere description. In each case, the medial woman represents the state of a temporary suspension of death and decay, and a temporary escape from a normal world of social interaction with its restrictions and restraints. Clarimonde is most clearly situated between two deaths: between her initial death following Romuald's ordination, and the final destruction of her body by the resentful advocate of Christianity. Antonia is equally trapped between two deaths. Her removal from the social world, from expression and love, and her sequestration in the isolation of her father's household, is a kind of suspension, an early death of which her final, physical death is the consummation. Her death, however, appearing as a terrifying wish fulfillment both in her father's dream of her wonderful singing and in the narrator's fascination with her voice and the frailty of her body, is removed from any easy moralizing access.

As if to comment on how we are to imagine the site for this kind of escape from the mortal body within the history of reading and writing, Poe's narrative specifics the strange suspension of, or escape from, a normal temporal and spatial order, through the details of the first person narrator's decoration of Rowena's sumptuous bridal chamber, which will be the locus of his contact with the medial woman, Ligeia. In the elaborate description of the arabesque interior, the cultural site of the fantastic is indicated as the space between the imaginary immateriality of the signifier—the transparency of the library that gives way to imagined vistas—and the imaginary materiality of the signifier: the ornamental and opaque, potentially three-dimensional characters of illegible signs.

NOTES

18. Poe, "The Philosophy of Composition" (1965), p. 201.

19. See Elisabeth Bronfen, "Risky Resemblances" (1992); Joan Dayan, "Convertibility and the Woman as Medium" (1987); Elmer, "Poe, Sensationalism, and the Sentimental Tradition" in *Reading at the Social Limit* (1995) pp. 93–125; and Clark Griffith, "Poe's 'Ligeia' and the English Romantics" (1985), pp. 71–80.

20. For a study of Poe's literary production and his attitude toward the changing book and magazine culture in America, see Kevin J. Hays, *Poe and the Printed Word* (2000). Though Hays does not mention "Ligeia," the text was written in that period during which Poe radically revised his position toward book culture: "The year the *Tales of the Grotesque and Arabesque* appeared, pamphlet novels began being published. The importance of the pamphlet novel to Poe's literary career cannot be underestimated. The new format forced Poe to question the value of separately published books[....] Poe's disgust with the pamphlet novel coincided with his growing uncertainty about the aesthetic value of the book-length narrative[....] Early on, Poe eschewed periodical publication, which others, including his own brother Henry Poe, took advantage of, but Poe eventually came to champion the periodical. To him, the magazine, not the book, became the vehicle for serious, important literature[....]" (p. 114).

21. Page references in text are to Poe, "Ligeia" (1965); this passage is on pages 248–49.

22. Gerhart von Graevenitz, *Das Ornament des Blicks* (1994), pp. 13–19.

23. Whenever writing is understood as a cultural technique of preserving and transmitting meaning, the materiality of writing is merely virtual materiality; although some material support is certainly needed to inscribe and preserve writing, its actual concrete nature is largely irrelevant. For writing to mean anything, it suffices that it partake of an internally coherent system of differential marks that can be read. Whether we are dealing with printed letters on paper, painted signs on silk or parchment, electromagnetic signals, or engravings in stone seems to matter little. Moreover, as soon as writing is linked with reading, as soon as the differential marks make sense, the external sensory perception of the characters can be replaced by merely imagined sense perception. The question of writing's material sensuousness is displaced when we attend to the sight, sound, taste, or feeling of the immaterial signified. One realm of senses gives way to another, and the text as such disappears. But this transparency is historical. It is especially within the domain of print culture that the activities of reading and sense-making tend to render the medium of writing transparent.

Oddly, perhaps, it is only when the materiality of the textual surface is flawed, wounded, or interrupted that we can think about it. Whenever writing is undecipherable, owing to some physical distortion or damage done to the characters or the surface of inscription, or thanks to the reader's ignorance of the code, the elements of writing are foregrounded in terms of their physical features. The written text might appear as a pattern or differentiated surface that nevertheless remains an enigma. In the case of undecipherability, when a particular artifact resists a decoding effort, we encounter writing as a specific instance. This particularity is, indeed, the materiality of the script. The aesthetic domain shares with the domain of the undecipherable a tendency to foreground instances of the medium's opacity. Under certain historical circumstances, this opacity becomes available for its own elaboration.

24. I owe this insight to the brilliant study by von Graevenitz about Goethe's poetics of the arabesque in his West-Östlicher Divan. Von Graevenitz traces the history of the ornament and the arabesque in the visual arts and relates it to the history of print technology. Whereas the first part of his book demonstrates how this history illustrates the imaginary materiality of the signifier, the second part proceeds to show how Goethe's poetics of the arabesque draws on and elaborates this history. See von Graevenitz (1994), pp. 19–24.

JOHN H. TIMMERMAN

House of Mirrors:
Edgar Allan Poe's
"The Fall of the House of Usher"

"The Fall of the House of Usher" is among those few stories that seem to elicit nearly as many critical interpretations as it has readers. More recent critical appraisals of the story have largely followed two directions: a reappraisal of the genre of the story as a Gothic romance[1] and a close attention to Madeline Usher as a type of Poe's other female characters.[2] But the tale presents the reader a multiplicity of problems that set it aside from Poe's other stories. Madeline is as enigmatic as a new language and as difficult to construe. While debates about Lady Ligeia have filled the pages of many journals, it is not hard to understand why.[3] Her contrarian social role, her purely gothic resurrection, and her defiant antithesis in character to Rowena sharpen her person from the start. But Madeline? This sylph-like creature, so attenuated and frail, seems to slip through the story like vapor, all the more mysterious for that and for her incredible power displayed in the conclusion.

Similarly, while the story is certainly Gothic in nature, here, too, we find exceptions and qualifications. In the majority of Poe's Gothic tales the narrative point of view is first person, and, significantly, the reader is also placed inside the mind of this leading character-narrator who is only a step away from insanity. In "Usher" we also have a creeping horror and the mental disintegration of the principal persona, but the story is in fact

---

From *Papers on Language and Literature* 39, no. 3 (Summer 2003). ©2003 by Southern Illinois University, Edwardsville.

narrated by an outside visitor (also representing the reader) who wants to find a way out of the horror. The only problem with this narrator is that, even having been given ample signs and warnings (as happens to Fortunato in "The Cask of Amontillado"), he is too inept to put the clues together. Poe has designed this deliberately, of course, for the reader is far more deductive than the narrator but has to wait for him to reach the extreme limit of safety before fleeing. However dull the narrator's mental processing, it is altogether better than being trapped in insanity.

One of the more penetrating of these studies of Gothic traits is G.R. Thompson's analysis of "The Fall of the House of Usher" in his *Poe's Fiction*. Thompson addresses the variations Poe creates with the Gothic tale by structuring a conflict between reason and irrationality. Particularly successful is his analysis of the decayed House mirroring Usher's mind so that "The sinking of the house into the reflecting pool dramatizes the sinking of the rational part of the mind, which has unsuccessfully attempted to maintain some contact with a stable structure of reality outside the self, into the nothingness within" (90). The analysis provides a lucid discussion of the process of that disintegration, of the dream-like qualities of Madeline as the devolution of the subconscious, and of the narrator's final infection by "Usher's hysteria." What Thompson does not explore, however, is an accounting for the loss of reason and what conclusion the reader may infer by the storm-struck house crumbling into the murky tarn.

To explore such issues, one must investigate beyond the confines of the tale proper, even beyond its generic home as a Gothic romance. The tale yields its full meaning as we turn to areas much overlooked in the study of this work; first, the influence of Poe's cosmology as set forth in other works but nonetheless pertinent, by his own telling, to his art; and, second, the historical context of his time when the effects of Enlightenment thinking of the prior century had not yet fully yielded (for Poe, at least) to the new spirit of Romanticism. The latter point in particular is crucial for an historicist appraisal of the story and of Poe, for it becomes evident that Poe did not reject Enlightenment thinking, that he was in fact suspicious of the newer Romanticism, and that at best he hoped for a tenuous harmony between the two. Keeping in mind such premises, we can observe the theory for unity, symmetry, and harmony emerging from *Eureka*, the aesthetic principles of the theory in his essays, and the application of those principles in a study of the conflict between Romanticism and Enlightenment in "The Fall of the House of Usher."

The casual treatment of Poe's cosmology no doubt springs from the conception that this is but one more entertaining hoax from the master trickster, somewhat akin to the elaborate architecture of "The Raven" described in "Philosophy of Composition." Undeniably, however, even Poe's most wildly Gothic romances, his most mysterious tales of ratiocination, and virtually all his poems, spring from some "idea" of order, a principle that this world can try to twist and break but can never quite succeed. Basically, his cosmology rests upon the philosophical principle that the very apprehension of disorder assumes an agency of order. Those familiar with the works of Aristotle will recognize the argument immediately. The essentials of Poe's cosmology reside in his essay *Eureka*, and there, too, he relies upon Aristotelian premises.

Since the work is less familiar to contemporary readers, I preface a discussion of it with a brief chronology. In 1843 Poe published the "Prospectus of *The Stylus*," the literary magazine he hoped to launch in July of that year. In late 1847, he had completed the lecture "The Cosmogony of the Universe"[4] that would be the introduction to *Eureka*, but also a lecture (nearly two hours) long that he could use to raise funds for *The Stylus*. The lecture had limited use. The only event we are certain of was an appearance on January 17, 1848, at Society Library where only 60 people showed up, most of them journalists. Poe finally prevailed upon Putnam to publish the work, asking for a print run of 50,000 copies and receiving instead a run of 500. It appeared in early July 1848.[5]

There appeared to be good reason for caution. The narrative guise of the learned scholar adopted for the lengthy third section absolutely confounds the casual—or even the very literate—reader.[6] Elsewhere, the narrator moves from humble observer to snide satirist. In addition to the shifting narrative poses, the work itself is simply such a strange miscellany of facts and thoughts and extrapolations that it is nearly impossible to find an orderly, fruitful, and singular thesis emerging in it. Every issue seems to lead to an ever-widening gyre of new questions. Admitting that, however, the work still constitutes Poe's fundamental cosmological view, and it does remain central to understanding his aesthetic principles. That essential element of *Eureka*, at least, may be rather clearly and conveniently summarized.

Preceding all existence is a deity functioning like Aristotle's Prime Mover. Humanity, and all physical nature, exists because this Prime Mover willed it to exist. Poe states that "'In the beginning' we can admit—indeed, we can comprehend, but one *First Cause*, the truly ultimate *Principle*, the Volition of God" (237).[7] We have then, a fairly traditional view of God's creation *ex nihilo*, that is, he willed all things into being out of nothing more than his will. As with Aristotle (and also the Judeo-Christian tradition) God is that being beyond which one can go no further.

But here Poe throws some of his own twists into the proposition. If the creator being is that ultimate first cause, it must represent unity. All the created order is individuated; necessarily, therefore, its source is not chaos but unity. Poe speaks of this as "Irradiation from Unity"—the primary creative act. Moreover, "This primary act itself is to be considered as *continuous volition*" (237). This is to say that God's creative impulse continues through the creative order, including humanity, that he has willed into being.

We arrive at the old religious and philosophical conundrum. If willed into being by God, and out of nothing, then what constitutes both our individuation yet also our unity with this God? Judaism provides the earliest answer with the story of the Edenic fall, where because of an act of transgression the unity was partially severed and, according to the Kabbalistic myth of "God in Exile," God withdrew into mystery. Nonetheless, as God's creation, humanity was still *mindful* of God. Plato provides the first coherent philosophical accounting in the western world with his concept of the Ideal Forms being transmuted by the earthly stuff of humanity. Only humanity, however, possessed the quality of mind to apprehend the ideal.

Poe, on the other hand, insists upon an ongoing volitional act of God apprehended by intuition. The idea led to his notorious concept in "The Poetic Principle" that the task of the poet is "to apprehend the supernal loveliness" (*Essays* 77) of God's order and that the best way to do so is through sadness. Poe reflects "that (how or why we know not) this certain taint of sadness is inseparably connected with all the higher manifestations of true Beauty" (*Essays* 81). This leads Poe, then, to the idea that the most sad thing, and therefore the most beautiful, is the death of a beautiful woman. The result is a body of work littered with female corpses.

It remains difficult, even for the most earnest reader, to take "The Poetic Principle" altogether seriously. Yet, herein lie many of Poe's seminal ideas and aesthetic principles. Many of those ideas, moreover, relate directly to the cosmology of *Eureka*. One has to remember that Poe desires to startle the reader into an awareness of the divinity within, for, he insists, we are all part and particle of the divine.[8] Necessarily so, since God willed all things into being out of nothing. What then are we but particles of the divine itself? Therefore in all created order there resides what Edward Wagenknecht called "the Shadow of Beauty."[9] Poe describes it as such: "An immortal instinct, deep within the spirit of man, is thus, plainly, a sense of the beautiful" (*Complete Works* 14:273). Therefore, Poe concludes that, since we are willed into being *ex nihilo*, since we are thereby part and particle of the divine, and since the ongoing volition of the divine rests among its creation as a shadow of beauty, symmetry that mirrors this unity of the universe is the paramount aesthetic quality of the work. Poe argues that the sense of the symmetrical "is the poetical essence of the *Universal—of the Universe* which, in the supremeness of its symmetry, is but the most sublime of poems. Now symmetry and consistency are convertible terms; thus poetry and truth are one" (*Complete Works* 16:302).

Poe takes the issue one step further, however. If indeed all things are willed into being *ex nihilo*, then not only all humanity but also all matter is part and parcel with God. Such a view Poe expresses as his infamous "sentience theory" in "The Fall of the House of Usher."[10] In particular the theory exerts itself twice. When Usher reveals that he has not left the mansion in many years, he describes the effect that the "mere form and substance" of the mansion has had upon him: "An effect which the *physique* of the gray walls and turrets, and of the dim tarn into which they all looked down, had, at length, brought upon the *morale* of his existence" ("Usher" 403).[11] Later, after Usher's rhapsody of creative expressions, the narrator and Usher fall into a conversation on "the sentience of all vegetable things" (408). Remembering Usher's description of this, the narrator describes the preternatural interconnectedness of mansion and family, and concludes, in Usher's terms, that "The result was discoverable ... in that silent, yet importunate and terrible influence which for centuries had moulded the destinies of his family, and which made *him* what I now saw him—what he was" (408).[12]

Careful readers of Poe will quickly understand that this use of a mental landscape is nothing new to Poe. It appears most prominently, perhaps, in the poetry. In "Ulalume" for example, the weird and otherworldly geographical landscape is nothing more than an objectification of the narrator's own mind. But so too it appears repeatedly in the short stories, particularly in the descriptions of the ornate and convoluted furnishings of a room ("Ligeia," "Masque of the Red Death") that mirror the mind of the narrator. In no other work, however, has Poe structured this sentience, or interconnectedness, between the physical world and the mental/psychological world more powerfully and tellingly than in "The Fall of the House of Usher."[13]

On the basis of his cosmological and aesthetic theories, Poe thereby constructs his architecture of mirrors to prop the movement of the story. Several studies have probed the pattern of mirror images, usually relating them to the rationality/irrationality of Usher or the physical/psychological tension between him and Madeline. Indeed, it falls beyond the space or provision of this essay to list them all, but in order to demonstrate the functions of pairing and splitting that the mirror images provide, a few central patterns may be noted.

The most evident, but eerily complex, of course, is the House of Usher itself. Roderick himself tells the narrator that over the centuries the mansion and the family had been so bonded as to become identified as one. Moreover, the diminishment of the Usher family, through years of inbreeding to this one lonely brother and sister, precisely parallels the physical collapse of the house, standing far apart from civilization as it does in some distant, lonely tract of country. The pairing between Roderick and the mansion is sustained in the careful detailing of descriptions, as the narrator observes first the one, then the other, and discerns unnerving similarities.

Although paired in matters of neglect and in physical description, both the Ushers and the mansion are undergoing a simultaneous process of splitting. The house is rent by a zigzag fissure that threatens its stability. In his letter to the narrator, Roderick admits to "mental disorder" that threatens his stability.[14] Similarly, the brother and sister are paired—not only by heritage but also by being fraternal twins. They, too, however, are simultaneously splitting apart, Madeline into her mysterious cataleptic trance and Roderick into an irrationally surrealistic world of frenzied artmaking.

Many other mirror images accumulate in the story. The house is mirrored by its image in the tarn and collapses beneath its waters at the close. Roderick's painting of the underground burial vault—at which the narrator marvels "If ever mortal painted an idea, that mortal was Roderick Usher"—preternaturally and prophetically mirrors Madeline's escape from the vault. The light with no apparent source in the painting may be referenced to Lady Ligeia's exclamation on the Conqueror Worm. "O Divine Father," Ligeia exclaims in a line that could be taken from *Eureka*, "Are we not part and parcel in Thee? Who—who knoweth the mysteries of the will with its vigor? Man doth not yield himself to the angels, *nor unto death utterly*, save only through the weakness of his feeble will" ("Ligeia" 319). Surprisingly with her glacial, ghostly demeanor prior to her entombment, Madeline possesses just such a will also.

"The Haunted Palace" provides another artistic mirror image. The work precisely traces the devolution of the House of Usher from a palace governed in orderly fashion by "Thought's Dominion" to a den of disorder in which demons flicker about like bats—except that these demons are in Usher's mind. An interesting submotif of the poem is the transition from spirits moving "To a Lute's well-tunèd law" to forms moving fantastically "to a discordant melody." With the demise of some structured order, artforms rampage into dissonance and cacophony.

This process of devolution forms the centering thesis of Gillian Brown's innovative study, "The Poetics of Extinction." Drawing upon Charles Lyell's *Principles of Geology* (1830–1833), in which he argues the diminishment and passing of "organic beings" over vast periods of time, Brown finds a model for the disintegration of both the House and lineage of Usher. The value of the essay resides in Brown's crisp demonstration of the relationship between the devolution of environment and humanity, predicated on Lyell's theory. As we have seen, moreover, that close interconnectedness between the physical and psychological, the external environment and the internal mind, is amply supported by *Eureka*, as well as by Poe's essays and art. Nonetheless one questions to what end this devolution exists in the fiction. Is it simply that all things pass away? Nothing could be further from Poe's writings, with their tenacious, almost frenzied grip upon the great mind that endures, as *Eureka* has it. Beyond anything Poe sought the physical incarnation of Hippocrates's incantation in his *Aphorisms: Ars longa, vita brevis*. To complete the careful construction of the story into an imaginative architecture that endures, however, one final set of mirror images bears scrutiny.

In order to create something of a mental theater that draws out the suspense of the story, Poe constructed a conflation of such images at the ending. To put Roderick's mind at ease, the narrator reads to him from "Mad Trist" by Sir Launcelot Canning.[15] Every step of Ethelred to force the entrance to the hermit's dwelling has its mirror in Madeline's clangorous escape from the dungeon. Meanwhile, a storm descends upon and envelops the mansion, mirroring the swirling collapse of Usher's rationality. Here, too, in the mirror of the storm and Roderick's mind, we find a clear use of the sentience theory.

Yet, the reader somehow feels dissatisfied if only construing the story as a clever construction of Poe's cosmology in his sentience theory. However carefully structured, the pairings and splittings of the mirror images point suggestively to a larger pattern than mere aesthetic architecture. Many directions to this larger significance have been offered.[16] It may be profitable, however, to relate the story to a larger conflict that Poe had been struggling with for some time: how to balance Romantic passion with Enlightenment order. By virtue of his work in the Gothic tale itself, many readers are quick to place him without qualification in the Romantic camp. But it is a conflict that Poe had struggled with previously that does, in fact, inhabit *Eureka* and comes to bear most forcefully in "The Fall of the House of Usher."

Although literary scholars generally date the Enlightenment era from

1660 (as a departure from the Renaissance) to 1798 (with the publication of *Lyrical Ballads*), all acknowledge the artificiality of such dating. All such periods consist of attitudes, ideas, and cultural dynamics that precede and postdate the era. Benjamin Franklin's fervid belief in perfectibility of self[17] gave way to romantic dissolution in order to feel life more passionately. Moreover, one could convincingly argue that the conflict between Enlightenment, with its heroic grandiosity of the mind, and Romanticism, with all its disheveled passions, continue in full force. Perhaps the conflict was only more heightened at Poe's particular point in literary history.

The Enlightenment presupposed the primacy of human reason, the ethical template of formal order, and the lifestyle of staid decorum. It may be argued that Poe's short stories eclipse reason by the supernatural, disrupt ethical values by gothic disorder, and blast decorum by the weird and grotesque. The argument would be wrong, for Poe sought nothing less than the delicate symbiosis between the two—and the key quality of symbiosis is in the mutual benefit one to another.

That Poe had struggled with the national literary shift from Enlightenment to Romantic thinking is evident long before 1839.[18] And while many of the early nineteenth-century writers embraced Romanticism passionately as the full outlet for an intuitive, imaginative, and story-driven art, Poe was by far more reserved. In his "1836 Letter to B___" Poe refers to the Lake Poets in quite derogatory terms: "As I am speaking of poetry, it will not be amiss to touch slightly upon the most singular heresy in its modern history—the heresy of what is called very foolishly, the Lake School" (*Essays* 6–7). The heresy of which Poe speaks, specifically in reference to Wordsworth, is that didactic poetry is seen as the most pleasurable. While admiring Coleridge's great learning, despite all that learning Poe is quick to point out his "liability to err." As for Wordsworth, "I have no faith in him" (*Essays* 8). Truly, the "Letter to B___" ends in a gnarled fist of contradictions (of Coleridge, Poe says he cannot "speak but with reverence"), and his attempt to define poetry is, in his own words, a "long rigmarole." But shot through the essay resides the governing belief that intellect and passion work together in art.

Such also became the central argument of "The Philosophy of Composition," a much better known, much clearer, but not necessarily more credible work. Here Poe lays his famous rational grid upon the composition of a poem of irrationality—"The Raven." For example, he states his (predetermined) scheme for rhythm and meter: "The former is trochaic—The latter is octometer acatalectic, alternating with heptameter catalectic repeated in the refrain of the fifth verse, and terminating with a tetrameter catalectic" (*Essays* 21). Poe's "The Rationale of Verse," moreover, might well be called one of the preeminent Enlightenment documents of the Romantic era. Surely, there were poets of Poe's time who followed fairly rigid verse forms, yet none of them that I am aware of would likely ever claim such an ornate, intellectual concept prior to the poem's composition. The fact is all the more telling in that the elegy, "The Raven," corresponds in many ways with "The Fall of the House of Usher," the singular exception being that in the former we are placed inside the disintegrating mind of the narrator while in the latter the narrator gives us some objective distance from the disintegration.

While "The Raven" remains one of the best known works in the western tradition generally, a second of Poe's elegies, "Ulalume," is perhaps of more critical importance to understanding the balancing act Poe was attempting between the Enlightenment and the Romantic. Upon a casual reading the poem seems archetypally romantic. We find the narrator wandering a strange landscape that ultimately is a mirror to his inner torment, if not his mind itself (his companion is Psyche). Similarly the time is more of a psychic state rather than the announced month of October with its withering and sere leaves. Into the groaning realms, he walks with Psyche his soul. Why? To what end? To discover the full meaning of the event for which they had traveled here the year prior.

The heightened, fantastic elements of the poem intensify throughout. The lonely season, the "dank tarn of Auber" (line 6), the unsettled and threatening landscape—all the essentials of the Gothic are here. Furthermore, supernatural figures enter—the ghouls who feed on the dead but also heavenly figures. The quarter moon rises, like twin horns hung in the sky. With it appears the figure of Astarte, Phoenician goddess of fertility and passion whose symbol is the twin horns of the bull. She is the consummate romantic figure, representing the outpouring of creative passion. The narrator observes that "She is warmer than Dian" (39), a reference to the Roman goddess of chastity and order. Strangely, and in spite of Psyche's caution to fly, the narrator trusts Astarte to lead him to the truth. Essentially, we have the old Appollinian-Dionysian conflict between order and impulse played out with two female goddesses—appropriate to the elegy for Virginia. In this case, and with the maddening desire to confront whatever lies at the end of his journey, the narrator insists,

> Ah, we safely may trust to its gleaming,
> And be sure it will lead us aright—
> We surely may trust to its gleaming
> That cannot but guide us aright.... (67–70)

Astarte, the goddess of passion, the fuel for the romantic flame, does in this poem lead him to the burning encounter with the fact of Ulalume's death. In this poem, Poe appears to recognize the enormous creative potential in romantic passion; yet, he remains wary of it, cautions that once unleashed it has the capacity to consume someone entirely.

This tension is similar to that which Poe takes to "The Fall of the House of Usher." Few other authors struggled as powerfully with that tension and with maintaining a balance between the analytic intelligence and the creative fancy. The possible exception is Nathaniel Hawthorne, whose "Rappaccini's Daughter" can very profitably be read as a clash between the coldly analytic Enlightenment man (Rappaccini) and the Romantic man (Baglioni). In "The Fall of the House of Usher" one notices the conflict already in the first paragraph, a masterpiece of prose poetry. The narrator possesses the initial rational distance from the scene, reporting to the reader what he sees and feels as he approaches the mansion. The organic form with which he reports his findings, however, allows the reader intuitively to grasp the sense of insufferable gloom. In the initial sentence, heavy, sinking, *o* and *u* vowels droop like sullen rain. The pacing of the sentences, with relatively brief, stumbling phrases in very long, heavy sentences, enhance the effect.[19]

The carefully ordered architectural grid Poe places upon the story, including the escalation of mirror images, is similar to the (purportedly) careful ordering of his poems. In this story, however, the balance between Enlightenment and Romantic itself is situated at the heart of the story. Roderick himself is emblematic of Romantic passion, while Madeline is emblematic of Enlightenment. Their genesis, as fraternal twins, is unified— a perfectly mirrored complementarity—but the story unveils their splitting to mutual destruction.

This way of viewing the relationship between brother and sister is not customary, to be sure. The common view is that the narrator, coming from outside the palace of horrors, represents rational order. An example of this view appears in Jack Voller's study of the sublime in Poe's tale, in which he states that "The narrator is associated with the rescuing force of reason.... Although he strikes few readers as cheerful, the narrator is suited to his task ..." (29). Yet, it is hard to find the narrator exercising anything like a force of reason. In the main, his role is limited to some musing observations, a rather slow study in horror, and a hopeless inefficiency to do much of anything about the divisive destruction of the tenants of the House, which seems to be precisely Poe's point. When Romantic passion and Enlightenment order divide, their mutual destruction is assured.

Madeline therefore becomes abstracted to little more than a mental evanescence—Enlightenment at its extreme, out of touch with reality. When the narrator first sees her passing in the distance, he is filled with unaccountable dread, so otherworldly she appears. She is, Roderick discloses, simply wasting away of some illness with no known etiology. At the very same time, Roderick diverges in the opposite direction. While Madeline disappears into a vaporific mist, Roderick flames into an unrestricted creative power, full of unrestrained, raw passion. He becomes the fiery polar to Madeline's cold abstraction. The narrator describes his successive days with Usher and his artmaking thus: "An excited and highly distempered ideality threw a sulphurous luster over all" ("Usher" 405). Usher thereby enters a creative mania, churning out songs, paintings, and poems against the coming dark.

That is precisely the point Poe makes in this tale. When split apart, as they are here, Enlightenment thinking becomes all cold, analytic, and detached; Romanticism, on the other hand, blazes into a self-consuming passion. Aesthetically and ideally they ought to be mirrors to each other, working in a complementary fashion to serve art. When split from each other, they become mutually self-destructive. Preternaturally charged with his Romantic instincts, Roderick hears, above the storm, the approaching footsteps of Madeline. She enters, falls upon her brother, and together they die. The splitting pairs have conjoined once again, but tragically this time. The separation had gone to the extreme, disrupting the sentient balance, destroying both. As the narrator flees, the house itself parallels the act of Roderick and Madeline, first splitting apart along the zigzag fissure and then collapsing together into the tarn.

If *Eureka* teaches us the design of unity, and the essays teach us Poe's efforts to integrate intellectual order into his aesthetics, then it may be fairly said that "The Fall of the House of Usher" is a cautionary tale, warning of a way Poe would not have artists go. While he did exult in the freedoms of the Romantic imagination, he was also highly suspicious of it. He needed, and called for, the orderliness of design inherited from the Enlightenment to contain that imagination. Without that synchronous working, as "The Fall of the House of Usher" demonstrates, both are doomed.

NOTES

1. Perhaps the most helpful study of this sort is Gary E. Tombleson's "Poe's 'The Fall of the House of Usher' as Archetypal Gothic: Literary and Architectural Analogs of Cosmic Unity" (*Nineteenth-Century Contexts* 12.2 [1988]: 83–106). Tombleson locates the place of the story—both its traditional and innovative elements— within the tradition dating to Walpole's *The Castle of Otranto, A Gothic Story* (1764). Also helpful is Stephen

Dougherty's "Dreaming the Races: Biology and National Fantasy in 'The Fall of the House of Usher'" (*Henry Street* 7.1 [Spring 1988]: 17–39). Of particular interest, and with a revealing twist on interpreting the story, is Mark Kinkead-Weekes' "Reflections On, and In, 'The Fall of the House of Usher.'" Kinkead-Weekes argues that the story is "not merely Gothick, but rather a 'Gothick' which at every turn signals a consciousness of its own operation" (17). This pattern includes, furthermore, an awareness of the writer of the Gothic.

2. See, for example, Cynthia S. Jordan's "Poe's Re-Vision: The Recovery of the Second Story" (*American Literature* 59.1 [Mar. 1987]: 1–19). Jordan sets forth the ways by which Poe differs from Hawthorne and pays close attention to such stories as "Berenice," "Morella," and "Ligeia," in addition to "The Fall of the House of Usher." In "'Sympathies of a Scarcely Intelligible Nature': The Brother–Sister Bond in Poe's 'The Fall of the House of Usher'" (*Studies in Short Fiction* 30 [1993]: 387–396), Leila S. May discusses the issue of the female persona with an interesting twist, arguing that the story represents Poe's vision of social destruction with the breakup of family structures in mid-19th century. That the relationship between Roderick and Madeline is aberrant goes without saying, but May provides insufficient evidence of a social meltdown at this time or support for Poe's holding this view.

3. It is nearly impossible to keep track of all the articles and dissenting opinions that "Ligeia" has engendered. In Poe's mind, at least, the story was his best to date. To Philip Pendleton Cooke he wrote, "'Ligeia' may be called my best tale" (9 August 1846 *Letters* 2:329). Readers don't always agree with authors on such matters. The story is, nonetheless, a fascinating document for Poe's revision process. In *The Collected Works of Edgar Allan Poe*, volume 2, Thomas Mabbott discusses these at some length.

4. Technically, a "cosmogony," the term Poe uses, is concerned with the origins and the evolution of the universe. A "cosmology," the more fitting term here, deals with the universe in total relativity—from the origin to the acts and consequences of all life in the universe. As we will see, Poe's theory clearly points in the latter direction.

5. For helpful discussion of the relationship between the lecture and *Eureka* see Burton R. Pollin's "Contemporary Reviews of *Eureka*: A Checklist" (*Poe as Literary Cosmologer: Studies on "Eureka"—A Symposium*. Hartford, CT: Transcendental Books, 1975. 26–30) in addition to standard biographies.

6. Frederick Conner demonstrates the plethora of contradictions and fallacies in the third section in his "Poe's *Eureka*" (*Cosmic Optimism: A Study of the Interpretation of Evolution by American Poets from Emerson to Robinson*. New York: Octagon, 1973. 67–91).

7. Quotations from *Eureka* are from volume 16 of the Harrison edition of *The Complete Works*. Page numbers refer to this volume. More recently, Richard P. Benton has edited a new edition of *Eureka* with line numbers, a compendium essay, and a bibliographic guide (Hartford, CT: Transcendental Books, 1973). The text is quite difficult to find, however, while the Harrison edition is in nearly every library.

8. Poe made this point in a number of places, perhaps most forcefully in his 2 July 1844 letter to James Russell Lowell: "But to all we attach the notion of a constitution of particles—atomic composition. For this reason only we think spirit different; for spirit, we say, is unparticled, and therefore is not matter.... The unparticled matter, permeating and impelling all things, is God. Its activity is the thought of God—which creates. Man, and other thinking beings, are individualizations of the unparticled matter" (*Letters* 1:257). Humanity is a part or extension of God. Since it is the nature of God to create, humanity's

closest affinity to the Deity lies in its creativity. To express its godliness humanity must create in its own unique, but divine, method.

9. Wagenknecht puts it as such: "For though the Shadow of Beauty may float unseen among us, we can never make much contact with it in human experience unless it can somehow be made to impregnate the stuff of human life ..." (151). It is precisely the task of the poet to make that "impregnation."

10. One should not be deterred from spotting similarities in cosmology by the fact that *Eureka* was published nearly a decade (1848) later than "The Fall of the House of Usher," which first appeared in *Burton's Gentleman's Magazine*, September 1839. The fundamental beliefs pulled together in *Eureka* were ones that Poe had been developing in part for years and in *Eureka* tried to systematize as a whole.

11. All quotations from "The Fall of the House of Usher" and "Ligeia" are from volume 2 of Mabbott's authoritative edition and will be cited as "Usher" and "Ligeia."

12. In his "Sentience and the False Deja vu in 'The Fall of the House of Usher,'" John Lammers makes a distinction critical to understanding Poe. Sentience, he points out, is a matter of shared awareness:

> Since the word "sentience" can mean "feeling with awareness" or "feeling without awareness," since everyone believes that plants at least have "feeling without awareness," and since Usher's theory is unusual because only four writers in the history of the world have agreed with him, then the meaning of "sentience" here must be the unusual one—"feeling with awareness or consciousness." In short, Usher believes that all vegetation has a mind. (21)

This view comports precisely with the "volitional" act of creation appearing in *Eureka*. For another discussion of sentience, see David L. Coss's "Art and Sentience in 'The Fall of the House of Usher'" (*Pleiades* 14.1 [1991]: 93–106).

13. For a consideration of the disintegrating mind of Usher, see G.R. Thompson's *Poe's Fiction*, 87–97. Thompson's views have been contested by many. See, for example, Patrick F. Quinn's "A Misreading of Poe's 'The Fall of the House of Usher'" (*Critical Essays on Edgar Allan Poe*. Ed. Eric W. Carlson. Boston: G.K. Hall, 1987. 153–59). In a study of "Ligeia" and "The Fall of the House of Usher," Ronald Bieganowski observes that "Reflected images double the intensity of beauty" (186).

14. Earliest published forms of the story use the term "pitiable mental idiosyncrasy" here. See *s2*:398. For a lengthier discussion of the house and the "divided mind," see Jack G. Voller's "The Power of Terror: Burke and Kant in the House of Usher."

15. In an unusual twist on Poe's notorious ending, Kinkead-Weekes views it as an ironic, comedic scene in which the affected superiority of the narrator is destroyed (30–31).

16. Several of these different interpretations explore the conflict between the natural and the supernatural, such as E. Arthur Robinson's "Order and Sentience in 'The Fall of the House of Usher'" (*PMLA* 76.1 [Mar. 1961]: 68–81) and David Ketterer's *The Rationale of Deception in Poe* (Baton Rouge: Louisiana State UP, 1979). Several studies explore the subconscious or the conflict between image and reality in the story. Representative here are Sam Girgus's "Poe and the Transcendent Self" (*The Law of the Heart*. Austin: U of Texas P, 1979. 24–36) and Leonard W. Engel's "The Journey from Reason to Madness: Edgar Allan Poe's 'The Fall of the House of Usher'" (*Essays in Arts and Sciences* 14 [1985]: 23–31).

17. "It was about this time I conceived the bold and arduous project of arriving at moral perfection. I wished to live without committing any fault at any time.... As I knew, or thought I knew, what was right and wrong, I did not see why I might not always do the one and avoid the other" (Franklin 1384).

18. For a more detailed analysis of Poe's relation with the English Romantics and the part they played in his aesthetics, see my article, "Edgar Allan Poe: Artist, Aesthetician, Legend" (*South Dakota Review* 10.2 [Spring 1972]: 60–70).

19. For linguists with an interest in quantitative rhetoric, the first paragraph is a treasure trove. Just dealing with the baseline figures, the first four sentences are 60, 22, 32, and 81 words in length, for an average of 49, an extraordinary average. But the proliferation of short phrases and clauses works as interior counterpart.

WORKS CITED

Bieganowski, Ronald. "The Self-Consuming Narrator in Poe's 'Ligeia' and 'Usher.'" *American Literature* 60.2 (May 1988): 175–87.

Brown, Gillian. "The Poetics of Extinction." *The American Face of Edgar Allan Poe*. Ed. Shawn Rosenheim and Stephen Rachman. Baltimore: Johns Hopkins UP, 1995. 330–44.

Franklin, Benjamin. *The Autobiography*. New York: The Library of America, 1987.

Kinkead-Weekes, Mark. "Reflections On, and In, 'The Fall of the House of Usher.'" *Edgar Allan Poe: The Design of Order*. Ed. A. Robert Lee. London: Vision Press, 1987: 17–35.

Lammers, John. "Sentience and the False Deja Vu in 'The Fall of the House of Usher.'" *Publications of the Arkansas Philological Association* 22.1 (Spring 1996): 19–41.

Poe, Edgar Allan. *Collected Works of Edgar Allan Poe*. Ed. Thomas Ollive Mabbott. 3 vols. Cambridge: Belknap Press of Harvard U, 1969.

———. *The Complete Works of Edgar Allan Poe*. Ed. James Harrison. 17 vols. New York: T.Y. Crowell, 1902.

———. *Essays and Reviews*. Ed. B.R. Thompson. New York: Modern Library, 1984.

———. *The Letters of Edgar Allan Poe*. 2 vols. Ed. John Ward Ostrom. Cambridge, MA: Harvard UP, 1948.

Thompson, G.R. *Poe's Fiction: Romantic Irony in the Gothic Tales*. Madison: U of Wisconsin P, 1973.

Voller, Jack G. "The Power of Terror: Burke and Kant in The House of Usher." *Poe Studies* 21.2 (1988): 27–35.

Wagenknecht, Edward. *Edgar Allan Poe: The Man Behind the Legend*. New York: Oxford UP, 1963.

Chronology

1809	Born in Boston on January 19 to itinerant actors David Poe Jr. and Elizabeth Arnold Hopkins Poe. Father abandons the family while Edgar is an infant.
1811	Elizabeth Poe dies on December 8 in Richmond, Virginia. John Allan, a Richmond importer, and his wife Frances take in Edgar, while his brother and sister each end up in different locations.
1815–1820	Travels with the Allans to England and Scotland, where John Allan hoped to expand his business. Attends boarding school in London, 1818 to 1820. Family returns to Richmond in 1820.
1824	Writes earliest extant verse.
1825	Meets and becomes romantically involved with Sarah Elmira Royster. John Allan inherits considerable wealth and property from his uncle, William Galt.
1826	Attends University of Virginia but does not return after the winter break.
1827	Goes to Boston, where he enlists in the army. Publishes first book of poetry, *Tamerlane and Other Poems*.
1829	While stationed in Virginia, Poe hires a substitute to serve for him and is discharged from the army. Frances Allan dies. Publishes *Al Aaraaf, Tamerlane, and Minor Poems*.
1830	With John Allan's help, attains an appointment to West

	Point and enrolls in May. Allan remarries and ends his relationship with Poe.
1831	Court-martialed and expelled from West Point for neglecting classes and drills. Publishes *Poems: Second Edition*. Moves to Baltimore, where he lives in poverty with his grandmother; his aunt, Maria Clemm; his cousin, Virginia; and his brother, William Henry Leonard Poe, who dies August 1.
1832	*The Saturday Courier*, a Philadelphia magazine, publishes five stories Poe submitted as entries in a contest. John Allan writes Poe out of his will.
1834	John Allan dies.
1835	Grandmother dies. Poe begins writing for T.W. White's fledgling *Southern Literary Messenger*, then moves back to Richmond with his aunt and cousin to edit the magazine. Contributes stories and often-scathing book reviews to the publication.
1836	Marries thirteen-year-old Virginia Clemm in May.
1837	Moves the family to New York City, after he is either fired by White or resigns.
1838	Moves to Philadelphia. Publishes *The Narrative of Arthur Gordon Pym*.
1839	Becomes co-editor of William E. Burton's *Gentleman's Magazine*. First twenty-five stories are published as *Tales of the Grotesque and Arabesque*.
1840	Leaves *Gentleman's Magazine*.
1841	Hired as an editor of *Graham's Magazine*.
1842	Virginia contracts tuberculosis. Resigns from *Graham's*.
1843	Travels to Washington, D.C., to win a government job and raise subscriptions for his planned magazine.
1844	Moves to New York City. Works as an editorial assistant at the *New York Evening Mirror*.
1845	Becomes co-editor of the *Broadway Journal* and later its proprietor. Publishes *Tales* and *The Raven and Other Poems*.
1846	*Broadway Journal* folds. Moves with family to Fordham, New York. Suffers severe illness when Virginia's health declines.

1847	Virginia dies in January. Poe is depressed and ill for most of the year and writes little.
1848	*Eureka* is published. Engaged to Sarah Helen Whitman; she breaks the engagement. Probably attempts suicide by overdose of laudanum.
1849	Negotiates with E.H.N. Patterson to establish the *Stylus*. Proposes to Sarah Elmira Royster Shelton. Falls into a coma. Dies on October 7 and is buried in Baltimore beside his first wife's remains.

Contributors

HAROLD BLOOM is Sterling Professor of the Humanities at Yale University. He is the author of 30 books, including *Shelley's Mythmaking* (1959), *The Visionary Company* (1961), *Blake's Apocalypse* (1963), *Yeats* (1970), *A Map of Misreading* (1975), *Kabbalah and Criticism* (1975), *Agon: Toward a Theory of Revisionism* (1982), *The American Religion* (1992), *The Western Canon* (1994), and *Omens of Millennium: The Gnosis of Angels, Dreams, and Resurrection* (1996). *The Anxiety of Influence* (1973) sets forth Professor Bloom's provocative theory of the literary relationships between the great writers and their predecessors. His most recent books include *Shakespeare: The Invention of the Human* (1998), a 1998 National Book Award finalist, *How to Read and Why* (2000), *Genius: A Mosaic of One Hundred Exemplary Creative Minds* (2002), *Hamlet: Poem Unlimited* (2003), *Where Shall Wisdom be Found* (2004), and *Jesus and Yahweh: The Names Divine* (2005). In 1999, Professor Bloom received the prestigious American Academy of Arts and Letters Gold Medal for Criticism. He has also received the International Prize of Catalonia, the Alfonso Reyes Prize of Mexico, and the Hans Christian Andersen Bicentennial Prize of Denmark.

BARBARA JOHNSON is the Fredric Wertham Professor of Law and Pyschiatry at Harvard University. She is the translator of a book by Derrida and has written a number of other titles, such as *The Critical Difference: Essays in the Contemporary Rhetoric of Reading* and *The Wake of Deconstruction*.

DAVID S. REYNOLDS teaches English at the City University of New York. He is the editor of an edition of Walt Whitman's *Leaves of Grass* and has written titles on Whitman. He is the author of other titles, among them *Faith in Fiction: The Emergence of Religious Literature in America*.

JOHN T. IRWIN teaches composition and writing at Johns Hopkins University. He was the editor of *The Georgia Review* and is the general editor of The Johns Hopkins University Press Fiction and Poetry Series. He is the author of a book on Faulkner and has written several other titles as well.

SHAWN ROSENHEIM has taught at Williams College. He is the author of *The Cryptographic Imagination: Secret Writing from Edgar Allan Poe to the Internet*.

SCOTT PEEPLES teaches English at the College of Charleston. He has written *The Afterlife of Edgar Allan Poe*.

HARRIET HUSTIS teaches English at the College of New Jersey. She has published pieces on Faulkner, Poe, Tolstoy, and Stoker among others.

LELAND S. PERSON teaches English at the University of Cincinnati. He has authored *Aesthetic Headaches: Women and Masculine Poetics in Poe, Melville, and Hawthorne* and other titles on Henry James and Hawthorne.

DOROTHEA E. VON MÜCKE teaches German at Columbia University. She is the author or co-editor of two titles on eighteenth-century literature.

JOHN H. TIMMERMAN teaches American literature at Calvin College. He has authored or edited numerous essays and books, such as *A Nation's Voice: An Anthology of American Short Fiction* and *Other Worlds: The Fantasy Game*.

Bibliography

Argerginger, Jana L. "From an Editor's Easy Chair: A Partial View of Prospects in Poe Studies." *Edgar Allan Poe Review* 4, no. 1 (Spring 2003): 42–50.

Blevins-Le Bigot, Jane. "Valéry, Poe and the Question of Genetic Criticism in America." *Esprit Créateur* 41, no. 2 (Summer 2001): 68–78.

Burwick, Frederick L. "Edgar Allan Poe: The Sublime and the Grotesque." *Prism(s): Essays in Romanticism* 8 (2000): 67–123.

Cantalupo, Barbara. "Interview with Daniel Hoffman (April 2002)." *Edgar Allan Poe Review* 3, no. 1 (Spring 2002): 95–112.

———. "Interviews with Poe Scholars: Eric W. Carlson." *Edgar Allan Poe Review* 1, no. 1 (Spring 2000): 54–60.

———. "Interviews with Poe Scholars: Roger Forclaz." *Edgar Allan Poe Review* 1, no. 1 (Spring 2000): 61–64.

———. "Interview with Richard Wilbur (May 2003)." *Edgar Allan Poe Review* 4, no. 1 (Spring 2003): 68–86.

Carlson, Eric W. "Poe's Ten-Year Frogpondian War." *Edgar Allan Poe Review* 3, no. 2 (Fall 2002): 37–51.

Dameron, J. Lasley. "Poe and Twain: Cooper Reviewed and Revised." *Mississippi Quarterly* 53, no. 2 (Spring 2000): 197–207.

Dern, John A. "Poe's Public Speakers: Rhetorical Strategies in 'The Tell-Tale Heart' and 'The Cask of Amontillado.'" *Edgar Allan Poe Review* 2, no. 2 (Fall 2001): 53–70.

Ehrlich, Heyward. "Poe in Cyberspace: Electronic Guides to Printed and Online Research." *Edgar Allan Poe Review* 4, no. 2 (Fall 2003): 93–97.

Foust, Ronald. "Poe, Pym, Postmodernism." *McNeese Review* 41 (2003) 13–25.

Freedman, William. *The Porous Sanctuary: Art and Anxiety in Poe's Short Fiction*. Sexuality and Literature 10. New York: Peter Lang, 2002.

Gervais, David. "After Poe: Poetics and Poetry." *PN Review* 29, no. 4 (150) (March–April 2003): 30–34.

Goddu, Teresa A. "Rethinking Race and Slavery in Poe Studies." *Poe Studies/Dark Romanticism* 33, nos. 1–2 (2000): 15–18

Gruesser, John C. "Madmen and Moonbeams: The Narrator in 'The Fall of the House of Usher.'" *Edgar Allan Poe Review* 5, no. 1 (Spring 2004): 80–90.

Guthrie, James R. "Broken Codes, Broken Seals, and Stolen Poems in 'The Purloined Letter.'" *Edgar Allan Poe Review* 3, no. 2 (Fall 2002): 92–102.

Harris, W. C. "Edgar Allan Poe's *Eureka* and the Poetics of Constitution." *American Literary History* 12, nos. 1–2 (Spring–Summer 2000): 1–40.

Hayes, Kevin J. *The Cambridge Companion to Edgar Allan Poe*. Cambridge, England: Cambridge University Press, 2002.

Hoffman, Daniel. "Returns from the Grave: The Spirit of Poe in Contemporary Fiction." *Edgar Allan Poe Review* 5, no. 1 (Spring 2004): 6–15.

Hovey, Kenneth Alan. "'These Many Pieces Are Yet One Book': The Book-Unity of Poe's Tale Collections." *Poe Studies/Dark Romanticism* 31, nos. 1–2 (1998): 1–16.

Hughes, John. "Poe's Resentful Soul." *Poe Studies/Dark Romanticism* 34, nos. 1–2 (2001): 20–28.

Irwin, John T. "Knight's Gambit: Poe, Faulkner, and the Tradition of the Detective Story." In *William Faulkner: Six Decades of Criticism*, edited by Linda Wagner-Martin, 355–75. East Lansing, MI: Michigan State University Press, 2002.

Jackson, Virginia. "Poe, Longfellow, and the Institution of Poetry." *Poe Studies/Dark Romanticism* 33, nos. 1–2 (2000): 23–28.

Jahshan, Paul. "The Deferred Voice in 'The Murders in the Rue Morgue.'" *Edgar Allan Poe Review* 3, no. 2 (Fall 2002): 78–91.

Jung, Yonjae. "The Imaginary Double in Poe's 'William Wilson.'" *Lit: Literature Interpretation Theory* 11, no. 4 (February 2001): 385–402.

Kearns, Christopher. "Rehearsing Dupin: Poe's Duplicitous Confrontation with Coleridge." *Edgar Allan Poe Review* 3, no. 1 (Spring 2002) 3–14.

Kelly, Warren Hill. "Detecting the Critic: The Presence of Poe's Critical Voice in His Stories of Dupin." *Edgar Allan Poe Review* 4, no. 2 (Fall 2003): 77–86.

Kennedy, J. Gerald, ed. *A Historical Guide to Edgar Allan Poe*. Oxford: Oxford University Press, 2001.

Magistrale, Tony, and Sidney Poger. *Poe's Children: Connections between Tales of Terror and Detection*. New York: Peter Lang, 1999.

Markley, A.A. "The Godwinian Confessional Narrative and Psychological Terror in Arthur Gordon Pym." *Edgar Allan Poe Review* 4, no. 1 (Spring 2003): 4–16.

Merivale, Patricia, and Susan Elizabeth Sweeney, eds. *Detecting Texts: The Metaphysical Detective Story from Poe to Postmodernism*. Philadelphia: University of Pennsylvania Press, 1999.

Moore, Patrick, Sir. *Eureka*. London: Hesperus, 2002.

Morrison, Toni. "Romancing the Shadow (1992)." In *The New Romanticism: A Collection of Critical Essays*, edited by Eberhard Alsen, 51–67. New York: Garland, 2000.

Mücke, Dorothea E. von. "The Imaginary Materiality of Writing in Poe's 'Ligeia.'" *Differences: A Journal of Feminist Cultural Studies* 11, no. 2 (Summer 1999): 53–75.

———. *The Seduction of the Occult and the Rise of the Fantastic Tale*. Stanford, CA: Stanford University Press, 2003.

Mutalik-Desai, A. A. "Edgar Allan Poe: Poetry and Metre." *Indian Journal of English Studies* 38 (2000–2001): 28–36.

Nadal, Marita. "Beyond the Gothic Sublime: Poe's Pym or the Journey of Equivocal (E)motions." *Mississippi Quarterly* 53, no. 3 (Summer 2000): 373–88.

Neiworth, James. "International Poe Bibliography: 1998–2000." *Poe Studies/Dark Romanticism* 35 (2002): 38–65.

Peeples, Scott. *The Afterlife of Edgar Allan Poe*. Rochester, NY: Camden House, 2004.

Polk, Noel. "Welty, Hawthorne, and Poe: Men of the Crowd and the Landscape of Alienation." *Mississippi Quarterly* 50, no. 4 (Fall 1997): 553–65.

Rainwater, Catherine. "Edgar Allan Poe (1809–1849)." In *Writers of the American Renaissance: An A-to-Z Guide*, edited by Denise D. Knight, 300–07. Westport, CT: Greenwood, 2003.

Renza, Louis A. "Edgar Allan Poe, Henry James, and Jack London: A Private Correspondence." *Boundary* 2 27, no. 2 (Summer 2000): 83–111.

Rudoff, Shaindy. "Written in Stone: Slavery and Authority in 'The Narrative of Arthur Gordon Pym.'" *American Transcendental Quarterly* 14, no. 1 (March 2000): 61–82.

Stockholder, Kay. "Is Anybody at Home in the Text? Psychoanalysis and the
    Question of Poe." *American Imago* 57, no. 3 (Fall 2000): 299–333.

Vines, Lois Davis. *Poe Abroad: Influence, Reputation, Affinities*. Iowa City:
    University of Iowa Press, 1999.

Whalen, Terence. *Edgar Allan Poe and the Masses: The Political Economy of
    Literature in Antebellum America*. Princeton, NJ: Princeton University
    Press, 1999.

Wright, Thomas. "Edgar Allan Poe's Tales of the Grotesque and
    Arabesque." In *American Writers Classics, I*, edited by Jay Parini,
    339–58. New York: Thomson Gale, 2003.

Acknowledgments

"Strange Fits: Poe and Wordsworth on the Nature of Poetic Language" by Barbara Johnson. From *A World of Difference*: 89–99. ©1987 by The Johns Hopkins University Press. Reprinted with permission of The Johns Hopkins University Press.

"Poe's Art of Transformation: 'The Cask of Amontillado' in Its Cultural Context" by David S. Reynolds. From *New Essays on Poe's Major Tales*, edited by Kenneth Silverman: 93–112. ©1993 by Cambridge University Press. Reprinted with permission of Cambridge University Press.

"A Platonic Dialogue; *Eureka* as Detective Story; Marked with a Letter; The Tetractys and the Line of Beauty; Letter as Nodal Point; A Shared Structure; Thematizing the Act of Reading" by John T. Irwin. From *The Mystery to a Solution: Poe, Borges, and the Analytic Detective Story*: 398–416. ©1994 by The Johns Hopkins University Press. Reprinted with permission of The Johns Hopkins University Press.

"Detective Fiction, Psychoanalysis, and the Analytic Sublime" by Shawn Rosenheim. From *The American Face of Edgar Allan Poe*, edited by Shawn Rosenheim and Stephen Rachman: 153–76. ©1995 by The Johns Hopkins University Press. Reprinted with permission of The Johns Hopkins University Press.

193

"Black and White and Re(a)d All Over; *The Narrative of Arthur Gordon Pym*" by Scott Peeples. From *Edgar Allan Poe Revisited* edited by Nancy A. Walker: 55–73. ©1998 by Twayne Publishers. Reprinted by permission.

"'Reading Encrypted But Persistent': The Gothic of Reading and Poe's 'The Fall of the House of Usher'" by Harriet Hustis. From *Studies in American Fiction* 27, no. 1 (Spring 1999): 3–20. ©1999 by Northeastern University. Reprinted by permission.

"Poe's Philosophy of Amalgamation: Reading Racism in the Tales" by Leland S. Person. From *Romancing the Shadow: Poe and Race*, edited by J. Gerald Kennedy and Liliane Weissberg: 205–24. ©2001 by Oxford University Press. Reprinted by permission.

"Ligeia: 'Her Large and Luminous Orbs'" by Dorothea E. von Mücke. From *The Seduction of the Occult and the Rise of the Fantastic Tale*: 180–96. ©2003 by the board of trustees of the Leland Stanford Jr. University. Reprinted by permission.

"House of Mirrors: Edgar Allan Poe's 'The Fall of the House of Usher'" by John H. Timmerman. From *Papers on Language and Literature* 39, no. 3 (Summer 2003): 227. ©2003 by Southern Illinois University, Edwardsville. Reprinted by permission.

Index

Characters in literary works are indexed by first name (if any), followed by the name of the work in parentheses.